Dear Reader:

The book you are about to read is the latest bestseller from the St. Martin's True Crime Library, the imprint the *New York Times* calls "the leader in true crime!" Each month, we offer you a fascinating account of the latest, most sensational crime that has captured the national attention. St. Martin's is the publisher of bestselling true crime author and crime journalist Kieran Crowley, who explores the dark, deadly links between a prominent Manhattan surgeon and the disappearance of his wife fifteen years earlier in THE SURGEON'S WIFE. Suzy Spencer's BREAKING POINT guides readers through the tortuous twists and turns in the case of Andrea Yates, the Houston mother who drowned her five young children in the family's bathtub. In Edgar Award-nominated DARK DREAMS, legendary FBI profiler Roy Hazelwood and bestselling crime author Stephen G. Michaud shine light on the inner workings of America's most violent and depraved murderers. In the book you now hold, DEAD ENDS, you will take a sobering look at a female serial killer, in an account written by Michael Reynolds, the reporter who broke the story.

St. Martin's True Crime Library gives you the stories behind the headlines. Our authors take you right to the scene of the crime and into the minds of the most notorious murderers to show you what really makes them tick. St. Martin's True Crime Library paperbacks are better than the most terrifying thriller, because it's all true! The next time you want a crackling good read, make sure it's got the St. Martin's True Crime Library logo on the spine—you'll be up all night!

Charles E. Spicer, Jr.
Executive Editor, St. Martin's True Crime Library

The black vulture cocked its raw head toward the intruders as they high-stepped through the dump, over shards of ruined Sheetrock, ghost-ridden mattresses, and eviscerated appliances. Fear overran the bird's hunger as it spread its mite-ridden wings and beat a retreat from the dirty red carpet runner shrouding its meal. The men it watched cringed as the septic stench of decay flared through the clearing. Expecting to find a dead deer or some other wildlife carrion, one of the men reached toward the carpet and froze.

Protruding from the remnant was a blackened crab-fingered human hand . . .

DEAD ENDS

MICHAEL REYNOLDS

St. Martin's Paperbacks

ISBN: 0-312-98418-9

Printed in the United States of America

Warner edition / October 1992
St. Martin's Paperbacks edition / January 2004

10 9 8 7 6 5 4 3 2 1

Acknowledgments

This book would not have been possible without the generous cooperation and assistance provided by the following individuals and agencies.

Captain Steve Binegar, Marion County Sheriff's Office
Sergeant Bruce Munster
Major Dan Henry
Investigator David Taylor
Investigator John Tilley

Sergeant Jake Ehrhart, Volusia County Sheriff's Office
Investigator Larry Horzepa
Sergeant Robert Kelley
Investigator Jim Lau

Investigator Tom Muck, Pasco County Sheriff's Office

Ward Schwoob, Florida Department of Law Enforcement

Detective Sergeant Leonard Goretski, Michigan State Police

John Tanner, State Attorney, Seventh Circuit
David Damore, Assistant State Attorney, Seventh Circuit
Sean Daley, Assistant State Attorney, Seventh Circuit
Rick Dilley, Investigator

Brad King, State Attorney, Fifth Circuit
Ric Ridgway, Assistant State Attorney, Fifth Circuit
David Eddy, Assistant State Attorney, Fifth Circuit
and especially, Karen Combs

Tricia Jenkins, Chief Assistant Public Defender, Fifth
    Circuit
Billy Nolas, Assistant Public Defender, Fifth Circuit
William Miller, Assistant Public Defender, Fifth Circuit
Don Sanchez, Investigator, Public Defender's office

The Honorable Uriel Blount, Jr., Seventh Judicial Circuit,
    State of Florida (Retired)

Steven Glazer, Gainesville
Arlene Pralle

Dayle Hinman, Florida Department of Law Enforcement

Steven Egger, Sangamon State University
Elliott Leyton, Memorial University
Candice Skrapec, John Jay College of Criminal Justice
Roy Hazelwood, FBI Behavioral Science Unit
Eric Hickey, California State University
Paul Gribben, Daytona Beach
Vera Ivkolivich, Harbor Oaks
Cannonball

Laura Kauffman, *Ocala Star-Banner*
Chuck Bartels, *Ocala Star-Banner*
Linda Sawyer
Mark McNamara

For extraordinary support, sometimes beyond limits of tolerance, I wish to thank . . .

Julie Vorman and Joanne Kenen (good idea, Joanne)
Reuters, Miami/Caribbean Bureau
James Quine
Jim Morgan
David Dowling

Special thanks to my fierce agent, Jane Dystel, my gracious and understanding editors, Fredda Isaacson and Rick Horgan, and the Legal Department at Warner Books, who came through when I needed them.

And to Rhonda, who kept it going when . . .

Author's Note

This book is the result of reporting that began in November 1990 for Reuters. I utilized scores of personal interviews with investigators, witnesses, prosecutors, defense attorneys, and crime-lab technicians, as well as thousands of pages of police reports, narratives, and interviews, plus criminal records, school records, psychiatric evaluations, prison documents, medical examiners' reports, and media accounts. I viewed Aileen Wuornos's videotaped confession numerous times prior to, and after, attending her trial. All this was filtered through sixteen years' experience in crime reporting, much of which involved serial and mass murder.

All circumstances and quotations throughout this book are directly from the record, excepting two chapters—"Predator" and "Two Days in November." These chapters are based on statements by Wuornos, Moore, and witnesses, and conversations with homicide investigators, medical examiners, and crime-scene technicians. Aileen Wuornos left no witnesses to the homicides she has confessed to. Only eight people had direct knowledge of what happened on those separate occasions. Seven of them are dead. Ms. Wuornos's public statements, including her confessions and courtroom testimony, often played loose with the facts and severely strained credibility. By incorporating her versions of the events with investigative and forensic evidence, it was possible to reconstruct those scenes to a reasonable degree of accuracy.

Aileen Wuornos did not cooperate in the writing of this book. My many attempts to interview Ms. Wuornos came up empty, except for one occasion in the Marion County Courthouse just after she had pled to the murders of Troy Burress and Dick Humphreys. For most of the period between January 1991 and May 1992, requests for interviews with Aileen Wuornos were reviewed by her adoptive mother, Mrs. Arlene Pralle. Mrs. Pralle refused my requests for an interview, perhaps because I offered no monetary incentive, perhaps because it would be in conflict with her own projects, perhaps because Mrs. Pralle and Ms. Wuornos feared this book would not be sympathetic to their interests.

—June 1992

Prologue

After the sheriff's deputy unlocked the restraints holding her thin wrists, she lifted her hands to her breasts, the sleeves of her cranberry-colored jumpsuit sliding down her pale arms as the deputy slipped the chain from around her waist. She looked up at the judge seated at the bench above her and gave him a loopy smile, shuffled a sheaf of notebook paper on the podium facing him, and squinted at the pages.

Here at the center of this small oval courtroom in Ocala, Florida, her back to her audience, she felt all eyes upon her—the eyes of the state prosecutors, the eyes of her former defense counsel, the eyes of the cop who had taken her confessions, the eyes of her victims' widows and children, the eyes of her new "mother," the eyes of the curious, the eyes of reporters, and, through the lenses of the cameras, the eyes of the big world beyond. She was in the center, at last. On the other end of the stick. They all wanted to listen to her now. Now she was on top, she was running things . . . *her way*. And she was going to let them all have it. Just like she did with those seven bastards she'd left in the woods.

". . . All I'd like to say is: I killed him. I straight-out killed him." Then she laughed, a short stacatto. "I just right flat-out killed him. I shot him with a .22-caliber nine-shot pistol. I straight-out killed this guy. . . .

". . . But if I wanted to· just go out and kill, there would've been hundreds. You see, everyone had taken off for Saudi Arabia, all my regulars, and I had no customers and I had to get strangers. . . .

". . . I'm not a man-hating lesbian who only killed to rob, robbed to kill. This is a downright fabrication, full of fairy tales and very far from the truth, all for a fast buck. A sick and vile made-up horror flick these law-enforcement officers have created. They've already set it up for a real profound box-office hit. I'm fed up with their slanders, libels just so the public would hate my guts for their multi-million-dollar movie deal. Trust me, this movie is a lie!"

She rambled on, laying the blame for the death sentences on her head at the feet of her family, her ex-lover, her defense team, the cops, the witnesses, the media, the prosecutors, the jury, the Gulf War, pollution, and bad luck.

"Before I'm strapped in the electric chair, please please listen, for I am speaking the truth . . . You are going to crucify me, which is exactly what you did. I knew they would lie, cheat, and twist everything around . . . total defamation and slanders galore. I am not a murderer . . . by definition, murder is willful killing . . . I didn't take their honor cards. I didn't keep their cars and fence them off. I'm not a serial killer. I've killed a series of men but it was in self-defense. It wasn't premeditated design. My only premeditation was to go out and make another dollar. It wasn't in my mind to go out and kill a guy.

"I'm just waiting for my Sherlock Holmes to crack this conspiracy wide open . . . I hope these no-good cops see prison in the near future. I will seek to be electrocuted as soon as possible. I want to get off the fucking evil planet. I've never seen so much evil. I was a nice person, I've been treated like dirt . . . I just can't wait to leave. I'll be up in heaven when y'all are rotting in hell."

ONE

Mallory

On December 13, 1989, under a cold sun fast escaping the western sky, three scavengers met in a clearing punched from the thick woods northwest of Daytona Beach, Florida. James Jano Davis and Jimmy Bonchi were scrounging for scrap metal or some other marketable debris. The buzzard was there to dine.

The three were trying to make it through the winter, which in Florida can be particularly cruel when those expecting its usual subtropical hospitality are surprised by sudden frigid temperatures. When the oranges frost, even migrating birds appear confused. Unprepared for arctic nights among the palms, they either wing it farther down the peninsula in hopes of warmth or simply shiver in Kmart parking lots, chirping for a handout.

The black vulture cocked its raw head toward the intruders as they high-stepped through shards of ruined Sheetrock, ghost-ridden mattresses, and eviscerated appliances. Fear overran the bird's hunger as it spread its mite-ridden wings and beat a retreat from the dirty red carpet runner shrouding its meal. Bonchi and Davis cringed as the septic stench of decay flared through the clearing. Expecting to find a dead deer or some other wildlife carrion, Davis reached toward the carpet and froze. Protruding from the remnant was a blackened crab-fingered human hand.

Twenty minutes after the call came in to the Volusia County Sheriff's Office, Major Case Unit Investigator Larry Horzepa bumped his Ford along the rutted trail squirreling off US 1 less than a half mile from Interstate 95 and through the thicket of pine and palmetto to where Davis and Bonchi sat in Deputy Melady's vehicle scrawling their witness statements. When his supervisor, Sergeant Jake Ehrhart, had called him with the report of the body, Horzepa had had an idea who the John Doe might be. The detective stepped out of the heat of his car, and his glasses fogged. He had to wipe the lenses before he was able to read the witnesses' statements Melady handed him.

The first, Bonchi's account, was an agitated parade of crude markings, peppered with exclamation points.

> I James A Bonchi & James Davis were out skraping mettle's and exploring throw the woods and seen a Buzzard and, trompeding through the woods we smelled stink! I was off troming through the Palms when my friend yelled for me and sed look! I saw a tarp with a hand hanging out of It!

Horzepa had to read it again. "What's 't-r-o-m-p-e-d-i-n-g,' do you suppose? 'Trom-ped-ing.'"

"Tromping," said Melady. "He said that. Tromping."

Horzepa read the second man's version.

Me and Jim B. were out looking in the woods for steel, iron, aluminum to take to the junk yard. We were walking around looking for scrap. We saw this buzzard and was wondering if it was a dead deer or somethin bonch walked by it and Is saw the tarp laying on the ground I didn't know what was under it at first and then I saw the hand I showed Jim and we ran for the trck and went to the gass station and called in. we wer 1 mi. north of US 1 and on the west side about 50 yards in the woods.

"I like Bonchi's better. More drama," said Horzepa. Melady smiled. Horzepa looked over his shoulder as two cars rumbled in, their headlamps tossing splashes of light over the darkening palmettos and dead refrigerators.

Sergeant Bob Kelley and Sergeant Jake Ehrhart, supervisor of the Major Case Unit, climbed out of the cars. Horzepa shivered as he noticed Kelley's heavy jacket. In the lengthening shadows, the temperature was rapidly falling. Ehrhart shook from the chill and said, "Look, let's get back in the car until the crime lab gets here."

"I'm fine," grinned Kelley, a second-generation cop. "You guys cold?"

Ignoring their partner's deadpan dig, Horzepa and Ehrhart climbed into the front seat of the car and closed the doors. Kelley shrugged and joined them.

"What do you think? Is it Mallory's body?" asked Ehrhart, turning to Horzepa.

"Could be. We'll have to wait and look at him when FDLE lifts the rug."

Twelve days earlier, a local resident out walking his dogs had noticed a Cadillac backed into a fire trail off John Anderson Drive in Ormond Beach, just north of Daytona. Suspicious, the man put in a call to the sheriff's office. Sergeant John Bonnevier arrived to find a 1977 beige Coupe de Ville abandoned among the palmettos. The Caddy had tinted windows, a University of Florida "Fighting Gators" tag affixed to its front bumper and a Florida license plate, GDH-34Q, on the rear. Bonnevier radioed in a DMV check and found that the car belonged to a Richard Mallory of Clearwater, Florida. There were no keys in the car, but just east of the Caddy were scattered a wallet, several papers, two plastic tumblers, a bottle half full of vodka, and some condoms. Apparently someone had tried to bury the items in a sandy divot but had failed to finish the job. In the wallet were Mallory's driver's license and invoices from Mallory Electronics, with a Palm Harbor, Florida, address. Bonnevier called for a tow truck and then contacted the Major Case Unit.

Horzepa got the call, gave it the case number 89-12-00185, and then teletyped the Pinellas County Sheriff's Office, the jurisdiction covering Mallory's home and business addresses, for a check on him. Detective Bonnie Richway took Horzepa's request but was unable to locate Mallory. She called back with a physical description, however, including his clothing, and Horzepa added the case to his list of headaches. Since October the Major Case Unit had had five homicides on its plate, and each investigator was handling nine or ten sex crimes, most involving children.

The lights from an approaching car bounced off the rearview mirror. "That's Lau," said Ehrhart. "Let's go ahead, get the pictures and do a canvass."

Kelley and Horzepa got out and ducked under the yellow tape surrounding the clearing and began searching the immediate area around the carpet runner. Ehrhart signaled Investigator James Lau to join him in the car for a briefing. Lau slung a 35-mm camera around his neck, picked up a Polaroid from the front seat, and walked over to Ehrhart's unit.

"Get what you can now," said Ehrhart. "The FDLE van that's coming has the lights, so just wait until it gets here to video. It's getting dark."

Lau, crime-scene specialist for the Major Case Unit, went about his work with his typical bemused alertness, inured as he was to the grisly and often nauseating circumstances surrounding a homicide. Systematically he documented the setting and its red-carpeted focal point with the Polaroid, the 35-mm, and a tape recorder.

Darkness had enveloped the scene by the time Florida Department of Law Enforcement agents Kelly May and Dan Radcliffe arrived. They parked their van and turned on the spotlights, washing down the clearing with brilliant white light. Lau retrieved his video camera from his car, hooked up its power pack, and joined May, who was photographing the scene while Radcliffe took measurements with a tape.

"That's it, Jake," said May, as he put his camera back in the van and took out two pairs of surgical gloves. "Let's take a look." He reached down and lifted the carpet.

A visible cloud of hissing steam rose up from the decomposing body as its gases struck the frigid air. Two pieces of cardboard covered the chest and hips. May carefully lifted each of them and put them to the side.

Lau rolled more video tape, then shut down the camera and returned to his tape recording.

"The body is facing east and the feet to the west. It is face down with the left arm under the body in the chest area. The head, neck, and portions of the left arm are decomposed and crawling with maggots and other bugs. There is no hair or skin on the skull."

May and Radcliffe crouched and together turned the body over onto its back. The skull remained connected to the spine; but their movement dislodged the lower jaw and a pair of dentures spilled out. From the collarbone up there was nothing but black decay. "He bled from there," said Horzepa, pointing to the upper chest. "And up. The insects follow the blood."

"You think this is Mallory?" asked Ehrhart.

Horzepa noted the clothing. White short-sleeved sport shirt, blue jeans with brown belt. Blue socks and brown loafers. The right shoe was off, lying next to the foot. He stepped closer and looked at the false teeth. "From the clothes and what Richway gave me, I'm at least ninety percent sure that this is Richard Mallory."

Lau began gathering evidence into brown paper bags. A hair sample near the body. The right brown shoe. Scraps of paper.

Horzepa noticed that the front pockets of the dead man's jeans were pulled out. "I sure as hell hope this is Mallory, otherwise we got a bigger problem."

"Okay," said Kelley. "There's nothing much more to do out here for us. Where's Jake?"

"Back in his car, where I should be," said Horzepa. "Damn, Bob. It's like fifteen degrees out here. Shit. We need prints and we're not getting those tonight. Lau?"

"Tomorrow. At the autopsy. Can't do it out here. Not in this condition. Gee, it's really getting cold."

"It's not so bad," disagreed Kelley. "Not bad. *This* isn't cold."

"Goddammit, Kelley, you're from Boston."

The three investigators walked back to Ehrhart's car to wait for the livery service to pick up the body. At seven o'clock a Cadillac hearse slid through the pines and palmettos at the direction of a uniformed deputy. John Doe was carefully bagged and lifted aboard. Horzepa left Ehrhart's car and carefully stepped through the trash and scrub oak to his own vehicle. He looked up to see the hearse's red taillights softly bouncing in the darkness as it left the killing ground for the county morgue.

The next morning Larry Horzepa was again on the phone to Detective Bonnie Richway back across the state in Tampa. He wanted everything else she could get on Mallory. He had been arrested for drunken driving, she told Horzepa, and there were latent prints that she would fax to Volusia immediately. Mallory, she said, wore wire-frame glasses and had a full set of dentures and gray hair. Horzepa asked Richway to secure both Mallory's home and business addresses as crime scenes should the prints confirm the identification.

Upon receiving Mallory's latent prints, Investigator Lau took them to the medical examiner's office in Daytona Beach, where Dr. Arthur Botting and John Doe were waiting in the autopsy room. The pathologist and his assistant removed the dead man's shirt, a dull parchment color shadowed with bloodstains, and Botting probed the chest area, noting three small-caliber bullet holes. Botting looked up through his bushy eyebrows and spoke to Lau in a broad New England accent.

"We already have a projectile. It was lying free in the shroud. We need X rays to find these others."

The body was then trundled off for pictures. This done, Dr. Botting scanned the negatives, opened the chest, and recovered three rounds. All three appeared to be .22 caliber. One round had ripped through the victim's right arm and lodged against a rib just below the armpit. A second bullet had torn through the right side of the chest, the third had entered the left side just below the nipple.

"The one through the arm didn't do much," Botting observed. "But these others tore his lungs. Tremendous hemorrhaging. The hole on the right side allowed pressurized air into the lung and his respiration went. The lungs collapsed. It would have taken anywhere from ten to twenty minutes for him to die. He was trying desperately to breathe."

"What about the other bullet?" asked Lau.

"Well, maybe somewhere up here in the neck. But there's no tissue left. No way of telling. There was no wounding to the spine, which is just about all there is now up here." Botting swept a broad, gloved hand across the shriveled neck of John Doe. "But you might check the shirt. It appears to have a bullet hole on the right side of the collar." The doctor tapped the location on the side of his neck.

While Dr. Botting completed the autopsy and labeled the crime a homicide, Lau collected the shirt and bullets and bagged them.

Getting the fingerprints was a more difficult problem. Due to advanced decomposition, the skin of the fingers slid from the tissue, so the doctor had to remove the hands, and Lau found himself bagging them, heat-sealing the bags to lock in the odor, and placing them in an Igloo cooler. After phoning ahead to FDLE agent Kelly May, Lau toted the cooler out to his car and drove the 120 miles to the FDLE lab in Orlando.

Lifting prints in such circumstances can be done any of three ways. One: carefully slipping the skin from the dead hand to leave a morbid glove into which the investigator can insert his own fingers and ink and roll a set of prints. Two: injecting water with a hypodermic needle into the slack finger to inflate it like a water balloon before attempting a lift. May chose the third option instead. Taking the hands from their bags he floated them in a heavy saline solution for a couple of hours to tighten up the skin, figuring that at least one print could be rolled from one of the severed hands. Since Lau had been the designated glove model, he was relieved when May succeeded in making a print with the first roll. Then May compared the latents from the body with those faxed over from Horzepa at the Major Case Unit.

"You got a match, Lau."

Lau immediately phoned Horzepa with the news, cleaned the ink off Mallory's hand, rebagged it with the other hand, and dropped them back into the cooler. He had to return them quickly to the medical examiner's office for reattachment, so that the body could be released to the funeral home. In an unmarked car, Lau sped up Interstate 4 and into the radar field of a Florida Highway Patrol trooper, who immediately pulled the investigator over.

Lau handed over his license and registration to the trooper, who then asked, "What's the hurry?"

"I've got these hands here. Got to get them back."

"What?"

"Here," the ever-friendly Lau offered, picking up the cooler from beside him and opening it in the trooper's face. "These hands here."

The stench flew up into the trooper's face.

"Good God!" The trooper took a quick step backward. "Jeez, you guys . . . get them out of here. Go on."

"Okay. Thank you, trooper." Lau smiled and shut the box of hands. He drove the rest of the way back to Operations just as fast as he thought necessary. If another FHP wanted to take a peek, he was welcome to it.

With the John Doe now positively identified as Richard Mallory, Horzepa and Kelley returned to where Mallory's car had been discovered, and canvassed the neighborhood. They learned from a local man whose daily morning walk took him along John Anderson Drive that Mallory's Cadillac had not been parked on the fire trail the morning of December 1. Sometime during that day whoever had killed Mallory must have driven his car to Ormond and left it parked in broad daylight until it was discovered at 3:15.

Horzepa went to the compound where Mallory's car had been towed. As no keys had been found, Horzepa called for a locksmith to open the trunk. Although there was nothing inside, Horzepa noticed in the carpeting near the spare tire an imprint of what could have been a toolbox. From inside the glove compartment, Horzepa pulled a bonding ticket that showed Mallory had secured the release of a white male by the name of Michael Rosenblum, arrested in Pinellas County for cocaine possession and carrying a concealed weapon. Horzepa phoned Detective Richway, described the bond ticket, and asked her to run a check. "I'll be over in a couple of days with Kelley," he told her.

On December 18, Horzepa and Kelley left the operations center outside Daytona and hooked Interstate 4 west to Clearwater and the Pinellas County Sheriff's Office. Detective Richway was ready for them. Horzepa and Kelley sat back as Richway detailed what she had on Mallory.

"This guy isn't easy to put together. Number one: he was very paranoid. He changed the locks at his apartment eight to ten times in the last three years. He didn't have any friends. But," said Richway, "he was very much into porno and the topless-bar scene. Flashed a lot of money when he was in these places. Big tipper. Heavy drinker."

"What about Rosenblum and this bond ticket?" Horzepa interrupted.

"He's got a string of arrests up and down the Gulf Coast. He says he worked for Mallory until six months ago. Says Mallory was mental."

"What about Mallory's girlfriend? Jackie Davis."

"Ex-girlfriend. She said she'd dated him for about a year and a half. Just broke up. Mallory told her he'd been arrested in Maryland when he was nineteen. Said he became involved with a woman who was separated from her Arabic husband. The husband came back and it ended. Then, Mallory said he was attacked by some guys and part of his ear was cut off. That's why he moved to Florida. Davis also said Mallory told her he'd been married five times and had a son, but never saw him."

Horzepa thought, This guy just isn't going to be easy to put together. There were too many options opening up. The bond receipt on Rosenblum suggested drug and gun connections. Then there was Mallory's paranoia, the locks, and the topless joints.

A steady rain out of the Gulf fell on the detectives as they walked up to investigate Mallory's apartment on Oak Trail in Clearwater. "That's one of his vans," said Richway, pointing to a maroon vehicle with yellow police tape across its doors. "He's got two of them." Horzepa, Richway, and Kelley waited as the Crime Scene Unit pulled their vacuum cleaners, Luma Lite, and print kits out of their van and lugged them up to the door. They slipped on their booties and white gloves and set to work. The unit finally came out with ten bags of sweepings and three latent-print cards. The Luma Lite had detected no blood. Horzepa and Kelley then went in.

While the apartment was being photographed, Horzepa and Kelley set about piecing together the habits of the man who had once lived here. In the living room they found a collection of X-rated videos, all of them dubbed, plus a stash of off-the-rack soft-core magazines and personal photographs of unidentified naked women. In the kitchen a Smirnoff vodka bottle, blackened from dusting, stood on the counter. Another fifth of vodka was found in the freezer. On the kitchen counter next to the wall phone was a scrap of paper with two scribbled phone numbers. Horzepa pocketed the paper while Kelley stacked the videos, magazines, and photographs. They bagged Mallory's checkbook, a set of keys, and miscellaneous papers and then toted the lot out to their car. The next stop was Mallory Electronics.

Jeff Davis, the son of Mallory's ex-girlfriend, and a

one-time Mallory employee, was waiting with the key
when the detectives arrived at the small shopping strip
where Mallory had his repair shop. A white van with a
sign reading MALLORY ELECTRONICS was parked directly
in front of the shop.

Inside, there was no evidence of foul play. The Crime
Scene Unit took photographs while Horzepa and Kelley
collected repair slips along with the customers' names
and telephone numbers. Richway remarked that there
had been a number of angry notes taped to the front
door of Mallory's shop when she first came by the
place, all of them from irate clients demanding to know
when their repairs would be done.

After collecting Mallory's papers, Horzepa and Kelley
canvassed the strip mall. A veterinarian told them he
had seen Mallory on the morning of November 30, driving off in his maroon van.

Back at the Pinellas County Sheriff's Office, the two
Volusia County investigators sat at a table cluttered with
the debris of Mallory's life. Horzepa shuffled through
the papers and found a service-call receipt to a customer
by the name of Franco, dated 11-30-89.

"What it looks like here," said Horzepa, "is that Mallory took the white van on the call, came back, dropped
off the receipt, then went home in the maroon."

"It also looks like he was seriously in debt." Kelley
shifted through a stack of Mallory's mail as he spoke.
"He owed thirty-eight hundred dollars in back rent."

Horzepa pulled up another sheaf of paper. "Repair
orders. Uncompleted. Let's see . . . one, two, three . . ."
As Horzepa counted, Kelley said, "Oh-kay. IRS. Well,
Richard doesn't have to worry about this audit now." He
waved the notices and put them aside.

"One hundred and twenty. One hundred and twenty back orders. The oldest is May 1989. Not diligent."

"Diligent? The guy's life was a goddamn disaster. He was floating. The only thing he was serious about was this." Kelley tapped the stack of porno videos. "The guy was pussy-crazed."

"Okay. Then that's where we look."

Horzepa and Kelley spent the next day taking statements from Mallory's employees and Jacqueline Davis. They learned Mallory had an unusually erratic business system. He would backlog repair orders and then hire a squad of repairmen to clear the shelves. They would work until all the jobs were done, and then he would pay them out and let them go. No one worked steadily, not even Mallory. From his former girlfriend they soon learned why.

"He would be gone for days at a time. Just take off and you wouldn't see him. Then, he would just be back. It was impossible. I couldn't deal with the porno and the strip bars. He drank heavily and smoked dope. He'd have a bottle in the car and two tumblers, you know? Not constantly . . . he'd be all right and then he'd go off on a tear. He'd be off to the strip clubs. I never went with him. A year and a half of that. I broke it off around Thanksgiving. He didn't trust anyone. Never. You know about the locks? Changing his locks? He was just weird about things. Always had this black briefcase. Never, ever went anywhere without it. Always had cash in it. We'd go to a restaurant. He'd put it in the trunk."

Horzepa interrupted. "Excuse me. I want to ask you about some things he might take with him besides this briefcase. You know, if he were taking off on one of his trips?"

"He had some cameras. One was a Polaroid. The other a 35-mm. He might have those. An electric razor. He used a hair dryer. And those tumblers. Vodka. If he was on the road he'd have those."

"Any idea why he might go to Daytona? Family?"

"No. As far as I know, no. I can't think why he'd go to Daytona. Look, he'd just take off. Nobody knew where he'd gone. And he never talked about it either."

In response to further questioning, Jackie reiterated the story they'd heard earlier about Mallory's former marriages and his estranged son.

"Is there anything else you can tell us about him?"

Jackie Davis shifted in her chair and looked away from the detectives. "Well, you know he was in trouble when he was younger. When he was around seventeen or eighteen. I don't know any of this but what he said. He said he did some dumb thing like go into this house once. There was a woman in the house and she got scared. He . . . ended up in jail."

"Where was this?"

"It was Maryland."

"He just went to jail?"

Davis sighed. "No. He said he was in prison. Burglary was the charge. But that was when he was very young."

Horzepa didn't show any concern as he made notes on a yellow legal pad.

"He went into some kind of hospital after that. Or when he was in the prison. He said it was an experimental program."

"This   program . . . like   a . . . alcohol   thing . . . drugs . . . or what was it?"

"No." Davis raised her head stiffly. "I think it was some sort of sexual . . . problem kind of . . . he was just very young."

Horzepa looked down at his notes and then gave Davis his reassuring smile, the one that said, "Oh, that's nothing. No big thing." He glanced over to Kelley. "Well, if Sergeant Kelley doesn't have anything more . . ."

Kelley shook his head.

"Thank you, Ms. Davis." Horzepa stood up and extended his hand to the lady.

"Are you seeing Jeff today?" Davis looked from one detective to the other.

"Yes, ma'am."

Davis's son, Jeff, had gotten his job with Mallory as a result of his mother's relationship with the victim. "I was probably the employee he had for the longest time. And he dumped me the day he left, after my mom broke off with him. Just left a message on my answering machine."

"When was that?"

"The thirtieth. The day he went off to Daytona. Had to have left somewhere between seven and ten-thirty that night. Just fired me. I wasn't really surprised. You didn't know what he was going to do, but I figured after they split up, that was it."

"Did you know a Michael Rosenblum? Worked for Mallory?"

"I don't know. There was a guy came in three days before Richard disappeared. Said he used to work there."

Horzepa riffled through an accordion file and pulled

up Rosenblum's booking photograph. "Is this the guy?"

"Yeah. He came in and talked to Richard."

"On the twenty-seventh?"

"Yeah."

"Any idea what it was about?"

"No, they went off and talked."

While Horzepa and Kelley retrieved Jeff Davis's tape from his answering machine and then had his photograph taken, Detective Richway managed to turn up Mallory's sister out in Amarillo, Texas. Dulcie Turbin was contacted by Texas deputies and advised of her brother's death. She told them neither she nor anyone else in the family had heard from Richard in years. He had just dropped off the planet as far as they could tell.

Back in Daytona, Lau was making the rounds of the pawn shops—a daunting labor since Daytona Beach seemed to have one every six blocks or so. The cops knew that Mallory had had a suitcase and briefcase with him as well as a Radio Shack Micronta radar detector. None of these were found in the abandoned vehicle.

Right after the New Year, Horzepa and Kelley drove back to Clearwater. They took a hair sample from Jackie Davis to check against the various hair fibers that had been collected from Mallory's Cadillac by the FDLE technicians. At the same time, they showed Davis a batch of Polaroids from the dead man's home collection. All were of white females. Davis identified one as a forty-year-old Clearwater nurse. The nurse told the investigators that she had met Richard back in 1988 through a local dating service, but had broken off with him when she learned about his relationship with Jackie.

Horzepa got the name of the dating service, contacted its president, and asked for a membership list.

Then a call came in from a Dunedin, Florida, police detective who advised Horzepa that Rosenblum had been involved in an arrest some time ago. A .22-caliber revolver had been taken from him.

Horzepa and Kelley spent the next day canvassing Rosenblum's apartment complex and a nightclub called New York, New York, where Rosenblum hung out. When the detectives flashed Rosenblum's photograph nearly everyone recognized him, but no one had much more to offer. On January 4, Maryann Beatty, president of the M.C.I. dating club, handed over a list of one thousand members. Horzepa and Kelley told Beatty to let the female members know that the sheriff's office would be in contact with them in the near future.

Out in the car, Kelley flipped the pages of the list. "It really is a thousand, Larry," he said, as his finger trailed down to the bottom of the last page. "One thousand. Easily."

"Well, given Mr. Mallory's habits, there is a distinct possibility he went out with at least half of them."

"Don't say that, Larry. That's not a good thing to even think."

"Okay. Two hundred and fifty. Piece of cake."

Their next stop was Jersey Jim Towers Electronics out on the south side of Clearwater, where Mike Rosenblum was supposedly employed. Jersey Jim led the detectives back to his office and pulled Rosenblum's time cards for November and December. Horzepa shuffled through the cards and pulled aside the critical dates.

11-30-89 (Thursday) 10:10 A.M.–6:48 P.M.
12-01-89 (Friday) 8:58 A.M.–7:14 P.M.
12-04-89 (Monday) 9:52 A.M.–6:44 P.M.

When Rosenblum came to the door, Kelley glanced over at Jersey Jim, who got up and left the room.

An hour later, Horzepa and Kelley walked back to their car with a plastic Baggie of Rosenblum's hair, and his handwritten statement. Kelley read while Horzepa took the wheel.

"It's not much. But with the time cards, it's enough for Rosenblum to skate off for the time being. Says he called Mallory about a job. Hired the same day. Worked for him six to eight months. Quit because of Mallory's erratic behavior."

"Think we've got a theme there, Bob?"

"The erratic Mr. Mallory."

"Well, Mallory bailed Rosenblum out on that coke charge and then fired him for getting arrested. Paranoid about the bust. Then Rosenblum says Mallory 'exhibited disgust with his personal life and business endeavors.' Says he left for Orlando and didn't come back to open the shop. Left Rosenblum in the parking lot waiting all day. Yes. The erratic Mr. Mallory. What's the deal with this guy? We're getting nothing dirty on him. He's just like . . . paranoid and pussy-crazy, with bad business habits."

"Yeah. And dead." Horzepa said drily. "It's a lifestyle kind of thing."

The weekend of January 6 and 7 the newspapers in Tampa and Clearwater ran a story on Mallory's killing. Horzepa had done interviews with reporters before leaving, in hopes some civilian might kick up a new lead. When he and Kelley returned to the sheriff's office in Clearwater on Monday, there was a payoff.

A Ms. Snyder had read the article on Mallory's murder and called in the name and phone number of Mallory's ex-wife. Horzepa immediately tapped in the digits, only to get an answering machine: "Linda Nusbaum is not at home right now . . ." Horzepa left a message, then began flipping through the box of evidence from Mallory's apartment until he came to a manila envelope. He opened it and shook out its clutch of papers, spreading them across the table.

There it was. A small page from a notepad that had been found on Mallory's kitchen counter. On it was a phone number and a name—CHASTITY. Horzepa checked with the phone company and found that the number was listed to Alicia Wright. Then Linda Nusbaum called. The former Mrs. Mallory told Horzepa that she hadn't seen Richard for several months, and then proceeded to support what the detective had learned from Davis— Mallory was obsessed with pornography, was extremely paranoid, drank heavily, and smoked a ton of weed. "Sometimes he would just hop in the car and take off for Maryland," said Nusbaum. "Wouldn't give it a thought. Just take off."

"Was he the type who would pick up hitchhikers?"

"Sure, he would do that. If they were female. You know?"

"Yes, ma'am. I think I do."

"I can't see Richard picking up some guy. He didn't even have men friends. You know about changing his locks?"

"Yes, ma'am."

"No way he'd pick up some strange guy. But he'd definitely stop for a woman. That was his problem. You know?"

Back in Daytona a witness came forward saying he'd seen a maroon car leaving the scene where Mallory's body was found. Bob Goodwyn told deputies he had seen a man driving the car out of the woods around December 1. He said that there had been a woman in the car and that they both had appeared nervous. Despite questioning, Goodwyn could not remember any further details. He agreed to hypnosis and came down to the Volusia County Sheriff's Office operations center on January 18. The session resulted in Goodwyn's recalling a maroon two-door Dodge Aries with a maroon interior, black-wall tires with wire-spoked wheels, and a Florida tag from Volusia County, numbered GFE 723.

A check through the computer revealed no such tag. Cal Eden, the hypnotist conducting the session, said the numbers were likely mixed up. "It's probably all turned around some way," said the Daytona Svengali. "On the whole, I'd say we had a huge success here."

Horzepa and Kelley were less enthusiastic. They knew this one was in for a long haul. The killer or killers were not going to be sprung from an entranced civilian's sublimated recall. Nothing but basics were going to break this case out. Somewhere in the scrambled array of Mallory's paranoid and porno-fixated lifestyle was the key. Horzepa called assistant state attorney David Damore and asked for a court order to obtain Mallory's mail. The young, intensely thorough prosecutor was known for having the instincts and demeanor of a

well-trained Doberman. He immediately responded.
Cops liked Damore's style.

On January 23, Horzepa and Kelley were back at the
Clearwater Embassy Suites. After checking in, they
drove to Mallory's local postal station to check on his
mail. Nothing was there. The detectives made arrangements to forward the victim's mail to their office in
Daytona and then headed for the Pinellas sheriff's headquarters. There they began calling numbers gathered
from slips of paper found in Mallory's apartment. All
the numbers were annotated with female names.

The first one up was for Kimberly Guy, Danielle. The
number turned up her stepfather, a Tampa cab driver
who gave Horzepa Kimberly Guy's new address. The
detectives were there within half an hour.

They arrived at North Bay village and were checked
out by a guard at the security gate. Kelley surveyed the
landscaped townhouses and gave a low whistle. "She's
not doing so bad for a topless dancer." When she met
them at the door and invited them in, Horzepa noted the
furnishings and stereo equipment. *No, not too bad at all.*
She led them to the living room.

Horzepa and Kelley sat on the couch and put a tape
recorder and their notebooks on a glass coffee table.
Guy took a chair across from them.

"Ms. Guy . . . is it Kimberly or Danielle?"

"Uh, Kim. Danielle is my stage name."

"Okay. Kim, could you tell us when you met Richard
Mallory?"

"I don't know . . . last year. He came into the 2001

Odyssey . . . that's where I used to dance. I don't work there now . . . but, okay . . . Mallory. The first time he spent about a hundred and fifty dollars . . . for dances. Wanted me to date him. I told him I was gay."

"Kim, when you say date you don't mean like go out for a drink or dinner or . . . "

"No. Sex. You know. Have sex."

"For money."

"Well, yeah."

"Okay. And then you said no. You refused."

"Yeah, I didn't want to. I don't do that . . . I mean, I'm gay. I live with somebody. I've got a girlfriend."

"You don't have sex with customers at the club. Is that what you're saying?"

Guy turned in the big chair and then sat back. She looked at Horzepa. His eyebrows were lifted. He waited for the answer he knew she had to give.

"No. I'm saying I didn't want to. I've done that. Sure. I'm saying, when he first asked me I said no. He kept at it. He said we could go over to his shop in Clearwater, some TV shop, and do it there. I said I'd do some lap dances."

"Lap dances."

"You know, get over them . . . you know, get them off in the club. They sit in a chair. Mallory was constantly hitting on me and the other dancers. He was like a permanent fixture. But, he always had cash. A couple hundred or so all the time."

"So, he offers you a hundred and fifty dollars."

"No, not this last time. The night you're taking about . . . November. Last day in November?"

"Yes."

"No. He said he'd give us . . . me . . . a TV and VCR for some dances at his shop. I said, 'Okay, if you bring some cash. So, he gave me fifty bucks and a nineteen-inch Magnavox and a Fisher VCR . . . took me out there and back here. I don't have a car. We went in his van. Kind of red or maroon. Then when we were done, brought me back here, hooked up the Magnavox and VCR. And left. Wasn't here more than twenty, twenty-five minutes. That was it. The last I saw him. I gave him my phone number. I guess that's how you got it, right?"

"Danielle . . . sorry. Kim." Kelley leaned forward and flipped through his notebook. "You know Chastity?"

"Worked at 2001."

"Wouldn't happen to be the other girl with you and Richard that night, would she?"

"Let's . . . I mean, if it was, I wouldn't want her to know I was saying anything about that, you know? I mean . . . Oh, well, Chastity *was* with us. I mean she was with him. I got let off first. We came back here. Richard dropped me off, set up the Magnavox and the VCR and then left with Chastity. But you know, I didn't have sex with him. Chastity did. I just danced. Gave him ten dances. We smoked some pot, drank some beer . . ."

"This was at Mr. Mallory's shop?"

"Yes. Then he got the TVs and VCRs, loaded them into the van, and drove me back. I came back first. He left with her. I never saw them again."

"Are those still here? The TV and VCR?"

Guy got up. "Yeah. They're back in the bedroom."

"Well, Kim, we'd like to take some pictures."

"All right."

"And we'd like to take one of you too, if that's okay."

Guy looked at Horzepa. "Whatever's right."

Horzepa smiled. "Good. And Chastity. You seen her lately?"

"I don't know. She was just there at the club. She's not my friend or anything. You ought to try the club."

"Yes, thank you. We will."

Kelley snapped Polaroids of Kim, the TV, and the VCR. He noted there were no serial numbers on the electronics. The detectives left their card and told Guy they would be getting back to her. With Kelley behind the wheel on the way back to the Pinellas sheriff's office, Horzepa watched the wipers slop rain across the windshield. "Bob, I think we've got a handle here with these two. With Mallory there's got to be a woman in it. Look at him. Out at the topless joints two or three or four times a week. Carries a roll. Spreads it. This is not a discriminating guy. He thought with his dick."

Kelley took the left lane and braked for a red light. "Mallory was a Part One waiting to happen. It's blind luck he wasn't done years ago." (On a police incident report, "Part One" designates the victim of violence.)

Horzepa pulled a pack of gum out of his black Members Only jacket, slipped two sticks, and handed one to Kelley. "Let's find this Chastity and see if she makes a noise."

TWO

Chastity

The scrap of paper with a phone number and the name Chastity that Horzepa had taken from Mallory's kitchen brought them to a woman named Alicia Bryant. Horzepa and Kelley met her at her apartment in Tampa. She told them she knew Chastity from the 2001 Odyssey club.

"I let her use my phone when she wanted to give out a number to customers. But I don't want any of this down on paper or tape or anything, you know? I don't want to be involved in any homicide thing. Okay? I mean, I'll do whatever, but . . . all right?"

"All right, Alicia. That's fine. Now, would you look at this picture please." Horzepa showed Bryant a photograph of Mallory, whom she immediately recognized as a regular at the 2001.

"Sure, he's the guy that gave Chastity a TV and VCR."

"Alicia, do you happen to have a picture of Chastity?" Horzepa slid Mallory's photo back into his accordion file.

"No, no way."

"Well, would you describe her?"

"She's maybe eighteen, twenty. Kind of thin blond hair, big boobs. You might find a picture at 2001. You ought to talk with Ronnie. She's the manager. I haven't seen Chastity since December, since she came back from Daytona."

Horzepa and Kelley had been in and out of some twenty topless joints between Clearwater and Tampa by the time they pulled up at the 2001 Odyssey club. They had shown Mallory's photo to dozens of dancers and bartenders. Everybody knew him. An incorrigible 'john,' Mallory could not get enough of the scene—an artificial twilight world of commercial sex, concocted from ruby-red spotlights, bass-heavy sound systems, coke-rattled flesh, and over-priced booze.

Horzepa and Kelley stood at the bar and waited for the manager to return with a photo of Chastity. Out on the dancers' runway, a young woman with garter belt and bustier worked to Madonna's "Vogue."

"Here's her picture." The manager handed Horzepa an eight-by-ten glossy across the formica. The blond in the photo not only had big breasts, but quite a number of tattoos. These weren't discreet butterflies or roses. A devil on the left leg. Unicorn on left shoulder. Dragon on inner thigh. "Property of Bruiser" right there next to the dragon. Horzepa handed the photo to Kelley, who looked it over and then raised an eyebrow. Both detectives were thinking the same thing: outlaw bikers.

"And here's her employee information."

Chastity Lee Marcus. White female. Date of Birth: 10-29-64. Twenty-seven . . . not eighteen or twenty. "You have an address for her? Telephone numbers?"

"Got a few. Right on the back of that paper. Try them, that one there . . ." He pointed out the name Doug Lambert. "I think that's one of her boyfriends."

Doug Lambert was not particularly happy to see two cops at his door. "Hey, I don't know where she is. Jesus, she's long gone. I haven't seen her in . . . weeks."

"Mr. Lambert." Kelley fixed his eyes on Lambert's and held his gaze until the man blinked. "We really need to speak with Chastity. We are very interested in this. We didn't drive all the way over here to bullshit, you know? We are conducting a homicide investigation."

Two hours later Lambert suddenly had Chastity in tow and agreed to bring her to the Embassy Suites for an interview.

Horzepa and Kelley arranged for a conference room in which to conduct the interview and then waited in the lobby for Lambert and Marcus. She looked nervous, obviously scared, clacking across the tiles in her high-heeled boots. Dressed in a tight pullover and even tighter jeans, Chastity was working the only advantage she'd ever known—her body. But it soon became clear that these two cops were not interested in her body, but in her statement. She reluctantly answered their questions.

"I met Mallory around early November at 2001 Odyssey. He'd ask for dances. Lap dances, and I did like five for him—you know, at the back of the club. For a hundred dollars. I met him through a girl. Pandora. So, the next time I see him was late November, and Danielle and I started talking to him about having a good time. We told him we'd each charge three hundred dollars for three dances. And we took him to a corner of the bar and danced. He asked us if we'd like a TV and VCR instead of the three hundred. And we accepted and left with him in a white van and headed for Clearwater. We smoked a joint on the way over and drank some beer. Stopped at a Jiffy Store, got some food, and went over to his shop. Went through and we picked out a TV and VCR. A Zenith. He loaded them up in the van and then we all got undressed in his office. Danielle had sex with him and then I went on with her. He took us back about four or it was five. He took me home first, brought in the TV and VCR. Hooked them up for me and left with Danielle. You know, I saw him about a few days later, standing at the bar at the club. There was Danielle and a few other girls standing around him. I ended up pawning the stuff at a pawn shop out on Hillsborough."

Throughout the questioning process, Chastity balked and whined, complaining that Doug would beat her if he found out she turned tricks, that Danielle was the last one with Mallory, that Danielle was the one who had sex with him that night. The women's stories did not match. Horzepa and Kelley now had a trio, maybe a quartet in their suspect pool—Kimberly, Chastity, Mike Rosenblum, and Dougie. If the times Chastity gave them were right, Mallory's murder occurred between five in the morning and three that afternoon when his car was found. But how likely was Chastity's story? Kimberly and Chastity had different tales. While Kimberly Guy was living quite well and still had the TV and VCR, Chastity had pawned hers two days after receiving them and didn't seem to have any permanent residence. Horzepa and Kelley agreed that of the two, Chastity was the less believable. They asked for some identification, but Chastity had nothing—no driver's license, no Social Security card. Horzepa requested a sample of her hair and handed her a pair of scissors. Marcus clipped a quarter-inch lock of blond which the detective slipped into a plastic bag. They left the conference room and the detectives watched Marcus stride across the lobby with Dougie in tow. Horzepa and Kelley packed up the next morning and returned to Daytona, where they began running background checks on their quartet of suspects.

By the time Horzepa and Kelley returned to Tampa on March 29, eight weeks had passed since their interview with Chastity Marcus. The Mallory case was one of six homicides the four-man Major Case Unit was dealing with in early 1990. They also had rapes, robberies, and sex offenses. Each investigator was working twelve to fifteen cases. When Horzepa and Kelley arrived at Doug Lambert's apartment it was high noon, and they were in no mood for anything but the facts.

Kelley made a point of looking Dougie in the eye, while Horzepa steered the interview in his usual laconic style.

"Do you work, sir?"

"Not right now," said Dougie.

Horzepa walked Lambert through his earlier statements regarding Chastity, through the interview with her at the Embassy Suites and what followed.

"After we had spoken to her about her involvement with our victim, Mr. Mallory, did you happen to have a conversation with her after we left the Tampa area?"

"Yes."

"What exactly did she say?" Horzepa asked.

"She said she told you what you wanted to . . . you know, you wanted to hear. What . . . what . . . you know, the information that she was . . . the questions you asked her. 'Cause I told her"—Lambert earnestly changed gears—"I said, If you didn't do it, tell 'em what they want to know. I kept expressin' that to her."

What a model citizen you are, Dougie, thought Kelley. *You're a regular lawman's helpmate.*

Lambert said that during the weeks following the interview at the Embassy Suites he'd tried getting Chastity out of his apartment. "I was telling her to call somebody to come and get her. I expressed this to her several times, come and get her. You know, call somebody. I was even gonna call her dad, tell him to just come and get her. Get her out of my life. And she goes, Well, I'm just gonna call those cops and tell them I did do those murders. And that was her exact words. She said that a couple of times."

Lambert nodded and looked from Horzepa to Kelley as if to make sure they appreciated his honesty in this difficult admission. He got blank expressions in return, so Dougie plunged on. "I told her, You don't want to do that, 'cause . . . you know. I . . . I . . . I . . . really believe that she didn't do it at the time. I don't know if she's done this now and that was her exact words to me. And she even . . . she even started dialin' the number at one time. I just wanted her out of my apartment."

"Did you believe her?" Horzepa and Kelley waited while Dougie dragged out his moment.

"At the time, no. If she said it now? Yeah. She lied. She lied on three occasions to me, and I caught her in three lies."

"Do you feel she's lying about this and that she actually

might have had something to do with Richard's murder, based on what you know?"

"Yeah, I'd say that."

Dougie went on to say even more. He said Chastity was "schizy." One minute she was nice, the next she was full of hate. She was violent. She hit Dougie. Maybe she would've killed him. Terrible mood swings. Born liar. Her father was a member of the Warlocks, a biker gang based in Orlando. Two months ago he had died in a motorcycle accident. Her mother lived somewhere in California. Chastity had been married once to the president of the Sons of Silence, another outlaw biker gang up in Indiana. Maybe he was called "Bruiser," like that tattoo of hers. He got killed in some hassle with the Outlaws, a much bigger biker gang. She'd been scared to death after talking to the cops. Said she'd gone to Daytona with Mallory.

"Do you know how long she was in Daytona?"

"I . . . I know it was like over a week. 'Cause I had seen her before she went and then I seen her when she got back."

"What time period was it before she went?"

"Well . . . before Christmas I was with her a couple of times. And then . . . and, let's see . . . Christmas we had the bad freeze, and that's the night she gave me her jacket. 'Cause I remember all the electricity was off. You know? And I forgot my jacket." Feeling Kelley's hostility, Lambert shifted in his chair and picked up the pace of his recollection. "Christmas Eve. So, it had to have been after Christmas that she went to Daytona."

"Okay." Horzepa opened his accordion file. "I'd like you to look at a photograph. I'd like for you to tell me who this person is."

Horzepa held the eight-by-ten glossy in front of Dougie's nose.

"That's Chastity."

"For the record, Doug has identified Chastity as the girl we've been talking about." Lambert couldn't grasp what the cops were up to, but whatever their game was, Dougie wanted no part of it.

"Is there anything else that you can tell me I might have forgotten to ask you?"

Lambert looked up at the ceiling as if he were taxing his memory. Horzepa brought him back down. "One of the questions . . . do you know where Chastity is at this time?"

Dougie quickly answered. "No, I don't. But I wish I did."

That night, Horzepa and Kelley were back at the 2001 Odyssey interviewing the night manager, Ronnie Poulter, and Devon Kirby, a dancer and friend of Chastity. The two women were ready witnesses. Poulter said she spent Christmas 1989 with a frantic Chastity.

"She told me: 'I'm as hot as a firecracker and I've got to get out of town.' Just like that. She said she was in 'big trouble.' 'I've seen and done it all in my short life.' "

Poulter told the detectives that Chastity had been dating a biker from Orlando known as "Wildman," and that they'd first gotten together around Thanksgiving 1989. Poulter was convinced that Chastity had truly been in some kind of serious trouble. Kirby agreed, but said Chastity had been making frequent trips to Orlando with a biker named Bob. Kirby added that Chastity had called her about three weeks ago from some place in South Carolina, saying she was coming back to Tampa because she couldn't make any money up there.

Later that night, Doug Lambert answered a knock on his door. The two cops didn't seem pleased to be there—in fact, the shorter one was downright irritable. They wanted to know if Chastity had phoned him. They wanted phone numbers. Their attitude was troubling to Dougie, and he began crying as he riffled through scraps of paper looking for the numbers. He came up with numbers for Chastity's father, her mother, the Warlocks' clubhouse, and a number in South Carolina. "She called me from up there three weeks ago." Lambert kept repeating that Chastity had said she knew about Mallory's murder. Knew all about it. They took a Polaroid of Dougie and left.

Driving back to their motel, Horzepa kidded Kelley. "You two are getting pretty tight there, Bob. I think you've found a friend in Dougie."

"I just have a . . . dislike for him, that's all. He was just wasting a lot of our time. He jerked us around."

"He's just trying to cover his butt. He's as reliable as any of the other players. And if outlaw bikers are mixed up in this, Dougie's scared shitless that they'll be down on him."

A check with the Tampa police found no criminal record for Chastity Lee Marcus. A cross-check on the phone numbers that Lambert had given them confirmed that one was for the Warlocks' clubhouse in Lockhart, Florida. The South Carolina number gave them a rooming house in Florence. A call to the Indianapolis Police Department's intelligence division didn't reveal a criminal history on Chastity Lee Marcus. Horzepa believed that Chastity Lee Marcus was a bogus identification, and asked IPD to continue their search in reference to the Sons of Silence and "Bruiser."

Horzepa and Kelley joined Sergeant Ehrhart in his cubicle, and the three agreed an arrest warrant for the murder of Richard Mallory should be issued for Chastity. Horzepa typed up an affidavit charging Marcus for "the unlawful killing of a human being, while engaged in the perpetration of a robbery." Volusia County Sheriff Robert Vogel signed the affidavit on April 5, and it was immediately taken to Circuit Judge Uriel Blount, Jr., who issued the warrant.

Copies of the warrant and photographs of Chastity and Kimberly Guy—who had dropped out of sight since she had been interviewed—were sent to Florence, South Carolina, sheriff's investigator Kenny Boone. At the same time, Indianapolis came back with information on "Bruiser." His real name was Robert John Carrier; he was former president of the Sons of Silence and most likely dead. He'd been arrested for homicide, assault, manslaughter, and resisting arrest, and had had a Colorado conviction for manslaughter. His main occupation had been running narcotics and firearms between Colorado and Indiana. According to IPD intelligence, Carrier had been done in by bigger competition, though no body had yet been found. The wife had left Indiana right after "Bruiser" vanished, supposedly on her way to Florida. Her name was Robin Carrier.

A cross-reference on the phone number Lambert had said was for Chastity's father revealed a Timothy Altizer. Horzepa and Kelley responded to the address in Orlando and were met by a woman named Sharon Nunn. Nunn told the detectives she had known Chastity for two years. Chastity danced in a lot of clubs around Orlando: The Circus, The Booby Trap, The Candy Bar. Her real first name was Jamie, and Marcus was the last name of an old boyfriend of Chastity's. She confirmed Chastity's relationship with a guy named Bob, a heavy-set screen installer with blond hair and a mustache, about forty-five years old. She said Chastity was also tight with the Warlocks, had even been inside their clubhouse out on Fourth Street in Lockhart. "Funny thing, though," said Nunn. "You know, I haven't heard from Chastity since before Christmas and that's just not like her. Her and me have always talked at least every few weeks or so. I guess she *is* in some trouble, huh?"

On April 10, Horzepa and Kelley were back in Tampa, visiting their favorite witness. Dougie was told they would be taking all the clothing Chastity left behind. He gave them a black plastic garbage bag stuffed with Marcus's fashion leftovers. The detectives tagged the bag and placed it into evidence. In the meantime, Investigator Lau, armed with the information out of Indianapolis, made an identification on Chastity from a 1988 booking report out of Orlando. Under the name Robin Carrier, she had been found guilty of cocaine possession and then had violated her probation. Orlando had an active warrant on her. Lau also received Carrier's booking photo and a set of latent prints.

Horzepa then followed up on the phone number for Chastity's mother by calling Inspector Art Gerrans of the San Francisco police. Gerrans found the number listed to Birgelio Perez. Horzepa told Gerrans he was sending a flier including the arrest warrant and photo, and to contact the Perez residence upon receiving them. Six days later, April 18, Horzepa got a call from Gerrans. The Perez couple had adopted Chastity when she was nine years old, but had given her up after two years because of her incorrigible violence and thievery. They had adopted her with the name Celeste. Though they had not seen her in over five years, Celeste had suddenly called them on Easter Sunday to tell them she was in Texas and had given Perez an address in Mansfield.

Horzepa then phoned the Texas Rangers, eventually reaching Sergeant Jim Morgan, who took the address and said he'd check it out as soon as he received the flier with the arrest warrant. Then a call came in to the Major Case Unit from Ronnie Poulter, the night manager at 2001. She advised Horzepa that "Bob"—the guy from Orlando who had dated Chastity—was there at the club with Chastity's fellow dancer, Devon Kirby. Ronnie gave the detective the tag number on Bob's 1990 Ford Ranger XLT, a two-tone blue pickup. She also said Bob had spoken to Devon about "Wildman," that his real name was Tim. Poulter even had a description for Tim—five feet six, gray hair, and numerous tattoos. Horzepa thanked Poulter and ran a check on Bob's tag number that turned up Robert H. or Patricia Cole with an Orange City, Florida, address. To Horzepa and Kelley, Bob Cole was likely the "Biker Bob" that Chastity had referred to in her Embassy Suites interview in January. The guy who took her partying in Daytona.

After running a criminal history check on Cole that showed no record, Horzepa called Cole into the operations center for an interview. Cole arrived at the Major Case Unit on May 16 and gave Horzepa a written statement.

Cole had met Chastity at the 2001 club on her birthday.

He took her over to Daytona sometime during the last of November or early December 1989, hitting Froggy's and Harry's, two local topless clubs. Cole then brought Chastity to Orlando and dropped her off at Tim Altizer's. She stayed there about two weeks and then returned to Tampa. Cole said the last time he had seen her was the first week in January, when he dropped her off in Tampa.

On May 25, the Jefferson Parish Sheriff's Office in New Orleans called Horzepa with good and bad news. Chastity had been arrested. However, she was back out on the streets. Before Horzepa could reply, the New Orleans detective—an eighteen-year-veteran on the vice detail named Couret—jumped in to guarantee Florida that if Chastity were in New Orleans he would find her. Couret's promise was golden. Forty-eight hours later Horzepa and Kelley were in flight to New Orleans, where Chastity was cooling her heels in the Jefferson Parish correctional facility.

Along with Chastity, Couret had collared her pimp. Upon finding himself facing two Florida homicide detectives, he quickly gauged the situation and agreed to cooperate fully. "You don't want me. The bitch is wanted for killing somebody in Florida. She made up this story about the killing and said her sister killed this guy, her 'sugar daddy.' Then she says she killed him." He said he knew her as Page Carrier, had picked her up in Myrtle Beach, South Carolina, where he was working as a driver for an escort service. "She told me she knew all about New Orleans, talked me into driving her over here."

The three detectives then drove to the Sleepy Hollow Motel out on Airline Highway, where Chastity had been arrested. Couret had sealed the motel room where he had picked up Chastity. Horzepa and Kelley went through the clothing she had left behind. Nothing was found that linked her to Mallory. No radar detector, no cameras, no briefcase. The three detectives went on to the jail, where Chastity met them in the office of Couret's captain. She had been sitting in a cell for twenty-four hours, knowing she was under arrest for murder. She was crying and shaking. She denied having anything to do with any murder. She hadn't killed Richard Mallory. She couldn't keep track of all the stories she had told. There were too many. When Horzepa jotted down one of her statements, ten minutes later she contradicted it. "This isn't working, Chastity," said Horzepa. "It doesn't fit. You better get it together and get it right. Look, we've got the warrant and we know what you said about being 'hot as a firecracker,' about how you've 'done it all now,' about you saying you killed Richard Mallory."

"No! No! No!" She sobbed and grabbed the corner of the metal desk where they were sitting, and raised it from the floor and brought it down. "No, I didn't kill anybody!"

The Florida investigators were running on a short leash. They didn't have the opportunity for an eight-hour interrogation. The captain would be wanting his office back. They pressed on, with Horzepa hammering away at Chastity's story while Kelley noted discrepancies. They would bring her up emotionally and then back off to calm her down. But she wasn't calming down. After an hour, Chastity was blaming Kimberly Guy. Horzepa and Kelley knew they wouldn't be getting much more until extradition on Chastity came through and they got her back in Daytona. With the clothing Chastity had left behind at the Sleepy Hollow bagged as evidence, Horzepa and Kelley took a flight across the Gulf to Florida and Kimberly Guy.

The last week in June, Kimberly Guy was found and agreed to a polygraph examination. On June 29, Jack Mehl, a polygraph examiner with the Thirteenth Circuit State Attorney's office took Guy through a session that revealed no deception patterns when the young woman was asked about Mallory's murder. Shortly after she was cleared, Guy and her girlfriend left Florida for Sacramento, California. By this time, extradition proceedings on Chastity were completed, and she was housed in the Volusia County jail. Horzepa, Kelley, and Ehrhart met with assistant state attorney David Damore in his office at the Justice Center on Ridgewood Avenue in Daytona. The cops wanted an indictment. But Damore, after reviewing the case on Chastity, couldn't comply. There simply wasn't enough evidence to carry an indictment—no weapon, no witnesses, no recovered property from the victim. Chastity had an alibi in the statement from Bob Cole. Her whereabouts could be accounted for on December 1. They had nothing but the conflicting hearsay from an unreliable witness, Doug Lambert. There would be no murder charge against Chastity Marcus.

Horzepa, Kelley, and Ehrhart left Damore's office, each fighting down a gorge of frustration, anger, and disappointment. They had to cut Chastity loose. Ehrhart returned to the operations center while Horzepa and Kelley drove west out of Daytona on Highway 92, past the Speedway, the jai alai fronton, and Interstate 95, to the Volusia County correctional facility and Chastity. After a six-month pursuit of Marcus that had taken the two detectives in and out of topless joints, biker bars, and motels from Tampa to Daytona to Orlando, across five states, and through a swamp of aliases, lies, and contradictions, Horzepa and Kelley now had to tell their hard-sought suspect she was cleared. Chastity received the news and bid farewell to Horzepa and Kelley with a single upraised finger before being transferred to Orlando, where she was wanted on probation violations. That was the last Horzepa and Kelley saw of Chastity Lee Marcus, aka Robin Carrier, aka Page Carrier, aka Celeste Perez. A few months later, Chastity skipped bail in Orlando and disappeared. The investigation into Richard Mallory's murder was now as cold as his bullet-riddled body, six months buried.

THREE

Missing, Endangered, and Murdered

Law enforcement agencies—no matter their size—are constantly engulfed by BOLOs (be on the lookout) for the missing. Reports of runaway teenagers, abducted children, lost wives and girlfriends, and strayed spouses stream over the teletypes endlessly. Investigators fielding these calls for help sometimes feel that half the population has taken a powder. All any jurisdiction can do is determine priorities and hope for the best. Children, young women and teenagers, and the elderly make the top of the list. White middle-aged males are almost always at the bottom. If there is no evidence of foul play, missing adult males are usually suspected of purposefully disappearing, fleeing marriage or financial disaster or both. Sometimes alcoholism and psychological breakdowns lead these men to simply drop out. A few fall victim to midlife crisis and succumb to the allure of the road, only to turn up after a few weeks as embarrassed prodigals. Some are undiscovered suicides and homicides. The rest end up in a medical examiner's final report.

On the morning of June 4, two orderlies at the Lake County medical examiner's office rolled a gurney laden with a John Doe into the autopsy room. The body had been discovered three days earlier, naked save for a baseball cap, sprawled on its back, arms outstretched, in the scrub woods abutting the Chassahowitzka National Wildlife Refuge on Florida's Gulf Coast, forty miles north of Tampa.

Dr. Janet Pillow stood aside as Citrus County sheriff's investigator Marvin Padgett unlocked the white body bag. Then Padgett and three fellow detectives watched as the petite forensic pathologist scanned the exposed body with birdlike intensity. In her exquisitely articulated speech, she summed up her observation. "The remains are those of a nude, Caucasian male. The remaining skin is firm, dry, tan-yellow. And parchment-like. The skin and soft tissue is absent from around the mouth and eyes. There is no external ear tissue present. The skin is absent from the anterior chest and abdomen, as is the vast majority of skeletal muscle and other soft tissues."

One of the cops whispered, "Looks like a bad mummy job."

Pillow ignored the comment and bent closer to the corpse. "The skin is absent from the back of the left hand." She reached between the arms, which had been taped together at the wrists by the cops prior to transportation. With delicate, latex-gloved fingers, the doctor probed gently along each limb. "The inside of each arm from the axilla down to the hands has exposed bone." Pillow continued her examination of the remains, discovering a small remnant of white mustache hair and a few tufts of brown and gray head hair on those patches of skin left on the skull. The teeth were natural and a dental print was made. The genitalia were missing. Pillow ordered an X ray.

The shadowy pictures revealed six metallic projectiles scattered throughout the body's chest and abdomen. Pillow began retrieving them. Small-caliber bullets. One buried in the clavicle. Three in the back, one of them imbedded in the spinal column. One on the left side. Two in the chest.

After recovering the bullets, Pillow took measurements of the body—six feet two inches in length, forty-five pounds in weight. She then made way for Dr. William Maples, the legendary forensic anthropologist from the University of Florida, who began disarticulating portions of the skeletal remains, including the head. Maples bagged and tagged the skull and bones for transportation to his lab at the university in Gainesville. The detectives bagged the hands for the print specialists at the FDLE. The rest of the John Doe—his skin, flesh, and feet—remained with the medical examiner.

Padgett and his partner, Jerry Thompson, left the medical examiner's in Leesburg with the bullets and Pillow's autopsy report and returned to their office at the Citrus County Sheriff's Criminal Investigation Division in Inverness. For the next three days, the two detectives focused their energies on the foul-mouthed surveyor who had found the body. Mathew Cocking had two things working against him—a bad temper and no apparent reason for being at the remote crime scene. When Padgett and Thompson came to interview Cocking at his place of employment, the detectives had already talked with Cocking's mother-in-law. They were advised that Cocking was soon to be divorced, and that he usually carried a pistol. Cocking's boss said the young man was a good worker, but that there was no job-related reason for Cocking to have been in those woods near Chassahowitzka where the body was found.

Cocking refused to shake hands with the detectives and began yelling. "All I did is find a fucking body and you are harassing the fuck out of me! You pulled hair out of my ass and everything else!" The detectives at the scene on June 1 had requested hair samples from the obstreperous Cocking, who at the time had given conflicting stories as to why he was at the site. "Get me a fucking attorney. Stay the fuck out of my life!" Cocking's performance in his boss's office didn't impress Padgett and Thompson. It only made him more interesting.

While the Citrus County detectives were trying to identify their John Doe, agents of the Georgia Bureau of Investigation were vainly seeking identification of the nude body of a white male left with two .22-caliber bullets in the woods of Brooks County off Interstate 75 just north of the Florida state line in Georgia. The badly decomposed set of remains had been found a month earlier, on May 5. Then, on June 6, in Pasco County, thirty miles south of where Citrus County investigators had found their murdered John Doe, another nude white male corpse was uncovered. This one had died from the effect of nine .22-caliber bullets, and had been left beneath a green electric blanket and scattered weeds just a few miles from Interstate 75. Because of the condition of the body, Pasco County medical examiner Dr. Janet Woods could only approximate a time of death. Five days to two weeks. The decomposition was so severe that even the .22-caliber projectiles had deteriorated. Detective Tom Muck, a seventeen-year veteran investigator with the Pasco County Sheriff's Office, immediately ordered a facial reconstruction following the autopsy. Muck could take no prints, all he could determine was that this was the body of a white male between the ages of twenty-seven and fifty, five feet ten inches tall, with light brown hair.

Though these three similar homicides had been discovered within a thirty-day period, they were in separate jurisdictions and across state lines.

On June 7, Padgett and Thompson succeeded in identifying their victim. They also eliminated the abusive Cocking as a suspect. The detectives picked up on a Missing/Endangered BOLO out of Sarasota that fit the general description of their victim. David A. Spears, a forty-three-year-old heavy-equipment operator from Bradenton, was last seen leaving his place of employment in Sarasota on May 19. Padgett procured the name of Spears's dentist from the Sarasota police, retrieved a set of Spears's X rays from him, and arranged to meet forensic dentist Dr. Thomas Ford in Orlando. While Padgett and Thompson were en route to Dr. Ford's, investigators Fred Johnson and Dave Strickland drove to Gainesville and picked up the victim's skull from Dr. Maples. With the X rays and skull, Ford proceeded to make a comparison. While the detectives were waiting, a message came for them to call detective Tom Muck in Pasco County, who had heard about Citrus County's homicide. Muck advised Padgett of the circumstances regarding the Pasco County John Doe and suggested they keep in touch. By this time, Dr. Ford had confirmed that the skull was that of David Spears.

Padgett immediately contacted Sarasota police investigator Dottie Young, who was handling the Spears case. "We've got your man. He's our victim."

"Too bad," Young sighed, then began briefing Padgett on Spears. "First off, Spears's boss—Robert Kerr—and his wife found Spears's pickup up on I-75. Totally off-the-wall. The Kerrs are driving back from Tennessee, about twenty miles south of Gainesville in Marion County, when they see the truck. They stop. Kerr notices that the truck has a flat tire, the passenger window is ajar, and the doors are unlocked. The license plate is missing. Kerr gets hold of Marion SO and they impound the truck. Marion checks and the vehicle is not entered as stolen."

Young went on to say that Spears was supposedly on his way to Orlando when he left Universal Concrete in Sarasota on Saturday, May 19. "He was supposed to be there the next day around two or three. Kerr said he had to chase Spears and some of the other employees out of the lot where they were drinking beer after work. Said Spears should have had around four or five hundred dollars on him when he left Sarasota. Had problems with his wife. That's Ima Dean Spears. She goes by 'Dee.' And, Investigator Padgett, she is going to make your life miserable."

Padgett and Thompson met Ima Dean Spears later that evening, along with Mrs. Spears's friend, Ruth Holley. In the course of the two-hour interview, the two detectives spent half their time trying to keep Mrs. Spears and Holley on track. They kept straying far afield with their suspicions, family histories, and personal animosities. Dee Spears began by having difficulty recalling the age of one of her sons and the exact relationship she had with David Spears. Married for twenty years, the Spearses had divorced in 1984. "He always liked to drink and party, and I'm a churchgoer. I thought that if I got a divorce that he would change. But he didn't. I couldn't stay away from him and he didn't seem to stay away from me." Spears visited his ex-wife nearly every weekend, bringing over his laundry, which Dee would wash.

David Spears had phoned Dee the morning of May 19, the day he was last seen. He'd told her he'd see her later that day. "He'd drive straight here. He'd go on 75 till he got to where you turn on I-4, there close to Tampa. Take I-4 to 27 at Baseball City and take it up to Clermont to Highway 50 and then, you know, come to my apartment. When he says he'll do something he don't just call me up and lie to me."

Dee Spears told the detectives that David usually dressed in blue jeans and pullover shirts with a pair of lace-up workboots and a cap. He carried a set of Craftsman tools with him in his truck along with a brown vinyl suitcase. He might also have had fishing tackle with him when he left Universal Concrete that Friday. He had no credit cards, no checking or savings account. On May 19, his son Jeff had picked up David's paycheck. It was never cashed. Spears drank Busch beer and smoked Swisher Sweet cigars with a plastic filter.

As Padgett attempted to establish David Spears's circle of friends, Dee's friend Ruth Holley suddenly interrupted. "What about that panther? Tell 'em about that panther."

"Excuse me. Please," said Padgett.

Dee abruptly jumped the detectives' track of questioning. "I used to wear a lot of—I still do—I wear a lot of gold. He bought me a lot of jewelry. I have, you know, chains and everything." Dee's hands swept up to her throat. Her bracelets twinkled as she fingered a gold necklace. "On my birthday he bought me a necklace, and it's a panther with diamonds in it. The reason why I knew for sure he was coming, was he was so proud of himself. Aside from the road, where do they sell all this stuff? You know, where do they have all these little things out that they sell?"

Thompson, a veteran cop with a face as blunt and imperative as a fist, blinked. "Umm," he murmured from beneath his black mustache.

"He found the panther," Dee declared, as if that explained everything. "He knows I like wild animals. I even like to go to the zoo. And he bought me a panther."

"A stuffed panther?" Padgett asked.

"I don't know . . . I don't think so. I think it's the chalk kind."

The detectives were beginning to understand detective Young's warning about Mrs. Spears. A chalk panther. "You mean like a plaster one?"

"Yeah, something like that. He said, 'Momma . . .' He always called me Momma. ' . . . Momma, you'll really like it.' And when he called, I said, 'Did you put my panther in the truck?' And he said, 'Momma, I got it wrapped up in a blanket behind the seat.' "

By the time Padgett and Thompson completed their interview, Dee had interjected her suspicions of David's boss, Robert "Red" Kerr, based on an involved scenario regarding a stolen company truck and Kerr's dislike for Dee. She also let the detectives know she was dissatisfied with the Sarasota police and their investigation. Dee and Ruth had plenty more to say, but Padgett and Thompson had had enough. When Padgett finished transcribing the interview later that night, there were sixty-two pages in the report and—despite Mrs. Spears's innuendoes regarding Red Kerr—no likely suspects.

Down in Pasco County, investigator Tom Muck was having even less success with his John Doe. Muck's opinion was that there was a homosexual angle in this homicide. The victim was naked, male, and overkilled. Passion, maybe hatred, was the motive. But without any identification, there was less than nothing for Muck to go on. He contacted the Georgia Bureau of Investigation and discovered they had had no more luck in identifying the body they had. It was as deteriorated as the one in Pasco County. The two cases, however, were so similar—naked white males, .22-caliber bullets, left in wooded areas near Interstate 75—that there could be a connection; but the tenuous links weren't enough to suspect a single killer. By July 20, that had changed.

Meanwhile, in Volusia County, Horzepa and Kelley, still hot on Chastity, had not seized upon the similarities the recent murders shared with Mallory's. Not until September, when three more men had died, would the detectives link up their separate investigations.

FOUR

Marion County

A few blocks south of the sandy trail where Richard Mallory's abandoned Cadillac was discovered in Ormond Beach, Highway 40 begins its route west from the Atlantic to the Gulf of Mexico. Banded by blaring signs, fast-food outlets, and automotive services, four lanes carry traffic west to Interstate 95 and beyond into farmlands. Twenty miles from Daytona's sprawl the highway crosses into Marion County, where it narrows to an undulating two-lane corridor through the Ocala National Forest. Native longleaf and sandy pine, scrub hickory, and Chapman oak bearded by Spanish moss shadow knife like palmettos and snaking wild grapevines. Clear, cold springs feed an array of lakes that attract bass fishermen, scuba divers, and boaters. Fish camps, campgrounds, and convenience stores make up the little communities scattered throughout the national forest.

On the Fourth of July, 1990, Rhonda Bailey was sitting on her porch near Orange Springs, one such community in the northwest quadrant of the Ocala National Forest. It was late afternoon when Mrs. Bailey, along with her husband and cousin, were startled by the sound of screeching tires. "There's been so many wrecks out here," Mrs. Bailey later reported. "'Cause of the sharp curve. I knew exactly what was happenin'. Another wreck." The Baileys and their cousin ran from the porch toward the brush across the road where the car had come to rest. "These women were screamin'. Cans of beer flying through the air. They were throwin' beer cans out in the woods. By the time we got there they were both out of the car and the blond one had blood runnin' down her left arm. She must have been the passenger 'cause she kept cussin' at the brown-haired one, sayin', 'I told you not to go so fast!' She was usin' *real* foul language."

Mrs. Bailey said the blond pleaded with her not to call the police, saying her father lived just up the road. "The brown-haired girl wouldn't talk at all. It was like the blond-haired girl was treatin' her like a little baby. Cussin' her out, callin' her every name in the book." When Mrs. Bailey offered the use of her telephone, the blond refused and began walking away with her companion. "We went back up and sat down and there wasn't just a couple of seconds later that they both came runnin' back down the road and they jumped in the car and got it out. It landed on a steel gate. They bent that thing like a horseshoe and went through the barbed wire. When they started it up, the noise! It was like the fan was hittin' something, makin' that tinny noise. I seen the blond-haired lady was drivin' and the windshield was busted out of it."

Later that holiday afternoon, Harmon Jeter was driving south on State Road 315 when he spotted two women carrying a red and white cooler between them. "I thought they was local girls and I was goin' to give them a ride," Jeter recalled. "The blond one did all the talkin'. She had blood all over her. She said they'd been in a real bad accident and they needed to get to Daytona. They wanted me to give them a ride over to 40." To Jeter it seemed the two were lost. When he told them he wasn't going all the way to 40, the blond got upset. "She got radical on me. Like, 'Gee whiz, thanks a lot! We're out here and had an accident and you won't take us nowhere?!' I went straight up to my brother-in-law's house and I called the fire department."

Hubert Hewett, chief of the Orange Springs Volunteer Fire Department, and his wife, Brenda, responded to Jeter's call. A light drizzle was falling as they drove up and down 315 until Brenda spotted the two women. "I asked them if they had been in an accident," said Hewett. "This blond, she let out, 'No! Where did you get that idea?' They weren't bloody when we found them. The blond did all the talking. She sort of got mad and did a little cussing. Said, 'Why do all these people tell lies about me?' She kept gettin' all high temper like. Everything you say would make her mad. People were telling lies about her, lies about the road. They just kept on. Whenever somebody says they don't want our help, you know, we kind of talk to them and then we leave. They seemed like they were anxious to get on down the road. In a hurry."

Marion County sheriff's deputies responded to Church Street in Orange Springs, following Hewett's report of the accident. Just down the road from the Baileys, the deputies found the damaged gray 1988 four-door Pontiac Sunbird abandoned in a field. Its windshield was shattered, and glass from the door windows had been broken out. Reddish-brown stains that appeared to be blood were on the trunk and throughout the interior. As the Pontiac bore no license tag, the cops ran the vehicle identification number through the computer. It came back with bells: the owner was Peter Siems, Missing Person/Endangered Adult.

Marion County sheriff's investigators Leo Smith and Bruce Munster brought transcripts of their interviews with the Orange Springs witnesses to Beth Gee, forensic artist for the MCSO. Gee quickly worked up pen sketches of the two women seen leaving Siems's wrecked Pontiac, and these were immediately telefaxed to the Jupiter police and the Florida Department of Law Enforcement.

Over two hundred miles southeast of Orange Springs, down in Palm Beach County, Detective John Wisnieski of the Jupiter Police Department had been working the case on his missing civilian since June 22. When he received word on Siems's recovered vehicle and the two women seen leaving it, he put out a nationwide teletype.

> MISSING ADULT . . . FOUL PLAY SUS-
> PECTED . . . VIC: W/M PETER SIEMS
> DOB: 05/21/25 5'7" 160 GRY/BRO . . .
> SIEMS LAST SEEN AT HIS RESIDENCE
> 115 W BEVERLY RD, JUPITER ON
> 06/07/90, WHEN HE LEFT TO VISIT
> RELATIVES IN ARKANSAS AND NEW
> JERSEY. SIEMS NEVER ARRIVED
> AT EITHER DESTINATION AND WAS
> REPORTED MISSING ON 06/22/90 . . .
> THE VICTIM'S VEHICLE WAS FOUND
> ABANDONED IN MARION COUNTY,

FL . . . BLOOD WAS FOUND ON BOTH SEATS AND THE TAG HAD BEEN REMOVED . . . TWO W/F'S WHO APPEARED TO BE LESBIANS WERE SEEN EXITING THE VEHICLE AND LEAVING SOUTHBOUND ON FOOT . . . SUBJECT #1: W/F 25–30 YOA 5'8"/130 BLN/UNK WEARING BLUE JEANS WITH SOME TYPE OF CHAIN HANGING FROM FRONT BELT LOOP, WHI T-SHIRT WITH SLEEVES ROLLED UP TO SHOULDER. SUBJECT #2: W/F 20'S 5'4"–5'6"/ VERY OVERWEIGHT AND MASCULINE LOOKING W/ DK RD HAIR, WEARING GRAY SHIRT AND RED SHORTS . . . ALL PERSONAL BELONGINGS OF THE VICTIM ARE MISSING FROM THE VEHICLE AND NO CREDIT CARD OR BANK TRANSACTIONS HAVE BEEN MADE SINCE THE VICTIM LEFT HIS HOME. VICTIM IS A DEVOUT CHRISTIAN AND FAMILY MAN AND HAS NO HISTORY OF MENTAL INSTABILITY . . .

Wisnieski had learned that Siems, a 65-year-old veteran merchant seaman who had retired just a year earlier, was devoted to a Christian outreach ministry called Christ Is The Answer. His wife had been abroad working with the ministry in Germany when Siems packed up his car on June 7, intending to visit his sister in New Jersey before traveling west to Arkansas, where his son, Stefan, lived. On July 5, while Siems's Pontiac was being processed by Marion County sheriff's technicians, Wisnieski entered Siems's home with a key provided by a longtime friend of the Siemses. The detective shifted through mundane paperwork including banking records, credit-card billings, and business cards, but found nothing out of the ordinary. A check through Siems's mail located a phone bill showing the last long-distance call being made to New Jersey on June 6. No unusual activity showed up in Siems's American Express transactions—nothing to indicate that Siems was planning anything other than his trip to visit relatives.

At the Marion County impound yard in Ocala, technicians were scouring Siems's car for latent prints. A bloody palm print from the trunk offered possibilities, but nothing conclusive. More bloodstains were found inside the Sunbird, with one on the armrest of the passenger door indicating another possible print. On the floor of the car, the cops found several bottle rockets, a firecracker, an empty Busch beer can in an orange and blue foam-rubber insulator, an empty Budweiser can in another insulator, and a full can of Bud. They removed from the driver's seat two sections of upholstery that tested positive for blood. On the driver's seat they found a decorative tag with a bald eagle, wings outstretched, clutching two American flags in its claws.

Wisnieski spent the rest of July following slender threads. When Ursula Siems, the missing man's wife, returned, the detective met with her and obtained further biographical details that he incorporated into a Violent Criminal Apprehension Program Analysis Report. The VICAP Report is a fifteen-page questionnaire developed by the National Center for the Analysis of Violent Crime, a program begun in 1984 by the Department of Justice,

in conjunction with the Criminal Justice Center at Sam
Houston State University. The program serves as a kind
of clearinghouse for law-enforcement agencies facing
atypical crimes of violence. Information is funneled into
VICAP's offices within the FBI's Behavioral Science
Unit in Quantico, Virginia, where it is processed for patterns of victimization, physical evidence, and modus
operandi. Though VICAP and the Behavioral Science
Unit have received much media attention as a kind of
"super sleuth" enclave, in reality VICAP does not function as an investigative agency. It is a tool that is only as
good as the information provided to it. Many of the
17,000 law-enforcement agencies in the United States do
not provide such information, due to constraints in man-
power and budget. Small jurisdictions simply do not
have the wherewithal to employ an officer to fill out
lengthy reports. Others just don't bother. Wisnieski did.
After completing the VICAP, Wisnieski telefaxed a syn-
opsis of his case along with the two sketches to the
Florida Criminal Activity Bulletin, an advisory commu-
nication of the FDLE. Given the circumstances and the
condition of Siems's car, the detective's gut told him
Peter Siems was not likely to be among the living.

On the morning of July 30, Troy Burress left the
Gilchrist Sausage Company in Ocala on his delivery
route, which would take him through the Ocala National
Forest. When the 46-year-old Burress failed to return at
four that afternoon, Gilchrist manager Johnny Mae
Thompson called the Salt Springs Grocery, one of Burress's last delivery stops. She was informed that Burress
had never arrived. Thompson waited until seven that

evening for the 1983 Ford track to pull into the company's lot. She left a note for Burress on the gate telling him to call as soon as he returned. Four hours later, with no contact from Burress, Johnny Mae and her husband set out backtracking their driver's route without any results. At two in the morning, Sharon Burress called the Marion County Sheriff's Office to report her husband as missing. Two hours later, the dark brown Ford truck carrying a silver refrigerator box with "Gilchrist Sausage Company" painted on both sides was spotted on the shoulder of State Road 19 just south of its intersection with Highway 40, twenty miles east of Ocala. After notifying Operations, Marion County sheriff's deputy Dennis Chessner ran his hand along the truck's hood. It was cold and covered with dew. The doors to the cab were unlocked, but the refrigerator box was secured. There were no keys inside the cab.

Investigator John Tilley, an affable mustachioed young detective, was assigned to the case by his commander, Captain Steve Binegar. Having issued a BOLO on Burress into both the National Crime Information Center and Florida Crime Information Center systems as missing and endangered, Tilley was on his way to examine the sausage truck when he learned that it had been returned to the Thompsons. The alarmed detective immediately contacted Johnny Mae Thompson, requesting that the truck be relinquished to the sheriff's evidence technicians. While Tilley hoped the vehicle hadn't been severely contaminated by the Thompsons, the detective knew it was too late. On that sour note, he contacted Burress's wife, Sharon.

According to Mrs. Burress, Troy had nothing in his medical history or behavior that would lead to his voluntary disappearance. He and his wife had been married sixteen years without a problem. Since wives are not always the best sources when law enforcement enters the picture, Tilley continued his investigation with Burress's other family members and friends. He was told that Troy had a girlfriend elsewhere in the state, and that Burress had been previously married and had had two children and had one day "just up and left and disappeared."

Meanwhile, a sheriff's posse under the command of Major Dan Henry was dispatched on horseback over a four-mile radius from where the sausage truck had been discovered. A helicopter called in from Volusia County took to the sky to assist the ground troops. At eleven o'clock that night the search was called off.

A follow-up interview with Mrs. Burress revealed a more detailed picture of her husband. A year before Troy Burress disappeared he had sold what Mrs. Burress called "a thriving swimming-pool business" in Delray Beach. "He couldn't stand all the people and the traffic," Sharon Burress told investigators. "So we moved here to Ocala. But we didn't get all the money we were owed for the business. The guy who bought it still owed us $24,000, and he was just running the business down and couldn't make any money. He just let it go to pot. I think all Troy got out of it was three thousand dollars." Mrs. Burress said she and her husband were a little tight financially, but not too badly off. She couldn't understand what had happened to her husband. "Troy's got habits you can depend on. He wouldn't just up and run off."

Troy Burress's sister, Letha Prater, called Investigator Tilley on August 1 with a breathless account from a psychic. According to the psychic, Burress stopped for a lady or two men. They went to Daytona Beach and bought drugs. The psychic saw the victim around Perry, some seventy miles northwest of Ocala. Maybe Tallahassee. He was in a black or turquoise Pontiac, possibly stabbed. The psychic saw his mouth moving. The Pontiac was in a ditch. The psychic also envisioned a sum of money—seven hundred fifty dollars. Tilley dutifully leaned into the receiver, took notes, and later entered Prater's urgent message from the ozone into his narrative report.

Investigators worked up an itinerary detailing Burress's movements on the day he disappeared. The itinerary showed him leaving the Gilchrist lot at 6:20 the morning of the thirtieth. From there he made his first delivery at the Publix supermarket in the Ocala shopping center and proceeded east through Marion County, stopping at various markets, where he made small talk with his customers. In interviews with the proprietors, who had spoken with Burress that day, detectives got conflicting reports—some said Burress seemed fine and in good spirits, others said he had "acted different," complaining about money lost in the pool-business sale. After driving all the way into Volusia County and Ormond Beach, Burress had tooled his Ford truck back west along Highway 40, heading for Ocala. He made his last stop at 2:24 at the Seville Grocery on the eastern edge of the national forest, where he chatted with store owner Don Birdwell for about fifteen minutes. Burress's next scheduled delivery was just fifteen minutes west, in Salt Springs. He never arrived. Records further showed he had collected $293.80 in cash.

Late that same evening of August 1, Tilley was notified of a witness who had picked up a hitchhiker near

Burress's abandoned truck. Jessie Singleterry told officers that he had picked up a shoeless man wearing shorts and a multicolored shirt around six-thirty on the evening of August 30 and dropped the fellow off at the Salt Springs campsite. A check with the campsite confirmed Singleterry's story. A man calling himself Blankenship had paid cash for a tent and showed an Alabama driver's license. He had said he was a truck driver. Tilley entered the name Blankenship along with the number taken from the Alabama license into the NCIC. It came back with negative results.

On August 4, a family out for an afternoon picnic just a few miles into the Ocala National Forest noticed a thick train of ants furiously advancing toward a scattering of palmetto fronds piled beneath a spindly sand pine. Within a few feet of the insects' destination, shock overtook the picnickers' curiosity—the ants were disappearing up the blue jeans on a dead man's legs.

Lieutenant Woody Guess had taken command of the scene by the time Tilley arrived. The body was in a clearing at the end of what locals called a pig trail, just off Highway 19. It was a little over eight miles from where Burress's sausage truck had been found. The body was lying face down. Guess said that the remains were covered with insects—ants, beetles, maggots, and flies. A ground search along the pig trail recovered Burress's credit cards, his clipboard, his receipts, and an empty zippered bank bag. The body was too far gone for a positive identification at the scene, but investigators were certain that it was Burress. Blue jeans, tan Hush Puppies, and what might have once been a tan shirt with the name Troy stitched above the pocket. A wedding band and a gold necklace. All matched up for Burress. Missing were the man's wallet and driver's license. Tilley asked for the wedding ring and had it cleaned by evidence technician Wayne Scroggins. He bagged it, went to his car, and made the trip all homicide detectives dread, the one that takes them to the door of a victim's family. Mrs. Burress identified the ring as belonging to her husband and gave Tilley the name and address of their dentist.

The next day the autopsy was done on the body. Two bullets were found by X ray. One in the upper chest, and the other in the lower left side of the back. The bullet to the chest had burst through the aorta, ricocheted off the spine, and come to rest in the left lung. The back shot had coursed upward through the diaphragm and left kidney.

The investigation then focused on the hitchhiker picked up alongside Burress's truck. He was soon identified as Curtis Michael Blankenship, a twenty-five-year-old white male. Blankenship had stolen a Ford pickup in Ocala and fled north to Indiana, where he was arrested four days after Burress's body was discovered. Tilley contacted the Indiana State Police and asked for a copy of Blankenship's prints and a hold on the stolen truck and its contents, advising them that Blankenship was a suspect in a homicide. For the remainder of August, Tilley worked Blankenship, tracking the drifter's movements through central Florida prior to Burress's disappearance and on to Indiana, where he interviewed Blankenship. All Tilley ended up with was the pathetic history of a small-time thief who had happened to be in the wrong place at the wrong time, when he stood alongside a murdered man's truck and stuck out his thumb.

FIVE

Predator

On Monday, September 10, 1990, Charles "Dick" Humphreys and his wife, Shirley, celebrated their thirty-fifth wedding anniversary in the back yard of their Crystal River home on Florida's Gulf Coast. A home video shows the grandfatherly Humphreys standing among family and friends, puffing on his pipe and squinting through his glasses. On Tuesday, Dick Humphreys said his last good-byes.

After packing some paperwork into his burgundy briefcase, Humphreys made his way around the Sumterville office of Florida's Health and Rehabilitative Services for the last time. A retired Alabama police chief, Humphreys had just been transferred to the state agency's office in Ocala after serving a year in Sumterville as supervisor of protective investigators specializing in abused and injured children. A fifty-six-year-old toting two hundred pounds on his six-foot frame, Humphreys resembled a clean-shaven Wilford Brimley. Around three that afternoon, he told fellow HRS worker Joyce McDonald that he was on his way to the Wildwood police station, just ten miles to the north, to check on the autopsy report of a young boy.

Before going to the police station, Humphreys stopped at the apartment of Gail Goodwins, who at one time was the subject of an HRS investigation. Humphreys said he was there on a social call, informing Goodwins of his transfer to Ocala. To Goodwins, the big man seemed depressed about his transfer, pacing about her apartment until her boyfriend, Michael Collins, arrived. As Humphreys was leaving, he turned and gave Goodwins a bear hug.

From Goodwins's apartment, Humphreys drove to the Wildwood police station, where he checked on the autopsy report and then left. At four o'clock, Humphreys was pulling through the parking lot of the Journey's End Motel when he spotted a small boy alone in a car. He made several passes through the lot, then parked his car and went into the motel. The desk clerk, Ruth Mathieu, was talking with two other women when Humphreys came up, flashed his HRS identification, and inquired about the car. "The girl that the little boy belonged to said it was hers," Mathieu recalled. "He told her that the boy shouldn't be left unattended in the car. So she went out to the car to get him. Humphreys didn't raise his voice or anything, but he acted kinda nervous, like he really had something on his mind and he was aggravated because he couldn't take care of whatever he had to take care. Like he was looking for someone." Humphreys walked out, got into his Olds, and drove across the parking lot to a Speedway convenience store. He bought a six-pack of beer and tooled his Olds onto State Road 44, heading west to Interstate 75, and home.

She was standing near the northbound entrance

ramp to 1–75 with her thumb out, a somewhat bedraggled blond wearing cutoff shorts and a floral T-shirt, a
tote bag over her broad shoulder. Humphreys' glance
caught a pleading in the woman's eyes. He pulled over.
She came up to the passenger door, peered through the
window, and smiled. Humphreys noticed the scarlet
splashes across her forehead. Burn scars, maybe a
birthmark.

"I really need to get up to Ocala. My kids are
with their sister up there and my car broke down."
Humphreys waved her in with his broad hand. She was
inside the car, the bag between her sneakers. Humphreys
drove up the incline and merged with 1–75's northern
flow.

She was talking, bouncing in the seat, waving her
hands and asking questions—Where was he from? What
did he do?

"An investigator? You mean, like a cop?" Her lips
curled up to show a crowd of sour teeth. "Really? Mind
if I have a beer? I'm wiped. I just need something to
drink." Humphreys looked over, but she already had a
bottle of Miller in her hand, removing the cap with a
quick twist. She took a long pull. "Thanks. You know, I'm
really stuck. They want all this money for the car. Damn,
I need to get a hundred dollars and there's no way . . .
just no way. I don't know what I'm goin' to do. See, see
here." She fumbled with the bag at her feet and came up
with a plastic business-card wallet, flipped it open, and
shoved it toward him. Humphreys glimpsed a color
photo of two blond children, formally posed atop a table.
One of those Kmart studio portraits. "All these cards
here," she gushed, "these are my clients. You see, I had
this pressure-cleaning business, but I got all ripped off.

*You know, I mean, I'm a Christian, but I sometimes do
some things. You know, like, I mean as a professional call
girl. Thirty for head. Seventy-five straight sex. Just off in
the woods."*

Humphreys waved her off and cut in. *"No, no. I'm on
my way home. I can give you a ride, but best not go on
anymore about any of that."*

The woman seemed either genuinely distressed or
was working up a scam, but the veteran cop let it pass.
On that Tuesday afternoon, Dick Humphreys was preoc-
cupied. The transfer to Ocala already had him down,
and that anniversary the night before had only added to
the weight of time. He didn't notice the woman's hands
as they set the bottle down between her feet.

"Hey."

A glance showed Humphreys the long barrel of the
revolver that had replaced the beer in her hand. Despite
a metallic rush of adrenaline, the veteran cop kept his
cool. The .38 service pistol he usually carried had been
left at home that morning.

"Just get off at 484." She punched the barrel hard
into his rib cage. *"And then make a right."*

"Are you sure you want to go on with this?"
Humphreys spoke as if he were cautioning a child about
to do something foolish. She shoved the revolver, dig-
ging into his heavy belly.

*"Just do what the fuck I tell you. Fat motherfucking
cop. You motherfuckers give me nothing but shit."*

He flipped the turn indicator. Over the rush of cool
air blowing from the AC, the signal beat like a metallic
heartbeat. Humphreys eased the car down the exit off
the interstate and came to a stop. *"Take a left, take a
left."*

Humphreys squinted into the facing sun and peeked at his watch. 4:45. She continued to work the barrel into his flesh. Simple highway robbery, he figured. Take the cash, maybe the credit cards if she was as dumb as she seemed. Probably take the car. Leave his ass up in the woods. Shirley's going to be scared silly. Goddamn, what kind of walk is this bitch going to leave me with?

"You get up here across from Marion Oaks, you make a right. Take it straight on up."

Humphreys made the right that took them into what looked to be a failed subdivision. The streets were laid out, but somebody had dropped the ball. The street went nowhere. Brittle weeds and spindly scrubs had reclaimed the unsold lots, a few still flagged by bedraggled survey ribbons of dirty orange plastic. And then there was no more street to drive.

"Pull it up here."

Dick Humphreys brought his car to a stop alongside a concrete casement holding a sewer grate. He figured they were at least a half mile from the highway. At least she hadn't taken him way out into the woods. It would be an easy walk to one of the houses in Marion Oaks after she was done. The sun was still up. Humphreys knew if he just kept it cool not much was likely to happen.

"Get the fuck out." *She opened her door and backed out, leaving her bag on the floorboard. Humphreys pulled his keys out of the ignition and picked up his briefcase. She was around the back of the Olds and standing at the rear fender. As he shoved his door wide, he looked up at the .22 she had in her hand. A cheap nine-shot revolver. Hell, he thought, even if she got a shot off there was a good chance it wouldn't be a kill* shot. He got out and carefully, slowly stepped away from the car and faced her, his back to the sewer grate. Humphreys held himself quietly, waiting, feeling the grip of the briefcase growing wet in his palm, feeling a bruised ache where she had shoved the gun. And then he knew. She was raising up her arm. She was taking a small step backward with her right foot.

The bullet hit him down there. In the gut. His hands were up. The briefcase dropped. His arm. He dropped to the ground. Make a small target. Roll. His back. And another. They were all over him. There was nothing but fire. Fires burning way down inside and getting bigger. There was no air down there in the grass. He needed to get up, was up. On his knees. Then up to his feet. But no. He couldn't. He fell back against the concrete. He was choking. His throat was full. If he could just spit it up he could breathe. It was hard to grab air. He felt her close. She was close. She was all bright white and red.

"Die, motherfucker."

He saw the gun coming in. The long steel finger against his chest. Funny how he felt that. Everything was cold and wet. But right there it was hot. And then there was nothing at all. Dick Humphreys was gone when her last hollow-point round rocketed behind his left ear and through his skull, spraying fragments of lead and bone through his abandoned brain.

SIX

Connections

It was just after nine o'clock on Wednesday night, September 12, when David Taylor reluctantly left his couch to answer the phone. Taylor knew it wasn't going to be anything he wanted to hear. Generally Major Crimes investigators only get the bad ones when they've gone off the clock. Thirty minutes later Taylor's hunch was confirmed as he stared down into the face of the dead man.

The brilliant pool of light bathing the scene heightened the blue and purple lividity staining the victim's broad, sagging face. A pair of glasses lay askew across the forehead. The white of the short-sleeved shirt gave way to heavy bloodstains across the chest and the stomach. Taylor carefully stepped to his right and noted more stains across the shoulder and back. The victim's brown pants had grass stains on the knees and crotch as though he had been rolling around. On the left wrist, he still wore a watch. On the left hand, a wedding band. The tops of a pen and pencil set showed in his front pocket.

Taylor lifted them and said, "Cross." Then the detective noticed the ants. A flurry of them. All over the body. Taylor's eyes traveled back to the pants. The front pockets were turned out as if someone had gone through them. The back pockets were empty: no wallet.

Gary Brock, the assistant medical examiner, came up behind Taylor as the investigator hunkered down alongside the victim. "I say it's second-stage rigor mortis, David. Sixteen to eighteen hours. Just like this." Although the floodlights from the evidence unit were more than enough for good exposure, technician Wayne Scroggins' 35-mm camera went off with a flash each time he snapped its shutter, methodically documenting every inch of the body and its surroundings. Taylor stepped out of the whiteness and waited until Scroggins finished up. Then he and Brock began examining the corpse.

"Got a clear shot to the heart here. Right there." Taylor tapped his finger at a nearly symmetrical perforation in the blood-soaked shirt. "I swear there's burns around that. Got the barrel on him. Let's turn him. Hey, Wayne, get over here for this." Brock and Taylor held the dead man upright so that Scroggins could close in for a shot of the chest wound. Then they laid their victim onto a white sheet.

"That's it. Let's just stop here now," said Taylor. "Secure the scene. I want to get Captain Binegar out here, and we need to find out who this guy is. I think it's that HRS guy out of Sumter County that went missing yesterday."

August wasn't the hottest month in Florida. The heat and humidity that build during the summer seemed to concentrate in September. Forty minutes till midnight and the temperature had fallen only to a damp seventy-five degrees when Captain Steve Binegar pulled up in his maroon Chevrolet.

Thirty-three years old, Binegar had commanded the Marion County Sheriff's Criminal Investigation Division for almost a year. A solid light heavyweight with a bulldog jaw somewhat softened by a set of aviator-style glasses, Binegar had left the Federal Bureau of Investigation after a three-year stint in Virginia. He had risen from special agent to relief supervisor in the Bureau, where he'd worked violent and white-collar crime, fugitive investigations, and foreign counterintelligence. Prior to the FBI, he had served with the Marion County Sheriff's Office for seven years. Even in high school, he had known he wanted a life in law enforcement, and after a stint in the Marines as a military policeman, he had returned to Ocala and signed on as a deputy. Rising through the ranks, from corrections officer through the patrol division, the no-nonsense young cop took a degree in criminal justice and then helped organize MCSO's drug-enforcement and vice squad. When he was passed over for a promotion, Binegar's stiff-necked temper led him to resign and join the FBI. His old friend, Major Dan Henry, in collusion with Binegar's homesick wife, Kathy, persuaded him to leave Virginia and the Bureau for the CID post with Marion County. Binegar almost immediately made his mark by busting an elusive team of violent armed robbers who had specialized in hitting mom-and-pop grocery stores around the county. The captain was known for taking a case by its throat and wringing it till it coughed up a perpetrator. He expected his men to do the same.

Binegar joined Taylor for a view of the body and its surroundings. Taylor had just finished briefing his captain when a Sumter County sheriff's unit arrived, blue and red lights flashing. The Sumter County officers had a civilian in tow. Ken Jones, a child protective investigator with HRS, immediately identified the body as Charles Richard Humphreys.

Taylor took a statement from Jones, who sketched out Humphreys's routine on Tuesday. Just after midnight, Taylor and Binegar sped to the Wildwood police station, where the assistant police chief tipped them to the Wildwood Commons and a woman named Gail Goodwins. A little before three o'clock, Gail Goodwins and her boyfriend, Michael Collins, answered an authoritative knock on their door. Facing the young couple were the Wildwood police chief, his assistant, Captain Binegar, and Taylor, who asked them to make a trip to Ocala.

Waiting at the CID offices in the Marion County sheriff's sleek headquarters was a bald-headed detective stirring sugars into a cup of coffee. Bruce Munster was the most experienced homicide investigator in Binegar's squad, a veteran of the Miami streets, where he had specialized in undercover scams and beachside street crimes. Marriage had brought Munster on the train up from Dade County's boiling gumbo of drugs, violence, and sleaze to the rolling hills, forests, and horse farms of Marion County. He had been looking for a laid-back place in the country, with a low crime rate. But it just wasn't working out that way.

Along with sex crimes and homicide, another of Munster's specialties was the interview. The big guy with the deadpan face and the easy patter prided himself on being able to slide his subjects into a garrulous mood. He also had outstanding ability at separating truth from fiction. Binegar asked Munster to join Taylor in taking the statements of Goodwins and Collins. "As far as we know, these two were the last ones to see Humphreys alive," said Binegar, before the two detectives left his office. "Find out why Humphreys went to her apartment."

Munster and Taylor took Goodwins first, and then Munster did Collins one on one. Each was videotaped. At five in the morning, the couple was returned to Wildwood, no longer considered suspects. Three hours later, Taylor briefed Marion County Sheriff Don Moreland's second-in-command, Major Dan Henry, on the investigation, then drove back out to the crime scene to assist in processing for evidence. By ten that morning, Investigator Ricky Deen of the state attorney's office had met with Taylor and was on his way to Humphreys's HRS office in Sumter County for background on the victim and his activities prior to his murder. Mrs. Humphreys said that her husband never carried more than thirty or forty dollars, did not usually pick up hitchhikers, and was at home every evening like clockwork. She also told detectives that her husband's missing Olds had two bumper stickers—one, a Fraternal Order of Police decal and the other a Florida Association of State Troopers decal. By Saturday afternoon Taylor had Ruth Mathieu's description of Humphreys's stop at the Journey's End Motel in Wildwood that Tuesday afternoon.

On Monday morning, Taylor was dutifully filling out an FBI VICAP report when Captain Binegar came to the door of his office and called the young detective in for a meeting. Taylor crossed the hall into the CID conference room to find Munster, Investigator Jay Manifold, and the Major Crimes supervisor, Sergeant Brian Jarvis, along with Binegar and three others. Citrus County investigators Jerry Thompson, Marvin Padgett, and David Strickland sat on one side of the long table, three fat file folders holding their work on David Spears's homicide. "Okay," said Binegar. "Let's see what we've got. Just go around the table. Jay, why don't you give us Burress first, and then David and Bruce can pick up with theirs, and then the gentlemen from Citrus."

By the end of the meeting, the eight detectives had concluded that the similarities were too striking to ignore. Counting these three murders, plus one in Pasco County with the same earmarks, even the most cautious among them felt that a serial killer was a real possibility. The meeting ended with everyone agreeing to get back together just as soon as more information could be gathered. As Taylor was leaving, Binegar signaled him down to his office. The young cop took a seat at the captain's desk. "David, you're doing a hell of job on this, and what I've got to do now has nothing to do with your work. But I've got to go with Bruce on this one. If this turns out to be a serial, Bruce has had more experience than any of us. He's going to take point." Despite his crisp black mustache, Taylor had a soft, open face most people would not associate with a homicide detective, and at this moment Binegar saw it shudder briefly and then recompose. "I want you to work with Bruce on this. It's got to be a team effort from here on out. And if it turns out that these are linked with Citrus and Pasco, all of us are going to have to leave our egos at home. All right?"

Binegar could understand what Taylor was going

through. He could still recall the hit his own pride had taken when he was passed over for promotion.

"Yes, sir," said Taylor. "I understand. Whatever it takes."

The kid's not smiling, thought Binegar, *but thank God, he doesn't have my temper.*

Dr. Janet Pillow's autopsy on Humphreys produced five bullets and multiple fragments from a sixth. A seventh bullet, the one through the victim's right wrist, was never found. All were .22-caliber hollow points. They had lacerated Humphreys's heart, lungs, stomach, diaphragm, liver, right kidney, colon, and brain. Testing showed negative on alcohol. Dr. Pillow pointed out a curious bruise on the body to Munster, who was attending the autopsy along with Sergeant Jarvis and the evidence officer, Carol Egger. A dark, symmetrical ring on the right side of the midline just below the right rib cage. "Looks like a pistol was shoved up on him. See there." Munster made a small circle with his finger above the abrasion. "An outline of the barrel opening. Carol, please take a picture of this." Egger's camera went off with a burst of light.

Driving back from the medical examiner's office in Leesburg, Jarvis listened to his longtime buddy tick off the similarities between Humphreys's homicide and those of Burress, Spears, and the John Doe in Pasco County. The two detectives were a study in contrast. Jarvis had the look of a homicide cop out of central casting—close-cropped dark hair that receded from a widow's peak, a tightly manicured mustache, steely eyes, and an athletic body. With his bald head, bland face, and light voice, Munster could pass for an easy-going high-school counselor. Jarvis looked like the kind of cop Munster actually was. But Jarvis, though supervisor of the Major Crimes Unit, preferred spending his time at the keyboard of the CID computer rather than out in the field, a fact Munster quickly brought up on the way back to Ocala. "We need to feed everything into your computer, Brian. Humphreys, Burress, Spears. Even that one Ocala PD has . . . Giddens. I know it was a .38, and only one shot to the head that killed that one, but he fits in the ballpark. Then there's that one in Georgia Jerry Thompson has a line on. And I think Volusia has another . . ."

"Didn't they make an arrest on that?" asked Jarvis.

"Yeah, but I think I'll still give them a call."

By this time, John Tilley in Marion County and Jerry Thompson had been comparing notes on their cases for almost two weeks. Thompson had gone off on the trail of a male suspect arrested in Manatee County, south of Saint Petersburg. Articles seized from the suspect's pickup truck appeared to match some of those missing from David Spears's abandoned vehicle. But this lead came to a fruitless end, and Thompson had written it off the day Humphreys's body was discovered west of Ocala. On September 17, Thompson and Padgett left Citrus County for Ocala and arrived at the MCSO, where Tilley, Munster, Binegar, and a weary David Taylor were waiting in the CID conference room.

The investigators threw open their case files and

began. What did they have? Taylor took a large drawing pad and charted the cases.

Date:	Victim:	Location of body:
April 5	Giddens	Marion County
May 5	Unidentified male	I–75 Brooks County, Georgia
May 19	Spears	Citrus County
June 6	Unidentified male	Pasco County
June 7	Siems, missing	Car found, Marion County
July 30	Burress	Marion County
September 12	Humphreys	Marion County

All of the known dead had been killed with multiple .22 bullets, except for Giddens, who had one .38 shot to the head. All of the vehicles, except for Giddens's, had been recovered far from the victims. All of the vehicles, except his, had had their tags removed, been wiped clean of fingerprints, and were missing their keys. All of the victims had been white males traveling alone; all were within the same age range.

Taylor picked up the rough chart he'd completed and rested it on an aluminum easel at the end of the long table. They all stared at it, doodled on the yellow legal pads in front of them, and looked around the table.

"Okay, guys," said Binegar. "Any ideas?"

"This Giddens doesn't fit." Thompson ran his pen across his mustache. "One shot, different caliber."

Binegar nodded. "Yeah, I can't nail it down yet. But

this guy's a peanut farmer. Came down from Georgia. Has folks around here. Indicators are he was down to Lauderdale, maybe was doing some pot deal. Went through the trunk and found over a grand stuffed in a work glove."

"The other vehicles were cleaned out," said Munster. "I mean, they could've missed the money, but the case just doesn't fit. All the others were torso shots. This one was like an execution."

"Why'd you say 'they'?"

"A couple of things. Major Henry said something when he saw Humphreys out there by Marion Oaks. He said he thought the killer was a woman. The shots to the body. Women shoot for the torso, not the head. When they do suicide, they shoot here . . ." Munster cocked his thumb and thrust his finger to his chest. "That's where the kill shot went on Humphreys. Burress took his in the chest and back."

"Same with Spears and the John Doe in Pasco." Thompson rolled his pen back and forth across the table. "The Homicide Investigators Association meeting is day after tomorrow up in Green Cove Springs. Let's bring our stuff up there and see if we got one."

"Got one what?" asked Tilley.

"A serial."

"Serial killer? But Bruce is talking about a woman!"

"Women," corrected Munster. "There were two of them in Siems's car when they wrecked it."

"Could be a team," said Binegar. "Lots of those. Male and female. Could be some guy working with these two. Or maybe the two women just got hold of the car."

Thompson slipped his pen into his shirt pocket. "See you in Green Cove Springs."

· · ·

The Florida Homicide Investigators Association meeting south of Jacksonville in Green Cove Springs raised no new leads, but Munster and Thompson left hoping that something might break soon now that their cases had played before other jurisdictions. On September 21, another meeting was held in Marion County. This time Larry Horzepa and Bob Kelley were on hand with their hefty Mallory file, which included Chastity Lee Marcus. Tom Muck from Pasco County detailed what evidence his office had on the still-unidentified victim with nine bullets in him. It was agreed that vacuumings and fibers from this case and the ones in Marion and Citrus Counties should be sent up to the FBI lab for comparison. Binegar said that was fine but suggested the bullets should go to the FDLE for analysis. "I know how long those guys up in Quantico will take. Months. They've got a hell of a backlog."

A short list of female suspects was tallied by Munster and Muck and put alongside Chastity. Muck had initially supposed his victim to have been somehow involved in some homosexual encounter and, despite the disagreement of the other detectives, continued to entertain the possibility. The investigators were not having an easy time with Muck, a graying little fellow with defensive eyes and an aggressive strut who seemed less than willing to get on board as a team member. "A loose cannon," said one detective. "No matter what idea came up, he was against it."

Homicide detectives are, by nature, highly protective of their information and their turf and have well-developed egos by the time they reach this level. When they are thrust together in a joint investigation that crosses jurisdictions and departments, a certain volatility results. Conflicts in methodology and personality, competition for priorities, and an unwillingness to function under leadership outside their jurisdiction's chain of command, all contribute to a multiagency investigation's downfall. In this case, all the detectives were aware of the notoriety the case would produce in the media. Who then was going to do the talking? Who was going to take the lead? Who was going to end up in the limelight?

Binegar saw all this developing before him as he sat in the meeting. The seeds of disaster were germinating. Circumstances had led them all to this office. Five of these cases were tied to Marion County, either by bodies or by vehicles. Sooner or later, thought Binegar, somebody is going to have to step in and call the shots. He had no doubts as to who that would be.

On into October the detectives tracked likely female suspects—hookers, topless dancers, check forgers, thieves, druggies—from one side of the state to the other. None of them paid off. On October 12, Munster got a call from Jarvis that the Ocoee cops had recovered Humphreys's badge case and identification in the Green Swamp area down in the far corner of Lake County, over seventy miles southeast of where Humphreys had been killed. The next day, Munster and Taylor, fitted out with high-top boots and jeans, were following a snake-hunter named Williams down a red-clay trail called Boggy Marsh Road. Williams had found the badge case and papers. "That badge case you got there," said Williams. "That was all wet 'cause it was down off there in that water." Williams pointed off in the direction of one of the scores of lakes that give the county its name.

Munster and Taylor, along with two sheriff's deputies, began a systematic search of the area. They found Humphreys's gold tobacco pouch, his pipe, some HRS documents with Humphreys's name on them, and a crumpled yellow bumper sticker that read: Florida State Troopers' Association. "After we get photos of all this shit, David, be careful when you bag that baby." Munster tipped the toe of his boot over the bumper sticker. "There's a wild chance we could get a print from it."

Two ice scrapers, one Miller Lite beer bottle, and a Bud can, both empty, were found. Then the two investigators heard a shout from one of the deputies. He held up an old, worn army jacket bearing a name: POOL. It had obviously been down in the sand for a long time. There were two bullet holes through the collar, surrounded by brownish stains. "We take that along," said Munster. "Looks like somebody got hit, sometime. Never know when it might come up." Taylor and Munster noted that the position of the discarded objects indicated they had probably been tossed from the windows of a moving vehicle onto both shoulders of the road.

Munster was at home having supper with his wife and small daughter when the phone rang later that evening. Communications advised that a Suwannee County sheriff's deputy, Tony Cameron, had called to say they had Dick Humphreys's Oldsmobile Firenza impounded up in Live Oak. "Good God, that's two hundred miles from where we found his stuff this afternoon!" Munster took Cameron's number and went to his den to make the call. While dialing he thought of his killer. *Really putting some effort into this, aren't you? You really know the game.*

Cameron told Munster that the car had first been spotted on September 19 but had not been towed in until the twenty-fifth. "We didn't have a tag on it," said Cameron. "And then they had two missing numbers off the vehicle identification. Came up with a Miami address. That was nowhere. I didn't get it coordinated until I saw your BOLO."

Munster, Taylor, and Bud Damron from the MCSO garage drove north to Live Oak on Monday, the fifteenth. Munster noticed that the Firenza sticker that had been on the right and left panels had been removed.

"Looks like they used something to wipe it down," said Taylor. "See these smears?" White streaks crossed the windows, the dashboard, and the doors. "And remember those bumper stickers? See where they were?" Taylor waved his finger above two discolored rectangular patches along the back of the Olds.

Munster peered through the driver's window and saw cigarette butts in the ashtray and a can of Busch on the seat. "Dick Humphreys didn't smoke cigarettes, and the beer he bought was Miller Lite." No keys were found. The seat had been pulled up as far as it would go. The rearview mirror had been adjusted at an angle. "Short driver," he noted.

A search of the area where the car was found yielded nothing in the way of evidence. It was less than a tenth of a mile from an exit ramp on Interstate 10. Munster and Taylor looked for the nearest business. A quarter mile away they found Parnell's United 500, a truck stop. Ida Parnell fetched two iced teas and sat down with the detectives. "The only female I can recall coming in here was about a month ago. She had a dress on and was carrying this tote-type bag. She sat down in that corner over there and then got up and went to the bathroom, come out wearing shorts. Nope, didn't talk to her. Then she walked off."

Before leaving Live Oak, Munster and Taylor interviewed the deputies who had found Humphreys's car and took a set of latent prints from them for elimination. Then Munster recalled there was a pay phone outside Parnell's. He contacted the operator of the company—People's Telephone, in Dallas, Texas—and requested all toll calls placed from the phone from September 11 through September 19. "Way the hell up here," he told Taylor, "she just might have had to call for a ride."

Back in Marion, the Firenza having already arrived ahead of him, Munster put in a call to Dave Strickland down in Citrus and asked for some help in processing Humphreys's car. The next morning, before meeting the Citrus County crew, Munster decided to take another look at Peter Siems's car. Munster strolled over from the MCSO garage to a covered barn, where the wrecked Pontiac had been gathering dust since July.

Munster made mental notes as he walked around the Sunbird. Its original nameplates and stickers were in place. But the dealer's sticker had been removed. The ashtray was filled with cigarette butts. He got in to remove the ashtray, then took a peek beneath the seat and found a Windex bottle and a full can of Bud. On the Windex was an Eckerd drugstore price sticker.

The pricing label was traced to an Eckerd's in Atlanta. Its date of sale was February 1990. A call to Siems's sister-in-law was made. To the best of her knowledge, Peter Siems had never been in Atlanta, and he certainly wasn't in Atlanta in February 1990.

At the same time, Strickland's team had found a receipt beneath the gas pedal of Humphreys's car. Emro Speedway, dated 9/11/90. A purchase for $3.99. The Emro Speedway was adjacent to the Journey's End Motel in Wildwood, the last place Humphreys had been seen alive.

Scraps of paper, cigarette butts, beer cans, a few condoms, abandoned vehicles, and six dead bodies were all the evidence the detectives had. But a pattern was emerging—not a pattern of robbery, but of killing. Stranger-on-stranger homicide. No apparent motive; the robberies seemed to be merely opportunistic. Following the killing, the murderer just took the money. The crimes had occurred almost monthly, with a "cooling off" period between them. They seemed calculated, enjoyed. Not content with one shot or two, the killer had lavished four, six, nine rounds on the torsos. This most recent one, Humphreys, had a new wrinkle, the shot to the head. There was a definite escalation in the killing. And Humphreys's close shot to the heart suggested an intimacy. Enjoyment, humiliation, control. All the red flags that mark a serial killer. Or killers. And this time, the suspects were female. This was new territory.

SEVEN

Two Days in November

Ty woke up beneath a 3-D reproduction of Jesus and his Last Supper, rolled over, and pulled the sheets up to her freckled nose. It was November 16, and her plane was leaving for Ohio tomorrow. From outside the little bed-sitting-room tucked behind the Belgrade Restaurant, Ty could hear late-morning traffic motoring up and down Ridgewood Avenue. She was alone. She was hung over, and Lee was gone. Ty remembered Lee getting up sometime earlier, had watched her as she padded from their bed to the bathroom and returned. The thin morning light had come filtering through the small windows facing north. Lee's body was so pale, her belly spilled over the waist of her shorts, and Ty had momentarily focused on the angry bullet scar Lee carried there. Ty recalled the first time she had traced the old wound with her finger and then kissed it. That had been a long time ago, back when they were having sex, but that had lasted only a few months. Back in 1986, back through all those beers and bars, back through the fifteen-dollar-a-night motel rooms and the trailer parks crawling with oily-backed palmetto bugs the size of mice and old geezers running out their string on union pensions. Back in the Zodiac Bar, where they had met.

Ty had been a regular in the Zodiac, a watering hole for Daytona Beach lesbians. She was a roly-poly redhead with a burgundy Suzuki motorbike and no restraints, who had fled her hometown of Cadiz, Ohio, three years earlier, when she was twenty-six. Cadiz may have been Clark Gable's hometown, but it was too small and too straight for Ty. Her homosexuality was a touchy subject in the family, and Tyria Jolene was very sensitive to her family.

. Lee had come into the Zodiac one afternoon, and it was as though they had been waiting for each other all their lives. Lee said she was sleeping in her car, had been ripped off down in the Keys by her partner and sometime lover. Some bitch named Tony had taken Lee's pressure-cleaning equipment and had left her high and dry. The more beers Ty and Lee knocked back, the more Lee spouted. Said she'd been popped for some screwed-up armed robbery that really wasn't a robbery. She'd been wasted on beer and Southern Comfort and Librium. She'd just busted up with her boyfriend, Ray, and she didn't mean to do nothing except maybe kill herself. "Look," she said and lifted her T-shirt, right there in the Zodiac, and pointed at this awful scar on her side. That's where she'd tried killing herself before, she said, back when this rich husband of hers, this old fart who had lots of money, had dumped her for no damned good reason. Used to beat her with his cane . . . All the time Lee kept talking bullshit, but so sweet and funny. That was the way she was, except sometimes. One minute she was just your best, best friend ever. The next, she could be at your throat. But then, she'd never had nothing all her life. Never had a family. They'd just dumped her. That's what she said.

Ty was thinking all these things—and more. Thinking of more recent things. Like all the weird stuff Lee was bringing home. All kinds of stuff. Tools and toolboxes. Electric razors. Cameras. Fishing gear. Watches. A goddamned spellchecker. And briefcases and clothes. And cars. Even another gun.

Ty was glad she was leaving tomorrow. Mom had sent a plane ticket for Thanksgiving. Things were really getting too weird. And scary. Something was going to happen. And Tyria Jolene Moore was smack in the middle of it. She'd been the one driving that Sunbird when they plowed through that fence out in the Ocala forest. Broken glass and beer cans flying. Blood running down Lee's arm and all over her face. Back there tearing that license tag off with her bloody hands and screaming, "Run, you dumb bitch! You're driving a murdered man's car! Stupid cunt!"

Now the door swung open and Lee pulled at her foot. "C'mon, Ty. Get up. We got to move our stuff out of here. I've had enough of that son-of-a-bitch Yugoslavian bastard. He's not getting a goddamned dime out of me. Cocksucker."

Lee had it in for Val Ivkolivich. She had hassled with their landlord almost continuously since they had moved in last month. She was constantly in the old guy's face, ever since he'd stopped giving her rides out to the interstate. Lee didn't know when to let things go. She didn't give a damn that they owed money to Val and his wife, Vera. Lee just kept at him, trying to pick a fight. That's what she really wanted. Said she'd shoot the motherfucker dead. So here they were—evicted.

"What're we doing?" Ty got up from the bed and coughed. "I'm going up to my folks tomorrow. Got my ticket up . . ."

"We're getting a room back down at the Fairview. I've got the money."

Ty pushed past Lee as she rounded the bed, heading for the bathroom. The tiny room was piled with tool boxes, suitcases, plastic milk cases stuffed with bath and kitchen items, stacks of newspapers, and empty beer cans. "*I'm* not getting a room. I'm going home. You get a room."

"Yeah, Ty. But you're coming back. You're coming back, right? I mean, I'll get everything all straightened out."

Lee was all sweet and bright now, talking about how everything would be different. How she would stop tricking.

Ty loaded toothpaste onto her brush and turned on the tap. She had heard all this shit for a good while. Stop tricking. Bullshit. Ty saw her eyes blink in the mirror.

Lee, why don't you just stop killing them? she thought.

Ty saw herself going pale. She felt queasy. A shiver ran up her neck, and she felt her scalp go cold. She didn't dare let that thought grab her for very long. Not for even a heartbeat. *I don't care what Lee says. She won't stop killing. That's just bullshit,* Ty told herself, *just more of her big badass bullshit.* That's all it had been for months, since way back in December when Lee had come in that morning all excited up at the Ocean Shores motel. She'd been drinking, but something else had had her going. There was a big old Cadillac parked out front of the room. Lee was all over the place. "We're moving," she said, "right now." Had this Cadillac she'd borrowed. But then, later on that day, sitting on the floor, watching "Wheel of Fortune," Lee had come clean. "I killed a guy last night. Shot him dead."

And that had been the first. Maybe it would all go away, Ty thought. Maybe if she could just get away. And stay away. What was left, anyway? No job. That had all been over with when she had popped her boss at the motel. That fucking Iranian. Surprised his ass. Ty left a little grin on the mirror before pulling off her T-shirt and underwear. She turned on the shower, and when it was nice and warm she stepped in and tried to think about home. But she couldn't. Her mind replayed an inventory of all that stuff, all those cars. She didn't let herself think too much about where they had come from. That was trouble. She could care less about those guys. They were dead. One night in September they had been watching Roseanne doing a comedy special on the TV. Roseanne was a hoot. She was doing this routine about serial killers, about how they were always men who were psychos; but if one of them turned out to be a woman, everybody would just call her a man-hater, and Lee had just burst out, "That's me she's talking about!"

Tyria Jolene Moore didn't want to know any more about it. Tyria Jolene Moore just wanted to get the hell away from Lee and her .22 nine-shot. Sooner or later it was all going to come down on Lee.

Ty would go up for Thanksgiving, get things squared away with her mom and dad, get a line on a job. Maybe her sister in Pennsylvania would let her stay with her. Then she'd come back down, get her stuff, and get gone. It was only a matter of time until the police caught up with Lee. She was full of shit when she'd say they ain't got nothing, that there was nothing to worry about. Ty turned around and let the hot spray massage her thick neck. Maybe one time, she thought. Maybe once. But not two, three, four times. No way. Lee was always saying how she was street-smart, that there was no way the fucking cops could put anything on her. Maybe. Maybe not. But Tyria Jolene Moore wasn't going to be around to find out. There wasn't enough love left between them to risk a lifetime in prison.

Lee stood in the early evening shadows of the interstate overpass. Shifting the blue plastic tote bag from her right shoulder to her left, she reached into the pocket of her shorts for the cigarette lighter. Her back to oncoming traffic, she clicked up a flame for her Marlboro Light. Ty was up in Ohio with her mom and dad and sisters, getting ready for Thanksgiving. Lee had put her on the plane yesterday. Turkey and all the trimmings for Ty. Standing in the broken glass, cigarette butts, and weeds that littered Highway 44 where it crossed I-75 west of Wildwood, Lee felt abandoned. Ty had said she'd be back in two weeks, but things were all different now. All fucked up. Again. Like usual. Nobody would give her a fucking break. All of them all the time fucking her over. She swung the tote bag off her left shoulder and felt the weight of the pistol. An old maroon Grand Prix moved toward her. Her eyes caught the single silhouette behind the wheel. Out went her left hand, and a smiling mask covered her face. The big Pontiac slowed and came to a stop a dozen yards ahead. She was at the passenger door, her head thrust through the open window.

"Where you headed?" Lee asked. She raised her eyebrows and saw her face faintly reflected in the old guy's tinted glasses.

"I'm on my way up to Birmingham, darlin'," he said. "What can I do for you?"

"Just let me ride along. I need to get my kids up in Perry. See here, I've got their pictures." She pulled up the brown card wallet and flashed the Instamatic photo of the two blond children. "You gonna take 19 north?"

"Yeah, thought I would. Hop in. Name's Gino. Gino Antonio."

Antonio accelerated the Grand Prix onto the asphalt and drove west toward a November sun lowering into the Gulf of Mexico.

Sipping brews, he loosened up as they gabbed, and flashed his badge. Reserve Police. She couldn't tell if he noticed her sneer when he handed her the shield. She ran her finger over it and laid it down on the seat. She stared at his profile. Little fucker. Just like all the rest, only smaller. Same as the last one. Another fucking cop. Always full of shit, always thinking how they had it all coming to them when all they did was hassle people, fuck them over. Push people around with their damned badges. Cocksuckers.

Somewhere between Chiefland and Cross City, deep into the darkness of hardscrabble Dixie County and a couple of six-packs of Budweiser, the sixty-year-old Gino Antonio found her desirable. Somewhere along lonely Highway 19 he agreed to some fun. She made it sound easy, actually worthwhile since she needed the money to get her car fixed up and her kids back home.

Hell, just another hooker down on her luck, it looked like to him. No big hurry getting up to that truck in

Alabama. Had his severance money from the security job in his pocket, had a job waiting up in Birmingham. Might as well have a little roadside R & R. No way Aileen Berry would ever know. Even so, Aileen had known him since 1963. Knew he was a truck-driving man and accepted all that. He fingered the ruby ring Aileen had given him just before he'd left his trailer down in Cocoa. Might as well take this broad up on her offer. She'd got the rubbers here at the last beer stop. He cleared his throat.

"So, you say you know a place we can get to? I mean, you sure you don't want to stop and get a room or something?"

"Oh, no, no," she told him. "I don't want nothing to do with rooms. I do it my way and I like it out in the woods. It's better that way and you don't have to put up any more money, you know? What's the use of all that? It's real nice out tonight. Look up right into the stars. Sex under the stars is just too righteous. Just stay on up this way and I'll tell you where to turn. I been up this way a bunch. Hell, I know every backroad from Cedar Key to Saint Augustine."

Once past Cross City, she told him to be on the look-out for a county road. She pulled the tote bag from against the seat and reached in, leaving it slightly open between her feet. "Here you go. Here. Here. Go right."

The headlights on the Grand Prix fingered into the darkness as it bumped along a desolate logging road and finally came to a stop. Outside, the whole world was damp and endlessly quiet.

"Why don't you get out and get your clothes off?" *She waited on the seat beside him.* "Here. Take 'em." *She handed him a foil packet of Trojans. He took them, opened his door, and slid out. She reached down to the bag and her pistol.*

"What're you doing now?" Antonio watched her as she came around the rear of the car. "Why don't you get ready, honey?" She had the .22 out in front of her as she rounded the fender and faced him. "What the shit you think you're doing?" He took a step to the side and backed across the dirt road.

"Just go ahead and strip down, fucking cop. You're a cop, right? Or just another cocksucker tryin' to fuck me out of a free piece of ass? You motherfuckers are all alike. Strip on down." She set her feet wide and covered the man's chest with the barrel. "Or you want me to just start shooting?"

Antonio cursed her and unzipped his pants. He pulled his shirt over his head and tossed it down. "I mean strip all the way down. Get a taste for it. You like it? Different from this end, huh? Get your shoes off, get your fucking pants off, your fucking underwear."

Gino Antonio stood under the stars with only a pair of white tube socks covering his small feet. "Take off your glasses. And turn around." The sixty-year-old sometime trucker and sometime security guard felt his sweat chilling in the November night. "If you're gonna take the car, just take it. Okay?"

Antonio was doing his best to sound reasonable, calm, and understanding. The bitch was likely drunk, maybe even loaded up on dope. He felt his voice quivering. "I mean, we're way the hell out here. You got nothing to be afraid of. Just take the money. Take what you want. Take it. I'm not going anywhere."

"No, motherfucker. You're not going anywhere at all. Get down on your knees."

And there he was. She took a step closer and considered. He was still jabbering on, but she no longer cared what he said. It sounded like begging. She wanted that. She focused on his white body. Real white, a pale soft thing. It seemed to kind of glow. "Not much without your clothes, you old fuck. You know that? No badge, no gun. You ain't much at all. You know that?"

She considered the first shot, aimed, and fired. The white body jerked. She cocked the hammer on the clunky Double Nine with her thumb and fired another right behind the first. He was down on his hands. She stepped closer, centered the five-and-a-half-inch barrel on the base of his skull. Cocked and fired. His head jumped. She could hear him make these noises, little grunts and moans. One more. She stood over him, lowered the pistol, sighted on the protruding disks of his spine. Cocked. Steady. And fired. His knees gave way immediately and he slumped to his left. She watched him fold slowly into a fetal curl. He made no more noises. She saw something glisten in the dirt to his right. She reached down and picked up a row of teeth, holding them gingerly between her finger and thumb. She had to laugh.

EIGHT

Going Public

Twenty-five minutes north of the Marion County Sheriff's Office, the biggest serial murder investigation in the country was taking place. During the final days of August, in the space of three days, the bodies of five college students—four females and a male—had been found in three off-campus apartments. The girls had been horribly mutilated, sexually assaulted, and stabbed to death. The female bodies were provocatively posed by their killers. One victim was decapitated and her head placed on a shelf. There were few clues, almost no evidence. The bodies had been washed down with cleansers. Fear gripped the Gainesville community, and reporters from as far away as Japan and Australia flooded the college town.

I had been covering this grisly set of crimes and the investigation for the Reuter news service and *Playboy* magazine since August. Since there had been no arrests in the student murders, I devoured state newspapers for reported homicides, missing persons, rapes—anything that might possibly be linked to the Gainesville killings.

Little came of that, but another string of homicides and missing persons caught my eye. The reports were tucked into the local sections of various central Florida newspapers.

Bodies of white middle-age males with numerous bullets in them were being found throughout central Florida. Their abandoned vehicles were located miles from where they were killed. Some were nude, some were not. Three of the victims had been discovered in Marion County.

With the media sharply focused on the sensational Gainesville murders, not much ink or videotape outside of Ocala had been spent on these seemingly unrelated killings of male travelers. Initially, Marion County sheriff's spokesman Sergeant Robert Douglas had gone out of his way to downplay any possible connections between the killings, despite all the little red flags that marked their similarities. Douglas brushed aside such notions by saying the sheriff hadn't even assigned a task force. Still it was apparent that *something* was going on down in Ocala. The investigators working the highway killings were cannily taking advantage of the Gainesville drama. They had seen the damage an aggressive media pack in a feeding frenzy could inflict on an investigation. But the time was fast approaching when the public would have to be alerted.

On November 6, choosing to skip Sergeant Douglas's official line, I telephoned the commander of the Marion County Sheriff's Criminal Investigation Division. I was put through to Captain Steve Binegar, and he listened when I talked about the similarity I'd observed between these killings in his county and some others in nearby counties. I detailed what I knew about the killings, "It's really difficult," I said, "to ignore the pattern here. I know what you've been telling the press so far, but I've got to report on this. Maybe you've got a serial killer; maybe not. Just let me know what you don't want mentioned, and I'll go along. But I hope you can say something for the record."

There was a pocket of silence before Binegar replied. It was obvious he was weighing options. I explained that a Reuter story would be going out on the wire. Depending on the timing and what he had to say, it might get some play.

"Do we have a serial killer here?" He hedged. "I'm not ready to jump on the bandwagon yet. But I'm still looking at these cases as related." Binegar was not about to slap "serial murder" on his investigation and invite a media circus like the one going on in Gainesville, despite the fact that that was exactly what he and the other investigators *knew* they were dealing with. The multiagency crew was already arguing about whether to go public. Muck and Thompson were dead-set against it. Binegar and Munster knew it was only a matter of time. Might as well get our feet wet, Binegar felt.

"We figure there may be a group or individual pretending to be broken down on the side of the road," Binegar told me. "The victim stops to help and then is taken in control."

"How do you suppose that happens?" I prodded. "Nobody seems to pick up people anymore; do you suspect a woman might be involved?"

Binegar fingered the composite drawing Beth Gee had worked up on the two females described in connection with the murder in July before answering. "Mike, I've no idea right now and I've got to go."

The next day I filed the story.

An eight-month string of unsolved murders has left investigators in north-central Florida facing the possibility of a serial killer—or killers—preying upon highway travelers throughout the region. Since early this year, five middle-aged white males have been discovered alongside roads and in woods dead from gunshot wounds. A 66-year-old evangelist, missing since January, is also feared murdered. The latest victim, a former Alabama police chief, was found in September . . .

Walter Gino Antonio, nude except for a pair of tube socks, was found on the logging road in remote Dixie County on November 19. Tampa Police Captain J. F. Small was out hunting when he came upon Antonio's crumpled and bullet-riddled body. Five days later, his old Grand Prix turned up near the victim's home in Brevard County, 215 miles southeast of the killing site.

Two days later I managed to get a call through to Binegar. He agreed to meet with me at the Marion County Sheriff's Office operations center at five o'clock the next evening.

With tinted plate-glass walls, comfortable couches, and large plants, the MCSO reception area seemed more like the lobby of a better hotel than a cop shop. From the window I could see the Marion County Correctional Units. The entire compound—sleek, modern, and manicured—spoke confidently of the kind of money and political clout the longtime sheriff, Don Moreland, was able to muster in this community of high-dollar horse breeders.

Binegar appeared from a corridor and ushered me through the network of offices to his lair at the center of the building. It was after five, and we encountered no one in the carpeted halls. Binegar indicated a chair in his windowless office, said goodnight to his secretary in the adjoining room, and then closed the door.

After fifteen minutes of small talk about the Gainesville case, the PBS series The Civil War, and motorcycles, Binegar turned the conversation to the business at hand. There was no question he had his reasons for this interview, but the former FBI agent was not putting them out on the table right away.

We went down the list of victims, Binegar answering questions about their physical similarities and backgrounds, itineraries, dates when bodies were discovered, cause of death, condition of the bodies, and vehicles and missing property. Then for the next hour we exchanged speculations on the possible perpetrators and how they got control of their victims.

"We've got a couple of plausible scenarios," Binegar began. "Some guys may have stopped to help somebody on the side of the road and then found themselves on the wrong end of a gun. Maybe we're looking for a prostitute. Or a team."

"I can't imagine any of these men would stop for some guy on the side of the road," I said. "Not some hitchhiker. The sausage truck driver? The HRS investigator on his way home? No way. But they might stop for a woman, right?"

"As a matter of fact," Binegar replied, reaching into a desk drawer and pulling out two photcopy sheets, "we are looking for two women." He slid the sheets across the desk and I picked them up.

One rough drawing depicted a woman with straight, stringy hair, thin lips, and narrow eyes. A typed description gave particulars: white female, 5'8"–5'10", blond hair, 20–30 years of age, last seen wearing blue jeans, white T-shirt with sleeves rolled up, and a chain hanging from the belt loops. It noted that she might have a heart-shaped tattoo on one of her biceps.

The other sketch was of a moon-faced individual with a ball cap pulled low over the eyes. A meager description followed, for a white female, 5'4"–5'6", with a heavy build and short brown hair.

"These two were seen leaving the car belonging to the missing missionary, Peter Siems, last Fourth of July. We put out the description here in the local paper and on the TV station, but nothing came of it."

I stared at the drawings for a moment. "Well," I said. "I guess that's why you allowed me to come down here. You need to get these two composites out."

"Do you think we can get some press coverage around the state on this?"

I laughed. "Oh, yeah. Serial killings with two female suspects? You'll have all that you want. More than you want."

Binegar smiled briefly, then leaned forward and tapped the drawings. "We're not calling them *suspects* right now. We just want to talk to them."

"What do you think?" I asked. "Are these two working together? Are some guys involved? I can't figure this as just a pack of armed highway robbers. You said they didn't get all that much from the victims."

Binegar rocked his chair back and forth, his big jaw working side to side, and then abruptly changed direction. "Things got really crazy with the media up there in Gainesville. Leaks, reporters crawling all over everywhere. What do you think we can do to keep that from happening?"

"Get out front on it. And be prepared. Call a press conference. It's only a matter of time. Anyone else outside the investigation bring up the possibility of a serial killer?"

"Just you."

"Well," I said. "It's only a matter of time before somebody else puts all this together. You don't want to wait around to read about it in the papers or see it on the six o'clock news. But *you* need to get the word out. If this is a serial killer or a team of killers, they're not going to stop. White middle-aged guys driving around Florida are just targets right now. Look, they've been leaving a body about once a month. There's a definite pattern here. Which reminds me, Douglas keeps saying a small-caliber weapon. What is it? A .22 or a .25? Got to be one or the other."

"I'll tell you it's a .22, but I don't want to see that anywhere." Binegar held my gaze long enough to make his point. He had just handed me the check that better not be cashed.

"I understand perfectly. You won't see that in anything I report. When are you going to call your press conference?"

"Tomorrow."

Not until January would I learn that Binegar had made the crucial decision to go public as we were talking that evening. Certain members of the investigative team were vehemently opposed to this. By going on record with me, the ex-Marine left them with a fait accompli the next morning. I filed my story with Reuters as soon as I returned to Gainesville, and it moved over the wire before midnight. As it turned out, Binegar had used me as the trigger to blow the case wide open.

—REUTERS

OCALA—Investigators from five Florida counties said Thursday they were seeking two young women for questioning in a string of unsolved killings of men driving through the state on business.

Capt. Steve Binegar, chief criminal investigator at the Marion County Sheriff's Office, said the bodies of five middle-aged men had been found in secluded areas of north-central Florida over the past seven months.

All the victims ranged in age from the 40s to the mid-60s and were traveling by car on business. Each died from gunshot wounds from a small-caliber weapon, Binegar said.

Authorities theorize that the victims may have been approached at a convenience store or roadside stop by women and solicited for automobile assistance or sex, in order to gain access to their cars.

"The victims are similar, the method and pattern of the crimes are similar and the frequency is similar, about one a month," Binegar said. "These victims seem to have been targeted by their age, their type."

The victims include a 56-year-old former Alabama police chief, two truck drivers, a construction worker and an unidentified male.

   Police said they were searching for two young
women seen in July driving an automobile belonging to a 66-year-old Florida man who has been
missing since June and is believed to be dead,
Binegar said.

   Police investigators from five counties along
with agents of the Florida Department of Law
Enforcement and the Florida Highway Patrol held
a meeting Thursday in Ocala to share information
about the north-central Florida slayings.

Soon after this report ran on the Reuter wire, a flurry
of stories erupted across Florida and the nation, each
featuring the two drawings and the provocative speculation about a female serial killing team. As it turned out,
Binegar got all he wanted and much more.

NINE

The Breaks

At the multiagency meeting the morning of November 29, Binegar informed detectives of his interview the night before. Investigators Tom Muck and Jerry Thompson were livid. By going public, the Marion County captain had essentially left no room for argument. There was no going back. The story would be out, and they must go along with the press conference scheduled for that afternoon. While Muck continued to fume and grouse, Thompson gathered himself and assumed a laid-back attitude. The new member of the team, Dixie County detective Jimmy Pinner, a tall rail-thin country fellow with sad eyes, just leaned back in his chair and took it all in. Horzepa and Kelley were in agreement with Binegar and were already annoyed by Muck's volatile opinions. Binegar had a very good point—the people of Florida needed the warning. At least seven men were already dead. These poor guys had each made just one mistake—they had picked up one or two female hitchhikers.

"Why don't we just put out some guys in civvies?"

Muck blurted. "Put 'em in some impounded cars or something and see if these gals score them? Just take their butts down."

For a moment this wild notion hung in the conference room like a toxic cloud. Binegar stared from his seat at the end of the table, then glanced over at Munster, who was tapping his yellow legal pad with a pen. They briefly exchanged glances.

"There's no way I'm putting any of my men out on the road not knowing what the fuck they're getting into," the captain began, calling up the tone he had learned in the Marines. "That's just bullshit. It's a fucking logistical nightmare. Where do we start? Just have them cruise back and forth across the state? No, what we'll do is gear up to receive all the leads this press conference can generate. When we get these composites out to every TV station in the state and every newspaper, we'll get some targets."

Binegar faced the press that afternoon and released the composite drawings, asking that information regarding the two unidentified females be directed into the Marion County Sheriff's Office command post. Within twenty-four hours the story went national, the sketches appearing in the pages of *USA Today* and on the network news. Sergeant Brian Jarvis was directed to funnel all the incoming leads into a computer data base. Jarvis, an avid computer addict, jumped on the assignment with relish. A flood of phone calls followed. Within three weeks, over four hundred leads came in over the lines to sheriff's personnel, who manned the phones from eight in the morning until midnight.

• • •

On December 21, Jarvis called Munster with an interesting development—four leads had come in naming the same individuals.

On November 30, a Billy Copeland of Homosassa Springs called to say the two composites were Tyria Moore and a woman named Lee. They had rented a trailer from him a year earlier and then moved to Florida's east coast.

On December 13, Kathy Beasman phoned from Tampa. Beasman said the two sketches resembled two women who had worked for her at a motel in Zephyrhills, south of Ocala. She said their names were Tyria Moore and Susan Blahovec. She thought Moore might have family in Michigan.

On December 14, an anonymous caller was even more informative. She believed the suspects were Lee Blahovec and Tyria "Ty" Moore. Blahovec had purchased a recreational vehicle from Clark Recreational Vehicles in Homosassa Springs. The caller said Blahovec was the more dominant of the two and prostituted herself at I-75 truck stops around Wildwood. In addition, the caller had a telephone number in Ohio for Moore's parents. The two women had left the area in September 1989 and moved to the Ocean Village RV Park in Ormond Beach. The anonymous woman said the two were "lesbians, were violent and had a hatred for men."

Four days later, a clutch of intriguing reports from the Port Orange Police Department landed on Munster's desk. On December 16, Port Orange cops had begun tracing the movements of Lee Blahovec and Tyria Moore throughout their jurisdiction south of Daytona Beach. It was learned that Blahovec used an alias, a Florida driver's license identifying her as Cammie Marsh Greene. With this as identification, she and Ty had registered at the Fairview Motel on Ridgewood Avenue in Harbor Oaks on September 29, 1990. They stayed in room 8 until October 14. Then they moved into a small apartment located behind the Belgrade Restaurant, just a few hundred feet north of the motel. The two women left there on November 17 and returned to the Fairview and room 8. On December 2, the women left again; but three days later, the woman identifying herself as Cammie Greene returned alone. She had stayed until December 10.

A check through FDLE computers revealed the driver's licenses and criminal records of Tyria Moore, Susan Blahovec, and Cammie Marsh Greene. Moore had been arrested in 1983 in Daytona for breaking and entering. The charge had been dropped. Blahovec had a trespassing arrest. There was no record on Greene. Munster spoke with FDLE, requesting copies of the drivers' licenses for the three women. An FDLE pilot flew the copies to Ocala that afternoon.

The next day Munster strolled across the hall separating his office from the conference room that was now command post for the investigation. When Dixie County investigator Jimmy Pinner lifted his weary hound-dog eyes from the lead sheets spread out before him, Munster stood in the doorway, slapping his thigh with a sheaf of papers, a playful smile on his face.

"Hey, Jimmy. Want to ride over to Daytona tomorrow?"

Pinner rolled his chair back from the table and looked

at Munster. "Well, Bruce, I don't know . . . think I'll like it?"

Munster handed Pinner the Port Orange reports and tossed the three driver's-license photographs down on the table. "I think we're all going to like it."

Late the next afternoon, Pinner and Munster sat down with Rose McNeill in her office at the Fairview Motel, a tidy but modest string of cement and stucco rooms facing Ridgewood Avenue just north of the Rose Bay bridge.

"They came in on September twenty-ninth, and they were walking," said Mrs. McNeill. "They had one of those, like, tall carts that you pull with all their belongings in it. Everything seemed to be packaged, like really nice. Either in boxes or bundled up. There wasn't anything that you could see."

Munster slipped two photo packets from his notebook and handed them to Mrs. McNeill.

"Can you identify either of the women who rented room eight from you last September in any of the pictures you see here?"

"Number five."

"Okay. Who is number five?"

"That was the girl who went by the name of Ty."

"All right. Now that's the packet I've identified on the back with the number one. Now the second packet . . ."

"Number four. That's the one who went by Lee." Mrs. McNeill had identified Susan Blahovec's driver's-license picture. Her records showed that this person had registered under the name Cammie Marsh Greene and had provided a driver's license as proof of identification. McNeill noted the DL number on the registration. It matched that of Cammie Marsh Greene, but the photograph on the Greene license was not of Blahovec.

The two detectives went on questioning Mrs. McNeill in detail. Did the women say where they had come from? Did they say where they were going?

"No, they just left. I didn't care if they were coming back. When she came back again she said they were staying at the restaurant over there." Mrs. McNeill pointed behind her to the north. "Just a couple places down, past the RV there."

Munster and Pinner wanted to know about cars, about cash payments for the room, about dates. Mrs. McNeill provided them with a record of payments but couldn't recall any vehicles. Munster reminded her that she had said something different the day before when they talked on the phone.

"I'm sorry. You're right. Okay. There was a car in November, right around Thanksgiving. When Ty went on the plane. I'm thinking it was around Monday, the nineteenth. After Ty left. It was only here overnight."

"Tell me about your conversations with Lee about this car?"

"She said she had a car parked in back and asked if it was okay. She told me a gentleman had left her the car and that if his wife saw the car then she'd have to give it back, and she wanted to hold on to that car until she went back to pick Ty up at the airport. I'm pretty sure it was going to be on a Sunday."

"Was there a tag on it?"

Mrs. McNeill shook her head. "There was no tag. I went and looked at it."

Munster reached into his notebook for another photograph. "Now keep in mind," he cautioned. "This shot was taken in the sunlight and it has a glare on it. Do you recognize this car?"

Mrs. McNeill studied the picture of Antonio's Pontiac. "I would say it was similar. But I can't swear it was the same one."

"But it looks like it?"

"It looks . . . yeah." She nodded.

Mrs. McNeill also said Lee had paid her ninety dollars on November 19, the same day she appeared with the car. "Yeah, I remember that. She paid me the money and then later she came back and borrowed two dollars from me. She told me she was sandblasting buildings down in Orlando. I mentioned that a friend of mine has a motel and I said, 'Gee, why don't you go down and talk to her, maybe she would be interested.' And she never asked me who . . . where . . . nothing. I thought, well that's strange."

Mrs. McNeill recalled some other odd bits about Lee. She had a business-card wallet filled with cards that she flashed one night when Mrs. McNeill was in her room. "She was very, very drunk. She had all these cards in it, held it up and said her business was personal. She had on a bra and panties, and I made a remark because she'd been complaining about being cold. I said something jokingly, 'Well I guess you're not . . . you're not cold.' She was rambling on and the next thing you know she took her bra off and threw it across the room and said, 'Oh, what the hell.' I just came back and I told my mother, 'Boy, that's strange.' The next day she came to the door and I don't think she even remembered the conversation, didn't seem to me that she was even aware of what she had done. Or, if she did, she ignored it."

"Okay," said Munster. "So they left on December 2, and you've got a notation that Lee came back on December 5 . . . can you tell me about that?"

"Well, she came back and asked for a room. She only

had a suitcase. She might have carried something else but it was very small. She said she didn't want the same room because it would bring back too many memories. She wanted a different room. So, I gave her room seven."

"What did she tell you, what happened?"

"She didn't really tell me anything, but . . ." Mrs. McNeill gazed past the two detectives through the window behind them. The late December sun fired off the cars speeding south over the bridge. "When I tried to talk to them when they were thinking about getting an apartment—they always talked about looking for an apartment—Lee called me into her room and Ty was there and she was talking about 'getting a place' and 'they'd be moving.'

"And I said, 'Oh, that's really nice.' I said, 'Where are you going? Is it close?' And Lee got very upset. I can't remember all the things she said. But basically it was that her business was *private,* and when she left she didn't want *anybody* to know where she was at. She just kept going on like that. And I said, 'Oh, fine. I'm just trying to be nice, but I'll tell you I couldn't care less.' She was angry. I went to the next room and she came over and apologized. She said her friend had told her to."

"Was Ty there when she was raising cain?" asked Pinner.

"Oh, yeah. She never said a word. But Lee was sort of . . . the one who said and did, you know? She'd get mad or uneasy and there was no reason. She's praising you up and down one minute and the next minute she was mad. And there really wasn't, you know . . . really any reason." Mrs. McNeill frowned, shook her head, and looked from one detective to the other. "Never really any reason."

• • •

While Pinner and Munster took Mrs. McNeill's statement, Horzepa and Kelley, along with other Volusia County sheriff's officers, were checking Daytona-area pawn shops. On December 6, Cammie Marsh Greene had pawned a 35-mm Minolta Freedom camera and a Micronta Road Patrol radar detector at the OK Pawn shop on Second Avenue. These were items that had belonged to Richard Mallory. Records at Bruce's Gun & Pawn on South Yonge Street in Ormond Beach showed Greene pawning a box of tools. The description matched those missing from David Spears's pickup truck. On the OK Pawn receipt was a right thumbprint of the person calling herself Cammie Marsh Greene.

Late that same afternoon, Kelley sped to Orlando and delivered the receipt into the hands of Jenny Ahern, the latent-print supervisor at the regional Automated Fingerprint Identification System. Ahern told Kelley that she and her assistant would stay late into the evening to match a name to that thumbprint. When she and her assistants came up empty, she drove from Orlando to the Volusia County Sheriff's Office and began a hand search of their fingerprint section.

"They got very lucky," Kelley later recalled. "They hit pay dirt within an hour. We had the Lori Grody arrest on a 1986 weapons charge with an outstanding warrant, and those prints matched." The arrest report showed Grody occupying a stolen vehicle in Tomoka State Park, north of Daytona. She had had a loaded .22 revolver hidden underneath the front seat and twelve additional rounds stashed in a shoulder bag. A check with the Volusia County branch jail's records showed Grody's photograph; it matched that of Susan Blahovec. With Grody's thumbprint matching that on the Cammie Greene pawn ticket, all routes came back to the woman called Lee.

The Grody print and that from Moore's 1983 arrest were forwarded to the FDLE lab in Tallahassee to see if either matched the few latent prints recovered from the victims' vehicles and items thrown out by their killer. Merv Stevens, FDLE's latent examiner, came back with a positive ID linking the Grody print to the bloody palm print left in Peter Siems's Sunbird. A more intensive search of Grody's and Moore's criminal history was run through the National Crime Information Center. Law enforcement responded from Michigan, Colorado, and Florida. The result: Aileen Carol Wuornos, white female, born 02-29-56, Rochester, Michigan. 5'2", medium build, light brown hair, brown eyes.

Juvenile records for truancy, being a runaway, shoplifting, and burglary paled beside her adult exploits.

May 27, 1974

Arrested by Jefferson County (Colorado) Sheriff's Department under the name Sandra Beatrice Kretsch for disorderly conduct, driving under the influence, and prohibited use of a firearm. She had fired a .22 pistol from a moving vehicle. Later charged with failure to appear.

June 14, 1976

Arrested by Antrim County (Michigan) Sheriff's Department for making disturbance of the peace, and simple assault. Fugitive warrants out of Troy Police Department for consuming alcohol in vehicle, unlawful use of driver's license, and no Michigan operator's license. Threw a cue ball at bartender's head. The ball imbedded in a wall of the bar. Witnesses said Wuornos had a pistol in her purse. Her address was Ormond Beach, Florida. She paid $105 fine on August 4, 1976.

May 20, 1981

Arrested in Edgewater, Florida, for armed robbery of a Majik Market. Convicted of robbery with a weapon. Sentenced to Florida Department of Corrections prison May 4, 1982. Released June 30, 1983.

May 1, 1984

Arrested by Monroe County Sheriff's Department (Florida) for attempting to pass forged checks at Barnett Bank in Key West, Florida.

November 30, 1985

Pasco County Sheriff's Department offense report on theft of Webley .38-caliber revolver and ammunition from pickup truck at bar. Lori Grody named as suspect by victim.

December 11, 1985

Florida Highway Patrol citation to Lori Grody for driving without a valid driver's license.

January 4, 1986

Arrest by Metro Dade Police, Miami, Florida, of Aileen Carol Wuornos for grand theft auto, resisting arrest w/o violence, obstruction by false information. Wuornos was driving a 1985 brown Chevy Blazer.

"Driver became nervous, said she had forgot wallet at the store and asked if she could leave. I said no and asked her to get out of car . . . we walked to my vehicle . . ." Wuornos gave officer Lori Grody identification. While arresting officer was out of vehicle, Wuornos repeatedly asked assisting officer to return to her car to get something. Wuornos then attempted to resist by running away, and trying to jump into a vehicle stopped by roadway. Wuornos told the driver to leave. Officer grabbed her and dragged her from vehicle, restrained her with handcuffs, and read her Miranda rights. Later the officer found a .38 pistol with a box of .38-special ammunition in the stolen Blazer.

June 2, 1986

Volusia County Sheriff's Office reports incident involving Lori Grody and Wayne Keith Fredrickson. Florida Park Ranger investigated an argument between Grody and Fredrickson that was occurring in a Dodge pickup. Truck was a stolen vehicle, and Volusia County Sheriff's Office was called. Grody and Fredrickson were placed under arrest. A .22-caliber revolver was found beneath seat of Dodge. Fredrickson said Grody pulled the gun on him and said he owed her $200. She claimed she "knew nothing about a .22" though the officers hadn't determined the caliber of weapon at the time. She then said it was planted on her. She had 19 rounds for the pistol in her possession at time of her arrest.

June 9, 1986

Florida Highway Patrol speeding ticket to Susan Blahovec, Columbus, Ohio, on State Road 8, seven miles southeast of Monticello, Jefferson County, Florida.

72 mph in a 55-mph zone. "Attitude poor. Thinks she's above the law."

July 4, 1987

Incident report by Daytona Beach police involving Susan Blahovec, Tina Moore, and Henry Martin. Assault and battery with beer bottle at Barn Door Lounge on Wild Olive Street, Daytona Beach.

December 18, 1987

Florida Highway Patrol citations to Susan Blahovec for walking on interstate, possession of suspended DL, failure to notify re change of address in Flagler County. "Defendant was stopped for trespass . . . Attitude POOR . . . defendant was .45 miles north of NO PEDESTRIAN sign . . . believes she is above the law . . ." Threatening letters from Wuornos (aka Blahovec) were sent to the clerk of the circuit court (January 11, February 9, 1988).

March 12, 1988

Incident report by Daytona Beach police. Cammie Marsh Greene victim of battery by Gary Thomson, Volusia County Transportation Company bus driver (black male). Thomson pushed Greene off bus following confrontation. Tyria Moore listed as witness.

July 23, 1988

Incident Report by Daytona Beach police. Criminal mischief charged by Brian Donely against Tyria Moore and Susan Blahovec. Donely charged Blahovec and Moore with ripping out the carpet from his apartment, which they were renting, and with painting the walls brown.

November 22, 1988

Zephyrhills police receive complaint of threatening telephone calls to Robert McManus, a Publix supermarket employee in Lakeland, Florida, from Susan Blahovec. McManus said he didn't understand the numbers requested by Blahovec for lottery tickets and asked her to repeat them. Blahovec became angry and started cursing him. He told her to go some place else to buy the tickets. She took down his name and said she'd have his job. "Suspect called the store several times, threatened him with bodily injury, told him she had a contract on him." Calls continued from November 22 to 28 (McManus's birthday).

Meanwhile, Volusia County investigators continued to hand-search pawn-shop records that were not computerized and found that Cammie Marsh Greene had pawned a man's ring at the OK Pawn on December 7, 1990. She had received twenty dollars. Bob Kelley picked up the item from the pawn shop, a diamond and ruby ring sized to 10¾. He turned the ring over to Jimmy Pinner, who drove to Cocoa and the home of Aileen Berry, the late Gino Antonio's fiancée. There, Ms. Berry and her daughter positively identified the ring as the one they had purchased to give to Gino. Pinner then showed the ring to the jeweler who had sold and sized it. She confirmed the identification.

In the early chill just after dawn, the day before Christmas, Binegar put on his sweats and quietly left the house for his daily run, taking care not to waken the kids. School had been out for a week, but he had barely seen the three of them. By the time he came in from the office, they were already in bed. It wasn't going to get any better in the next few weeks, he thought, as he loped off down the street. The case was breaking fast. As he hit his stride, he anticipated the meeting scheduled that morning. Everything was in place, everything locked on to these two women, Wuornos and Moore. They could be found in Daytona, Munster and Thompson were convinced. But there were problems. Always. Not everyone wanted to play *together.* Muck was still dragging his heels, but that didn't mean a damn. Binegar's problem was much closer to home. His Major Crimes supervisor, Brian Jarvis, wouldn't move from in front of his computer. They had data processors to do that job, but Jarvis couldn't give it up. *He* had to be the one doing the program. It was a power trip. Four days ago, when deputies found that middle-aged guy shot full of bullets, all hell had broken loose. The victim fit the profile of the men in the other cases and had been found out in the woods. Binegar had been on the crime scene all that night with David Taylor and Major Henry sorting things out. The next morning he'd called a meeting with Jarvis, but his Major Crimes supervisor hadn't shown up. That had been the last straw. If Jarvis wasn't going to get out in the field with his investigators, Binegar decided, he could cool his heels out on road patrol. Everybody's ego was going over the top with this case. Hell, Hollywood and New York had been on the phone to the office almost daily since they'd had the press conference. Movies, TV shows, books, magazines. Deals. He'd already done "America's Most Wanted" in order to generate leads, but there was no way he was going on "A Current Affair," "Inside Edition," or any of the other tabloid shows. This was the big time, he thought, a once-in-a-lifetime case; but he had to keep all that out of his mind, had to keep it focused. Binegar rounded his maroon Caprice parked in the driveway and entered the still-slumbering house. He glanced at his watch. In an hour and a half the surveillance strategy on Wuornos and Moore would be decided. *This is when it gets hairy,* he thought. Out on the street, anything that *could* go wrong *would* likely go wrong. The big problem was never knowing where trouble was going to come from.

That morning Binegar got together with Major Dan Henry, and the two decided to pursue Tyria Moore. Information developed to this point placed Moore's family in Cadiz, Ohio. "While Bruce and the rest of them are working the Daytona area on Wuornos, you and me should get up to Ohio," Binegar told Henry. "We've got to nail both of them, and from what Bruce and Jimmy got from the lady at the motel, Moore took off for Ohio in December and hasn't come back. Hell, for all we know, Wuornos could be up there or on her way."

Henry squinted and smiled. "Then let's get in that ol' Chevy of yours and take a nice drive up to Ohio. Don't mind leaving on the twenty-sixth. Get up there in a day. Easy going."

When Binegar and Henry arrived in Cadiz on December 27, a light snow was falling on a bust of Clark Gable. The statue marked the screen legend's birthplace which stood next to an abandoned building. To keep a low profile in the little town of five thousand, they parked in front of the Harrison County sheriff's office, a little storefront displaying a hand-lettered sign that read NOTICE NO LOAFING OR TALKING TO PRISONERS.

"This is like Mayberry," said Binegar. "I expect to see Barney Fife come walking up the street."

"Let's be cool," chuckled Henry. "We've got to get this sheriff on our side."

Within minutes of meeting Sheriff Richard Rensi, the Florida investigators were impressed by his professionalism, despite his humble surroundings. The sheriff and his wife lived on the premises of the jail. It was a far cry from the ultramodern Marion County facilities. Binegar and Henry made no more jokes.

Ohio Bureau of Investigation Special Agent Gerald Mroczkowski, who was assisting in the investigation, joined them for the meeting, and Rensi agreed to do everything in his power to keep the presence of the two Florida officers undercover, but they hadn't been in town five minutes before Rensi started getting calls about "that car from Florida." Rensi knew the Moore family quite well. In fact, Tyria's father, Jack, was doing some work at the jail.

The sheriff took Binegar and Henry to the local school superintendent's office, where they examined Tyria's school records. She appeared to have a normal school history with no disciplinary problems. A "C" student, Tyria had attended the Harrison Hills Vocational School. Jack Moore was a hard-working carpenter and brick mason who was highly respected in the Cadiz area. Moore's sister, Twyla Jean, lived out of state and was married to an ex-deputy from Harrison County. Tyria had three brothers, Rensi said. After Tyria's natural mother, Janet, died, Jack had married his present wife, Mary Ann.

Later, Binegar and Henry met with Mroczkowski, who was investigating the background of Susan Blahovec in Berea, Ohio, and asked him to check the travel agency in Saint Clairesville, Ohio, to confirm Tyria's travel dates from Florida. Things got dicey at the agency when Mroczkowski overheard one of the agents say she was from Cadiz. He decided not to pursue the matter. Later, he learned that the office manager there was a close friend of the Moore family. However, through airline records, it was confirmed that Tyria Moore had traveled from Daytona to Ohio on November 17, thus putting her out of state when Antonio was killed. Henry's observation in his field notes read, "This development contributes to our belief that Tyria may be the 'weak link' in this investigation and may not even be directly involved in the slayings. However, she is still classified as a suspect in that we believe her to be one of the two females seen leaving the Siems vehicle."

Leaving Major Henry to pursue background on Moore and Wuornos, Binegar caught a plane to Florida. Obviously Wuornos was not in Cadiz. All indicators pointed to the streets south of Daytona. It was time to tighten the net.

TEN

Dropping the Net

At 9:45 on the morning of January 4, Citrus County sheriff's detectives wheeled past the Marion County correctional facility west of Ocala and turned south into the MCSO parking lot. Jerry Thompson led Sergeant Mike Joyner, and Investigators Mike Imperial and Dick Martin through the operations center's rear entrance and into the conference room.

An easel held a large map of the South Daytona area; the map was dotted with red and yellow stickers. On the corkboard lining one wall, three large color blowups of Wuornos, Moore, and Greene stared out into the room. Two large Florida maps were pinpointed with the locations of body and vehicle recovery sites. Next to these was a chart featuring enlarged photographs of the victims and accompanying details. A pattern chart detailing similarities among the homicides rested on another easel standing in a far corner of the room.

Binegar stood and shook hands with Joyner, Imperial, and Martin before Thompson introduced his three partners to the others. Along with Binegar, Munster, and David Taylor, four other MCSO investigators were now aboard—Don Chapman, John Tilley, Eddie Leady, and Art King. An FDLE agent, Lee Schneider, flipped open his notebook. "Since Steve requested that we not get into Volusia County with radios on this thing, we'll provide cellular phones and beepers for this operation. We'll also have personnel."

"Whoever you bring along," said Binegar, "they've got to have some seasoning. We need investigators on this, people who know what they're into."

"No problem," said Schneider.

"Sergeant Joyner and Investigator Martin are from our street-crimes unit," Thompson said. "They do the Bad Boy things. Working undercover on our drug surveillance."

Thompson's remark was unnecessary. One look at the detectives' beards and long hair was enough to identify their kind of beat. Munster smiled. "There's no way any son of a bitch in those Daytona bars is going to make you two. This is perfect."

"You think we look like shit now? Wait till you catch our act over there." Joyner combed his fingers through his red whiskers and scowled.

The next day the crew traveled to the Volusia County Sheriff's Office, where Horzepa, Kelley, and Ehrhart were waiting. A total of thirty officers from six agencies was now involved in the operation.

Ehrhart had made arrangements at the Pirate's Cove motel for a set of rooms to be used as a command post. Located on the beach, the pink, three-story tourist facility was just across the bridge east of Port Orange. Adding a bizarre bit of theatricality to the hunt, a ten-foot painted statue of a buccaneer leered over the entrance to the motel.

"It's far enough away from Harbor Oaks not to attract attention but still close enough," Ehrhart said. "We put two or three cellular phones inside the command post and pagers in one room. The rest of us will be spread through other rooms. Since we know Moore had something to do with housecleaning for the motels around here, we don't tell anybody anything. I'm sure they know we're police officers but not why we're there."

"You know these damned phones FDLE brought over? They're all 813 area code for over in Tampa," groused Thompson. "We've got to dial up long distance every time we use them to make a goddamned call! I sure as hell hope Schneider has some good people coming in on this."

Surveillance began at two o'clock on the afternoon of January 5. Horzepa and Mike Imperial were teamed in one car, a confiscated 280 ZX. Don Chapman and Eddie Leady cruised the Port Orange streets in a rental car brought over from Ocala. Mike Joyner and Dick Martin, posing as a couple of Georgia drug dealers down for a score, hit the bars along Ridgewood Avenue. At eight that evening another shift began with Jimmy Pinner joining Horzepa, and Art King and Tom Tittle relieving Chapman and Leady. Joyner and Martin continued on until two the next morning, when surveillance was shut down for the night. There were no sightings.

On the next day's shift, Mike Imperial called in at 10:40 with a tip from a bartender at a joint called Our Place.

The woman identified Moore and Wuornos from a photo pack, saying the two had been in her bar the day before. Martin joined Imperial at the Ridgewood Avenue location and hung out the rest of the day waiting to see if the suspects showed up. The women were no-shows.

ELEVEN

At the Belgrade

On January 7, Jimmy Pinner and Thompson drove to the Belgrade Restaurant, where Wuornos and Moore had rented a room for three weeks in November. They sat down with the owner, Mrs. Vera Ivkolivich, a thin bird-like Yugoslavian with large liquid eyes. Beneath a cloud of cigarette smoke, Vera sat at one of her vinyl-covered tables and recalled her boarders, straining her story through a thick Eastern European accent.

"I met Lee many years ago, ten years. She worked around here for a while and used to be my customer. Then she disappeared. So last year in September, one day she walk in the door and say, 'I come back. Again.' I say, 'Welcome home.' She say, 'I gonna stop for break-fast.' She's come alone. A few days later she come in with a girl for breakfast. The next day she's coming for lunch and she ask me, she say, 'Vera, uh, we lost busi-ness, we lost house, we lost property, everything we got. Do you know some place cheaper? They charge us in the motel one hundred twenty-seven dollars a week. That's too much money.' "

Vera flicked the ash off her filter tip. "I say, 'Lee, I got one beautiful bedroom here if you want. I gonna charge you fifty dollars a week. To cover water and electricity.' And she say, 'Can I see?' When she see room, she say, 'We gonna move tonight.' 'All right,' I say. She say she got cleaning pressure business."

"She started on a credit. First, lunch. Dinner. She paid twenty dollars, thirty dollars. She come over, take my husband thirty dollars. She paid first week. Also she pays second week too. She started on a credit and one day it went, come over one hundred twenty dollars' credit. And I can't afford it. Business slow.

"One day I say, 'Listen, honey, I'm sixty-five years old. I working seven days a week, eighteen hours a day. You working one days a week. I can't afford it anymore. She started to give money back. Ten dollars. Fifteen dollars. 'I get job tomorrow. The next day, this next day . . .' But also she start to fight with Vil, my husband, every day. She's ask for a ride. She's asking one time for Vil give her a ride to 95 and 44. 95 and 40. Give her a ride. She asking this.

"Second time, she's ask again. She say, 'Vil, I gonna pay you. Gimme ride.' All right. He gives her ride. Same exit. A little bit further north. When he's give her second-time ride, he says, 'Vera, that lady doing some kind of monkey business. I don't think she's got any business; she into dope or prostitution.'

"Ty stay home, inside all day. When Lee not home she don't even come for cup of coffee. All the time in her room.

"She's a talk, everything so nice but don't coming out when Lee gone. Ty don't show up. You don't see her. Every time I knock on the door and say, 'Ty, you want a cup of coffee?' 'No, Lee gonna be home. Soon.'

"Well, Lee beginning to fight with my husband, Vil, every single day. For everything. For everything she's fight. She knock on the door one night and fight with Vil. Knock on my door. To fight with Vil because he don't give her no ride to Winn-Dixie. She against men because she's lesbian.

"On a Wednesday she say, 'I got three jobs, I got . . . blah blah blah . . . and tomorrow a lot of money.' Next day she's sleeping all day. She's no go to work at all. On Friday morning she's finally go to work. When she's go she goes to the property and go by Magnolia." Vera points north to the street running west from Ridgewood. "Never go on the front, you know? She never show up on a US 1. She don't want people to see her. I beginning to think, what's up?"

"How was she usually dressed?"

"She wear shorts or pants. That's all they got. Got a lot of tools, a lot of razors, shaving razors. They got a lot of everything, but no clothes. They got one little TV set. I don't know wheresabout they got it. I go knock on the door. She got tools and I don't understand too much about tools, but got plenty tools. I say, 'For what you needa that, Lee?' She say, 'Whenever I working for people and people no have any money to give me, I take tools.'

"So, Vil come home and say, 'Lee bring money?' I say, 'Ten dollars.' He say, 'Oh no, that's enough, that's enough, we don't need that anymore.' He's a knock on their door, and Ty say, 'Who you are?' He say, 'Ty, you know very well who I am. I want tomorrow morning to be empty.' She say, 'Oh, no.' He say, 'Oh, yes. I'm gonna have come and help you put belongings in middle of highway.' So the next day the lady from the next-door motel come with car and everything that they have they move. They move back in the motel.

"So about three, four days I see Lee early in the morning before I open restaurant. She go in the station . . ."

Vera waved her cigarette toward the window and a Speedway gas and convenience store just across a small parking lot north of the restaurant. "Get a coffee and take a newspaper. About six, six-thirty.

"So one day Vil see her in station, and he say, 'Hey, lady, when you gonna give me money?' She say, 'Fuck you. You lucky you still alive by now.' We don't pay attention. We think she's mad we kick her out. Two day later, Vil say, 'Look at that on television. I see Lee and Ty sketch on a television, I say, '*Oooh*, yeah' "

Vera rolled her eyes.

"Can you describe a little more how she would dress when she'd go out?"

"She don't wear makeup. I don't see her with makeup. All the time she's got hat on, got hat down on her head. A cap. She's got hair tied up like me now . . ." Vera pulled at her thinning gray ponytail, tied high on the crown of her little head. "And then put the cap on.

"She carry only one plastic bag, like a shopping bag. Justa plastic, you know. I don't see her getting purse. Not even one. She wear slippers or those where you play . . . what you call?"

"Sneakers?"

"Sneakers, yeah. Running shoes, yeah. Or sometimes flops like a me." Vera raised a little foot and waggled a rubber thong.

"Port Orange police come in. Ask question after

Thanksgiving. I see sketch on TV. Vil say Lee and Ty. And I say, 'Oh, no, that's impossible,' but when I look further I see yes, Lee and Ty. They say 'serious killer.' I say, 'Oyyoyoyoy' . . . Police come in, I think it's next day, after seeing pictures. They ask me, 'Did they leave anything in the room?' I say, 'No, not even one paper, no place, nothing. Nothing nothing nothing.' Also, she's a put one picture of Jesus. That's my picture, but she's put it on the wall. They say don't touch those, they want to take a fingerprints before they catch her."

"Ever see her drinking?"

"Ohhh, boy! Oh, boy, she's can drink two case of beer a night. When she's home night."

"She make much noise?"

"No . . . well, once in a while after middle night, she's got big fight with Ty. Lee and Ty, yeah. Because I was sleeping in the house, the first room over here, and they fight like a gypsy. Just a Lee, just a Lee. I don't understand what she's saying, but she's screaming at Ty like a crazy."

"Fighting?"

"No, no fighting. Lee screaming at a Ty. One time I ask Ty why she's screaming. She say, 'Ah! She's crazy!' "

"Did Ty seem to be nervous or afraid?"

"No, so far. She's quiet, she's sit inside. Couple times she say she not have any cigarettes. I don't smoking that time. I steal from Vil a couple cigarettes and give to her. Sometimes I don't have chance to steal cigarettes . . . she sit all day till Lee come in. When Lee come in they go to Winn-Dixie. They bring food. Sneak over to station, they bring six-pack beer. They go again, six-pack. And again. And the next day you got two cases of beer, empty."

"Did you ever see Lee drunk? Staggering?"

"You never see Lee really drunk. But only when she's drinking a little bit over she's yakking too much . . . quack-quack-quack-quack-quack. Not like a normal person when she's drinking. First time she say to me she's born over here in Florida. Then, Pennsylvania. First from Pennsylvania and her family from Holland. Then she say she's born in Florida. And she's confused. Also I got one package Pennsylvania apples, you know? To me. From Pennsylvania. I know somebody from Pennsylvania. Best apple in United States . . . And Ty home and I receive apple. Big box. Lee don't let me alone till I show her parcel, address, and what they say in letter! She say she want to know . . . I say, 'Why you want to know? That's for me' . . . 'I want to see.' 'Here, you don't trust me?' "

"Who did she think it was from?"

"She knows it's from Pennsylvania."

"Did she think it was from Tyria's family?"

"I don't know why. She don't say why. But she want so bad to see. I show her letter, I show her parcel, and she stop bothering me. This before Thanksgiving Day."

"Did you ever see Lee with a gun?"

"Yes. Yeah. I walk in the room one day and she's clean up gun."

"What did it look like?"

"I don't understand very much about gun. Like this long." Vera spread her sinewy little hands about ten inches.

"Was it a revolver? Had it a cylinder?"

"Oh, sir, she hide it when she see me in the door. She come over here one day and ask Vil, 'Vil, do you got gun?' He say, 'Oh, yes. In every corner. I got in house, I got in a car.' We don't have any guns . . . he's lucky . . . he say, 'Oh, yeah, in every corner I got guns.' When I heard first time on the television and saw the sketch, I was surprised. And I say to my husband, 'You lucky you still alive.' Because here I pick up how she's knocking on the door to fight with Vil, how she's going to garage to fight with Vil, when she's come over here and see Vil, fight with Vil and ask Vil for favor, to ride to Orlando . . . yeah, I don't think he's going to come back if he's going with her.

"You know one night she's come in, a little bit late from her work, you know? And I seen her really, really excited."

"How do you mean?"

"She's come in and she's trying to explain me how her pressure blew up and she's explaining how it blew up . . . 'I can't stop it!' . . . and this and a that. And she's so nervous and she's talking. I believe that day she's killed somebody.

"She's come in about nine o'clock evening. Yeah. How her cleaning pressure exploded. Ohh! and she's trying to fix it . . ." Vera stood up and waved her arms. "Ooh! . . . ohh! . . . so excited. She's not dirty, but she's sweating. And waving her arms around. And I say, 'Vil, what's wrong with her?' He say, 'I don't know. Okay, cleaning pressure exploded. Why she so nervous? Like a . . . a . . .' "

"When was this?"

"Maybe four, five days before she left from here. Before Thanksgiving, yeah. She was so excited, had a red face and sweating. Not normal. Okay, if my pots exploded, why I have to panic that much? Exploded, exploded. You know? It was panic that night. Panic. Vil say, 'What's with her?' Then she go to station, take six-pack beer, and go to bedroom. All the night, television on. All the night, television."

Vera sat down and stubbed out her cigarette.

"To be honest with you, I was from poor family. In World War II I was starving and hungry, and feel sorry for them. Even when they left, I never think they are killer. No Ty. I don't believe Ty. I think she's working under Lee."

"Do you think she was afraid of Lee?"

"I believe it. One day Ty come outside and take a chair, and I sit down, and talking, she looking for job and this and that. She working in Ormond Beach motel and some Iranian guy fire her, and she beat him and this and that. They say they gonna find job and gonna make money, get house, buy car, everything normal. And Lee come in. 'What you talking about with my girl? She's my lover.' I say, 'Sorry, you can be my son. I not lesbian, I don't care. I regular woman. If I talking with Ty, I, like, talking with my daughter. Nothing wrong.' Never Ty come again talk to me. I say, 'Oh, boy, I got a big problem now.'

"One more problem. They come over here. Nobody's here. They order breakfast or lunch. When somebody come, they pack in hurry their plates. They say, 'We gonna go finish in our room.' And I start to think, Why? People start to think something's wrong. Take food and everything, they go into room. They eat omelet. Sand-wiches. But they like appetizer, mushroom appetizer, more than anything else. This all on credit."

"Why did you do that?"

"I don't know, to be honest with you. I trust them, that's why. I knew Lee from before. She come in like a regular customer. She lived some place around. She regular customer. She pay every day. Nice. Nothing wrong. She's wearing dresses, blouses. No shorts. She come with the girls sometime, sometime boys. Everything's normal. A regular person. In 1981, 1982.

"I don't understand, sometime, really. Also, I don't understand her. She pretending she been used. Everybody using her. But I don't think so, that's not the reason, sir. No. If she don't want to hear something, she say, 'I don't understand you.' I say, 'You understand me very much. Okay. I got broken language, my accent. But you understand me very well. How you understand me yesterday and this morning, you don't understand me now? Because you don't want to hear what I say. That reason you don't understand me. Don't play too smart, Lee. Okay, you traveling and you pass a lot of your life, but don't forgot one things, I pass a lot into my life too. But only difference between us, I passing honestly. But you try to be crookey.' "

"What did she say to that?"

" 'Ohhh, no! I not crookey. I got bad life. I no have any parents. I grow on the street. Everybody using me.' I say, 'Okay, when you young they using you. Why they using you now? You thirty-three years old, why you no find reasonable job and start to work and be lady? Why you always have to be crookey all the time?' "

"She don't say nothing. She don't like that at all. I don't care she like it, she don't like it. I like honest people. I like good worker. I don't like any monkey business."

TWELVE

The Last Resort

On the evening of January 8, Joyner and Martin were
cruising Ridgewood in their Jeep when they spotted a
blond standing in the doorway of the Port Orange Pub.
They wheeled right, pulled up in the parking lot, and
went in. Going by the names Bucket and Drums, the
undercover cops sidled up to the bar and ordered a couple of beers. The blond standing by the juke box had
scars on her forehead, matching the description given
by witnesses to the Fourth of July wreck near Ocala.
Bucket nudged the patron next to him and asked if he
knew the blond.

"That's Lee."

Bucket went over to the box, threw some quarters in,
and asked the blond if she'd like to dance. She would.
Drums watched the action over his shoulder and smiled.
Things were falling into place.

Five minutes after nine, Martin called into the command room at the Pirate's Cove and spoke to Thompson.

"Jerry, we're with her. Sitting over here in a dump

called the Port Orange Pub, knocking back a few brews. Joyner's dancing with her. 5602 Ridgewood. I'm going back in."

Thompson grabbed a cellular phone, punched up the Tampa area code, and relayed the news to all the mobile units.

Then the room phone rang. He stretched his free arm and picked it up. It was Martin.

"The shit's hit the fan!" Martin's voice was high-pitched. "Some Port Orange cops just came in and rousted her. They got her out in the parking lot; what the fuck's happening?"

"Take it easy, sit tight. Let me see what I can do."

Thompson stared for a moment out the window facing the Atlantic. A few lights winked in the distant blackness. If those Port Orange cops hauled her in and started questioning her, the whole investigation could go up in flames. There were still too many loose ends. They didn't have Moore. They didn't have the gun. Thompson punched up the Volusia cellular number, reached Kelley, who was driving south on I-95, and advised him of Port Orange's bust.

"They already have her out in the car!" Thompson's voice crackled over the phone. "Bob, is there any way you can stop them?"

"I don't know what I can do. Let me think a minute." Only the surveillance team knew anything about the operation. Volusia County sheriff's deputies, Daytona Beach PD, the FHP—all were in the dark; even the Port Orange Police Department. The effort to keep any leaks from spouting had definitely been successful. Now, it was backfiring. Who to call? What was the goddamned phone number at the Port Orange headquarters?

Kelley would later call it "divine intervention," but, Jake Ehrhart recalled, "The phone number just popped into Kelley's little head."

He called the Port Orange Police Department and told the dispatcher who answered, "This is Investigator Robert Kelley with the sheriff's office. Two of your patrol officers are at the Port Orange Pub. They've taken a white female out of the pub. There is an arrest warrant for that girl, but they are *not* to arrest her. If they look at the warrant, they'll see that it says, 'Upon contact notify Investigator Kelley of the sheriff's office.' And that's me. *Do not arrest her.*"

The dispatcher happened to be holding a teletype of the hit in her hand and had not dispatched it to the officers yet. But it was all too confusing, too strange. She freaked, blurting, "I don't know what to do! I don't know what to do!"

"Get a supervisor on the phone," Kelley said quietly, but with force. A female sergeant came on the line. Kelley advised her of the operation, repeating his instructions not to arrest this woman. With Kelley still on the line, the Port Orange sergeant radioed her officers and told them to back off. Although the Port Orange uniforms had apparently drawn the name and date of birth and it had come back with a hit . . . Cammie Greene . . . they gave her a song and dance, and released her. "What the shit was all that?" Bucket asked her when she went back into the bar.

"Aww, they were fucked. You know what?" she brayed. "They thought I was that serial killer goin' around shootin' all those guys. And then they started hasslin' me 'cause I ain't got no place to stay. Fuckin' cops."

1 Body of Richard Mallory, 51, found in Volusia County on December 13, 1989

1A Car of Richard Mallory, 51, found in Volusia County on Dec. 1 1989

2 Body of David Spears, 43, found in Citrus County on June 1, 1990

2A Truck of David Spears, found in Marion County on May 25, 1990

3 Body of Charles Carskaddon, 40, found in Pasco County on June 6, 1990

3A Car of Charles Carskaddon found in Marion County on June 7, 1990

4 Peter Siems, 65, reported missing June 22, 1990

4A Car of Peter Siems found in Marion County July 4, 1990

5 Body of Troy Burress, 50, found in Marion County on Aug. 4, 1990

5A Truck of Troy Burress, found in Marion County on July 31, 1990

6 Body of Dick Humphreys, 56, found in Marion County on Sept. 12, 1990

6A Car of Dick Humphreys found in Suwanee County on Sept. 19, 1990

7 Body of Walter Gino Antonio, 60, found in Dixie County on November 19, 1991

7A Car of Walter Antonio found in Brevard County Nov. 24, 1990

Map of the body and vehicle recovery sites.
(Courtesy State Attorney's Office, Seventh Judicial Circuit, Deland, Florida)

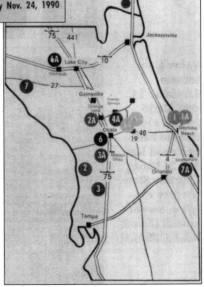

The murdered men, the cars they drove, and where they were found. *(Courtesy State Attorney's Office, Seventh Judicial Circuit, Deland, Florida)*

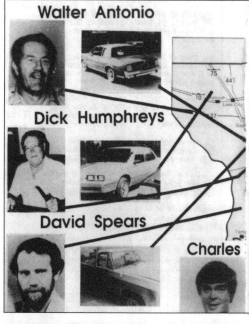

Walter Gino Antonio, November 19, 1990, Dixie County, Florida. Antonio had been dead less than 24 hours. *(Courtesy State Attorney's Office, Seventh Judicial Circuit, Deland, Florida)*

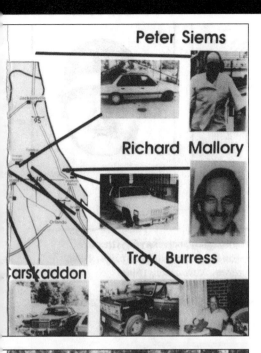

Peter Siems

Richard Mallory

Troy Burress

Carskaddon

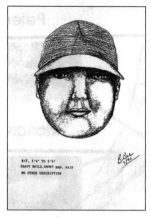

W/F. APPROXIMATELY 5'6"- 5'10''
BLONDE HAIR, 20-30 Y.O.A.
LAST SEEN WEARING BLUE JEANS.
WHITE T-SHIRT W/SLEEVES ROLLED UP
CHAIN HANGING FROM BELT LOOPS
POSSIBLY HEART TATTOO ON ONE
OF HER BICEPS.

W/F, 5'4" TO 5'6"
HEAVY BUILD,SHORT BRN. HAIR
NO OTHER DESCRIPTION

Composite sketches of women seen leaving the car belonging to the missionary, Peter Siems, July 4, 1990. *(Released by investigators, November, 1990.)*

The murder weapon. High-standard "Double Nine" .22 caliber, nine-shot convertible revolver. When recovered from the waters of Rose Bay, the pistol was loaded with nine CCI .22 hollow-point bullets. (*Courtesy State Attorney's Office, Seventh Judicial Circuit, Deland, Florida*)

Tyria Moore, Aileen Wuornos's companion, in the baseball cap witnesses remembered. *(Courtesy,* People *magazine)*

Aileen "Lee" Wuornos, March 31, 1992, Marion County Courthouse, Ocala, Florida. *(James Quine, Photographer)*

(Left to right) Volusia County Sheriff's Major Crimes Unit investigators: Larry Horzepa, Sgt. Jake Ehrhart and Sgt. Bob Kelley.

Mrs. Shirley Humphreys (second from left), Dick Humphreys's widow.

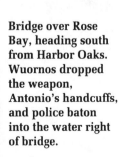

Bridge over Rose Bay, heading south from Harbor Oaks. Wuornos dropped the weapon, Antonio's handcuffs, and police baton into the water right of bridge.

The Last Resort, Harbor Oaks, Florida. Wuornos was arrested on the front steps, January 9, 1991.

"The Wall of Fame" at the Last Resort. Cannonball (second from left) served Wuornos her last beer.

Car seat outside the Last Resort where Wuornos slept the night before her arrest. Note "tribute" with knife slashes.
Photographs by James Quine

DEFENSE

Lee declares, "I'm not a serial killer. I only killed a series of men." She is being finger-printed for her return to Death Row.

Wuornos's public defenders who represented her in the Mallory trial. (Left to right) Billy Nolas, Tricia Jenkins and William Miller.

Mrs. Arlene Pralle, Wuornos's adoptive mother and press liaison.

Lee with "Dr. Legal," Steve Glazer, Gainesville attorney representing her and Arlene Pralle. He replaced Wuornos's public defenders in March, 1992.

Photographs by James Quine

"Yeah? No shit. Well, hell. Come over here and let me buy you a beer. Meet ol' Drums."

She told them her name was Lee Blahovec, but that she had given the cops a phony—Cammie Marsh Greene. It was obvious to Joyner that Lee had been drinking for quite a while, long before he and Martin had shown up, and grew louder and more garrulous as they kept drinking.

"Look, here." Lee shoved back the sleeve of her black jacket. "Look at that scar. Got that in a wreck."

"Mmm-hmm."

"Yeah, well that ain't nothin'." She jerked up the front of her blouse, exposing a white paunch marked by a narrow ragged scar. "Got shot with a .22. I've done some shit."

As Lee pulled down her shirt, Bucket noticed a diamond and gold pinky ring winking on her finger. Then she said she had to go, had to get down the road. Bucket said he'd be glad to give her a ride. Lee refused.

"Naw, it's just down the way." She got up off the stool, went to the restroom, and came back with a beige suitcase. Martin and Joyner watched her walk out the door.

At ten o'clock she was walking south along Ridgwood Avenue wearing a black Members Only jacket, a T-shirt, and blue jeans, the suitcase in her grip. A beige late-model car came up behind her, turned its lights off, and followed.

"What the hell do they think they're doing?!" Kelley snatched up his cellular phone and rang up Thompson. "We've got two female FDLE agents out here crawling behind Wuornos in their agency sedan. With the lights off! If she wasn't bombed out of her skull she'd make them in a heartbeat. Get them the hell off the street. Quick!"

Following in a vehicle when the subject is on foot is a basic surveillance violation, especially with the car's lights off. Within minutes the two inexperienced agents were off the street and on their way back to Tampa. That made two close calls in one evening. The tension among the team ground their nerves to a high whine. Curses were batted back and forth across the cellular phones until one wag tossed up the question—"How many FDLE agents does it take to screw in a light bulb? Four. One to screw in the bulb and three to get the equipment."

The Last Resort, a brick and plywood shack slapped on the west side of Ridgewood is a quintessential biker bar marked by the Harley colors—Halloween orange and black. A worn spread of sandy gravel serves as a parking lot for the clientele's hogs, pickups, vans, and late-seventies Detroit dinosaurs. Its front door opens to two pool tables, a cement floor, and a small bar beneath a low ceiling from which an array of dusty bras and panties hangs like dormant bats. The walls are plastered with yellowing snapshots featuring bare-breasted women, motorcycles, beery guys with beards and pigtails, and a dead man in his coffin. The customers wear blunt expressions of defiance, injury, mistrust, stupidity, and manifold grievance. They are a closed society of hard-eyed, rough-handed working stiffs, ex-cons, felons, and deadbeats in gimme caps, black T-shirts, and green GI grunt jackets emblazoned with declarations of allegiance to the Vietnam Vets, Harley-Davidson motorcycles, American beer, and the Stars and Bars. Deals go down, dreams go

nowhere, and blood gets spilled. Dope gets smoked and
people get fucked. The Last Resort means what it says—
there is nothing new to be had, just alcohol, weed, and
crank and talking trash while waiting for something to
happen. At ten minutes after ten, Lee Wuornos came
through the door. At ten-thirty Joyner and Martin walked
in, waved to Wuornos, and bought her a beer.

Thompson called Ehrhart. "Do you think we ought to let
our two undercover guys give her a ride home?"

"No, Jerry. She's too dangerous. We'd be letting two
guys who aren't wired get into a vehicle with her without any contact—even if they are armed."

"Then how far do we go with it? We can keep control
of her, and if we sense she's going to leave the bar with
somebody we can go ahead and arrest her. We still don't
have Moore though."

Counting Martin and Joyner, who'd just walked into
the bar, there were five units surrounding The Last
Resort, each with two officers. Kelley pulled his car into
a residential driveway just off Ridgewood that gave him
a direct view of the side of the bar. After twelve years on
the Daytona streets, he knew The Last Resort, inside
and out, front to back. The place was fenced all the way
around. The only way in or out was through one of the
two front doors. Two units were staked out behind the
joint.

Kelley also knew the scene, knew how the bikers oper-
ated. With their own little things to do, they wouldn't pay
much attention to what the cops were doing or why they
were out there. They wouldn't be surprised to see cops
hanging around.

Martin and Joyner left The Last Resort just after midnight. The bar shut down at two, and by three o'clock it had become obvious Wuornos was not coming out. She was bedded down somewhere inside for the night. Kelley told the team that there were several old trailers behind the bar where she could crash.

He had been up sixteen hours straight, with only four hours' sleep the day before, when he dialed Horzepa's home number and told him it was time for fun. "Come on down to The Last Resort, Larry. I've got a spot all ready and warm for you. I really hate to leave, but you know . . ."

During the night different strategies were projected and analyzed by Thompson and Ehrhart in Daytona, and Binegar and Munster, who were over in Ocala. One scenario was to wire an officer and let him pick her up. Thompson didn't want to put one of the men in that situation. "We can't control what would happen or keep an envelope of safety around the man. If he leaves the bar with her, we can't guarantee him complete surveillance. We wouldn't do it over in Citrus, so I'm not about to do it here."

"I wouldn't leave one of my own people out there, either," Ehrhart agreed. "Not with her in a car."

The game plan they decided upon for the next day was to put wires on Martin and Joyner, but not to let them take off with Wuornos to any unknown destination. Tyria Moore still hadn't been located, and the police had no certainty about how these two women were operating. Martin and Joyner were just to make contact with Wuornos and get her talking.

The Marion County surveillance van, a $90,000 unit equipped with a video camera, tape recorders, and a wireless receiver, would be positioned in front of the tattoo parlor north of The Last Resort. This van would monitor the undercover team's wireless microphones and video the exterior of the bar. Two units were left at the front and rear of The Last Resort, and everyone else went back to the Pirate's Cove for a few hours' sleep.

At 11:45 the next morning, Wuornos was seen moving around the interior of The Last Resort. By this time, Binegar and Munster were on the scene, having driven over from Ocala that morning. Just before two o'clock, Joyner and Martin parked their Jeep at the side of the bar and went in.

Five hours later, Terry Brevard was scrunched up in the back of the surveillance van monitoring the wires on the two Citrus County undercover guys who had been sent inside. His partner manned a video camera trained on the front door and patio. The two had been in position since eleven o'clock that morning. Through the video monitor the neon beer signs inside The Last Resort were coming alive in the growing twilight, while the mini-mikes on the undercover cops sucked up beery conversation, juke box music, and barroom clatter, and relayed the muddle of sound three hundred feet to the surveillance van. From the van, the monitoring cop advised four other units in the surveillance action—two in stationary positions, two others cruising the perimeter. In addition, the van was in contact with the operation's command center, improvised in the beachfront motel room across the Intracoastal. The cooling evening air along Ridgewood Avenue was bristling with invisible voices, each carried by a cellular phone routed through a station on the other side of the state. Though the cops were less than a mile apart, they were essentially making long distance calls to one another.

Brevard pressed his headset to his ear and listened . . .

THUB-thump THUB-thump THUB-thump THUB-thump THUB-thump . . .

The bass and drums laid down a hard, flat country two-beat beneath Randy Travis's taut leather twang.

"Last night I dug your picture from out our dresser drawer . . ."

Lee Wuornos started rocking her broad shoulders and stared wearily into the glow from the juke box. When Randy sang the chorus, so did she, whapping her thick denim-clad thigh to the beat.

"I'm diggin' up BONES . . . diggin' up BONES . . . ex-HUMin' things better left A-lone . . ."

With her thin blond ponytail wagging, she splayed out her elbows in her black jacket and sashayed across The Last Resort like a drunken black-winged hen. "I'm RES-urrectin' mem-o-ries of a love that's DEAD and GONE . . . tonight I'm sittin' . . . diggin' up bones . . ."

She lurched against the bar.

"Pitiful." The three-hundred-pound bartender set down two beers and glanced at her without a smile.

"Fuck you, Cannonball," she said flatly. "I put my quarters in there just like anybody else. What the fuck you care? I lost my best friend." Her voice rose. "I don't need this shit. I work my ass off up and down the fuckin' state. What do I get? I loved him to the max and he split and left me. What the fuck you know about pitiful?" She cocked her head back, abruptly brushed her stringy blond hair past her ears with both hands, and thrust out her chin.

"Whoa." Bucket tapped her shoulder with the back of his hand. "No big shit. Listen, I've got something for you."

She turned around to see a motel key dangling from the redhead's hand. She smiled. She knew this son of a bitch was likely. Some shit always happened when you needed some good shit to happen, and now it looked like it might be right here in front of her nose. She listened to him talk. She could go over to the motel, get cleaned up. She could get it together and help them out—him and Drums. There was some business to do if she looked like a stand-up chick.

Who the fuck were these two? She remembered now. They were a couple of dealers down from Georgia she had met the day before. Bucket and Drums. Jesus, but she could use the rest after last night here on that funky car seat out back. She studied the key. Her hand went to her jeans and she fumbled around in the front pocket. "Look here," she mumbled. She held up a single key. "See *this* key? I'll tell you something . . ." She turned the silvery key and it caught the neon from behind the bar, throwing tiny ruby digits of light as she twisted it in front of his beard. "This key . . . this key is my whole life." Then it fell to the floor. She bent down quickly and picked it up. "I mean it. This is my whole goddamned lie. I mean, life." Bucket looked carefully at the key. It was an Eagle brand key, the kind issued to a locker or padlock. He also noticed that pinky ring he had seen on her finger the night before was missing.

"Bucket, that bastard left me, stole everything I had when I was out on the road. What is it you guys need doin'?"

"Shit, Lee. You know . . . whatever. Might even have to whack some son of a bitch before we're through." Drums laughed.

"Yeah?" She bobbed her head, curled her lip, and rapped the bar with her palm. "I'll tell you, man, when I was down in Mexico, some fucker just touched my bike—I had a motorcycle down there. This shit fool kept fuckin' around and I got pissed. Pulled out my .22 and let a few off. Shit. I don't even know if I hit him. But I've done some shit, you know? You guys gonna stick around for the barbecue out back?"

Cannonball folded his enormous belly over the bar and joined the conversation. "Yeah. It's gonna be a big one tonight. Got a band playing out back. Build one humongous fire. And party."

"Look, I'll be back in a minute," said Drums, turning to Bucket. "I gotta make that call. Just hang here with Lee. Get another beer."

Martin went out the door, where the video camera caught him in the dirty light from an overcast sky. He moved quickly to the Jeep sitting at the far end of the parking lot and began talking into his mike as soon as he was behind the wheel. Two motorcycles rolled up into the lot, their engines obliterating the undercover's words. He waited until the bikers had shut down their hogs, and then resumed talking into his chest. "This bonfire pig-roast number is going down when it gets dark. You just heard a couple more come in. The place is going to be crawling with bikers when the sun goes down. I would advise making a call real soon."

Outside, a blue Oldsmobile Delta 88 cruised south on Ridgewood past The Last Resort, the surveillance van and the undercover cop. Inside the Olds, four men with cellular phones at their ears were intently engaged in four separate conversations, each man endeavoring to shut out the hectic babble filling the car. The driver made a right through a Li'l Champ convenience store parking lot, spinning the wheel with one hand while he held his phone with the other. He whipped the car back onto Ridgewood and drove north toward the bar. The sad-eyed man with the mustache sitting next to him turned from his cellular phone. "The undercover wants to know what to do about this pig roast. The bikers are coming in."

The police had known about the pig roast since early afternoon. It was going to be a real kick-ass affair behind The Last Resort in a yard shut off by an eight-foot-high wooden fence. The bikers called it the Japanese Hanging Garden. It was like a fort with nine Honda motorcycles strung up in the branches of a big oak and a stack of firewood six feet high waiting to be torched. A howling catastrophe of alcohol, drugs, fire, and craziness was coming down before this Wednesday night was over.

Binegar rolled his big jaw and looked over at the sad-eyed detective. This affair was Jake's jurisdiction. This was Volusia County's call. The Olds slunk past The Last Resort once again, taking the far inside lane, away from the bar. The driver glanced to his left and saw a red Harley turn in to join the string of bikes next to the bar. About ten of them were lined up on the oil-stained lot.

"Captain," warned Ehrhart. "She gets on the back of one of those bikes, she's gone. That can't happen. If she gets out of this and whacks somebody else a week or two from now, I can't live with it."

"Neither can I," said the captain. "This is going down. Take her."

• • •

Inside The Last Resort, Bucket sidled up to the blond. He had a twenty-dollar bill between his fingers. "Here you go. You can get a room over where we're staying." She bobbed her head and took the money. "You guys are straight up. All right. I mean that, thanks."

"Well," said the redhead. "Why don't you ride over there with me and Drums, get your room, then we can get back here for the party? You could get yourself a shower. Be feelin' a whole lot better."

"Sounds good. Let's do it." She upended her Budweiser, then pulled on her jacket. The three of them headed for the door.

Across Ridgwood, the Oldsmobile sat with its headlights staring toward The Last Resort. When Lee and the two undercover police came into view, the Volusia County detective's laconic voice broke the silence inside the car. "Okay, Larry. Do it."

On the north side of the bar, patiently waiting in the 280 ZX, Horzepa took the order and dropped his cellular phone into its cradle. He accelerated across the two hundred feet to the parking lot. He and his partner, Bernie Buescherr, were out of the car, shields in hand, just as a marked sheriff's unit pulled in from the opposite direction. In seconds, five officers were in the lot, walking toward the trio.

What the shit? She made herself stay calm. *The fucking cops already hassled me last night. The motherfuckers are so damn dumb they don't even know . . .*

"I'm Larry Horzepa with the Volusia County Sheriff's

Office." This wide-eyed bastard was in her face with a badge. "I'm with the warrants division and I have an outstanding warrant for Lori Grody. Concealed weapons charge, back in 1986." The cop looked at her and held up the warrant. "We got a report from the Port Orange police. I believe you spoke with them yesterday."

She heard herself saying, "I don't understand. I don't know what's goin' on." She wrinkled up her eyebrows, shook her head as if it was all just too bizarre. She was just going to give them whatever they thought they wanted. No big deal.

"You got a warrant? . . ." The cop held the sheet out for her to read. "Oh, yeah! . . . I remember. Well that concealed weapons thing was all a mistake. That wasn't even my car. I don't know anything about that gun . . ." She heard herself talking, she saw the cops nodding; she heard the redhead badmouthing the cop; she saw two uniforms roust the redhead down, and then there was Cannonball asking the cops if they wanted her stuff, and then there was this cop saying she was under arrest, and then this bitch was putting the cuffs on her. She just kept it cool. It was just routine. Nothing about the cars. Nothing about two girls wrecking that Sunbird out in the Ocala forest. Nothing about any killings. They didn't have a clue. They didn't have nothing. There never was a print or a witness. *Put me in jail, motherfuckers, you'll never know the half of it. It's like none of those bastards ever happened.*

THIRTEEN

Pirate's Cove

Munster was waiting at the Volusia County Sheriff's Department when Horzepa and Buescherr brought Wuornos through on her way to the county jail. Everyone kept his cool, kept up the front that this was just a routine bust on an outstanding warrant. While Horzepa made a phone call to Terry Moore, director of the Volusia County correctional facility, Munster approached Wuornos. Without identifying himself, he asked if she'd like a cup of coffee and a cigarette. She said she would, and Bruce went off to get them. He brought her a pack of smokes and the coffee, smiled, and said, "Well, I got to go. See ya." Bruce left the sheriff's office and headed back to the Pirate's Cove, where a party was under way.

Arrangements were made with Moore to have a female Pasco County officer placed undercover in the cell with Wuornos. Other than Moore and supervisor Dan Cassidy, no one else at the jail was aware of this ploy. It was a shut-down from the top. Meanwhile, a local newspaper reporter had picked up word of the arrest over a police scanner and had phoned the sheriff's office. His call set off a momentary panic.

"He put two and two together," Ehrhart recollected. "He asks, 'Did you arrest this woman for the murders?' I just flat lied. 'No . . . nothing to it at all. Routine warrant arrest.' He didn't know the name on the warrant. I made a split decision—the safety of the officers and the integrity of the investigation versus the public's right to know. At that particular time my concerns were the investigation and the safety of the officers. We had an officer undercover in the jail."

Out at the jail, Bob Kelley, Larry Horzepa, and Bernie Buescherr were working Wuornos through processing. Kelley brought in the undercover officer as if she were a prisoner he had just arrested, leading her in just ahead of Wuornos.

While the correctional officers went through Wuornos's belongings, Horzepa and Buescherr stood by. "That's when we came upon the key," Horzepa recalled. "When it was taken out and placed down in the inventory log, she says, 'Don't lose that key! That key is my life.' And at that time, we saw she had a card for Jack's Mini-Warehouse. An investigator went over there and found that Cammie Marsh Greene had rented a unit and had the same type of key, an Eagle key."

In her purse they found a plain piece of paper letterheaded Jack's Mini-Warehouse, an IOU for twenty dollars, several condoms, a photograph of Tyria Moore, photographs of two blond children—later it was learned these were her sister Lori Grody's children—and two advertisements for vanity presses that had been torn from the pages of magazines. Had Aileen Wuornos a book on her mind, perhaps the true story of a female serial killer? By the end of January her media ambitions would range much further than self-publishing memoirs.

Over at the Pirate's Cove a party was going on. The surveillance team was packed into one of the rooms, knocking back beers and vodka, a bone-weary pack of cops burning up excess adrenaline. They had done it! They had walked the high-wire in a windstorm, despite the Port Orange PD's premature bust, despite the fiasco with the two FDLE agents trailing Lee in their car, despite the wrong cellular phones, despite the near headlines from that enterprising Daytona reporter, despite the fact none of them had ever worked together before, despite everything—they had nailed her!

Into this raucous blowout walked Brad King, the state attorney from the Fifth Judicial Circuit, accompanied by his assistants, Ric Ridgway and Tony Tatti. The lawyers weren't smiling and they were sober. The cops were several hours into the juice. It was bad chemistry, and as a former cop, King was aware that one wrong word could explode the room. Nonetheless, the prosecutors were annoyed. They hadn't wanted the arrest to occur this soon. They did not have enough evidence to present an airtight case. There were too many loose ends. King tried to keep his misgivings low key, but Tatti couldn't contain himself. He stepped right into the crowded circle of 100-proof camaraderie and let loose.

"You guys blew it! What the fuck did you think you were doing? You just fucked everything! You don't have the gun! You don't have Moore! You don't have shit! What the hell did you think you were doing? It would've been better if she'd gotten away."

For what seemed like five minutes no one spoke or moved. Then Munster came out of his corner like a bear on amphetamines. Before Ridgway, King, or anyone else could react, Munster was all over Tatti. "What the shit do you know? What exactly do you know about any of this? Where the fuck were you? You little shit . . ." Joyner and Martin were now on their feet, still in their funky street denims, closing in on the lawyer. Tatti tried to step back. Ridgway and King moved to his side. The overcrowded motel room rattled with curses, shouts, and clattering glasses.

Upstairs, Binegar was now on his feet. He'd been lying back on the bed, propped up on some pillows, sipping a vodka, when he heard the racket beneath him. When he arrived downstairs, Munster and Ridgway were nose to nose, and Tatti was trying to make himself smaller. Binegar took one look at Munster's beet-red face and balled-up fists, and knew the next word would be followed by a punch. Binegar stepped between them, gently pushing Bruce back with one hand, and put his big jaw under Ridgway's.

"Back off." The Marine sergeant in him was talking. "This was my call. I'm running this investigation. Not you, not the state attorney's office, not anyone but . . ." He stabbed his finger into his chest. "We weren't letting her go, not letting her get on some damned bike and disappear and go out and kill another poor son of a bitch just because you don't have an airtight, walk-through case. You do your job . . . your job is to prosecute. You let us do our job . . . our job is to get her off the streets and charge her. Leave surveillance and law enforcement to *law enforcement.* You don't like it, well, that's just too goddamned bad. Quit whining and get on with your job." Binegar glanced around the room at the surveillance team, a furious knot of alcohol and anger. "Brad, I think it would be best if you and your guys just went back to your rooms."

King stepped up to Binegar. They had served together as young deputies, both at the jail and on patrol. "Okay, Captain. But . . . Tony's right. You don't have the gun. You don't have Moore. And if the shit hits the fan, it's not going to be me standing in front of it. Good night." The lawyers left, the cops went back for another round, and Captain Binegar made the long walk back up the stairs, thinking of Major Henry up in Ohio—*Dan, you better have something, you better have her damned soon.*

FOURTEEN

Collect Calls

The next day, January 10, Binegar got a call from Pennsylvania. Major Henry had located Tyria Moore after meeting with her father, Jack, on January 8, twenty-four hours before Wuornos's arrest at The Last Resort. Even though Ty's father was cooperative, Henry made sure a pen register was operative on the Moores' telephone in Cadiz, just in case Jack Moore decided not to work with them.

After learning that Tyria was living with her sister in Pennsylvania, Henry immediately contacted the Pennsylvania State Police and gave them an update. Given the urgency of the situation there was nothing for the flight-shy major to do but board an airplane for Pittston, where he was met by investigators from the PSP. En route to the motel where the Pennsylvania cops had Tyria, they told Henry that Moore would talk only with Florida authorities. The major felt that Munster and Thompson should be the ones on hand for the interview since they were the most familiar with the details of the murders, so he called the command post in Daytona to request that they come too.

When he met Tyria, Henry found her "tired, apprehensive, but otherwise in good shape. After she was reassured that she was not under arrest, could make phone calls, and leave if she so desired, she seemed to relax. She wanted to stay, she said, and she felt she could trust me.

"I told her it was late, and she looked very tired, and all I wanted her to do was get some sleep. I asked her if she would speak to my investigators when they arrived in the morning and help us 'clear up' the problems in Florida. She said she would."

Henry checked into the room next to Moore, gave her his phone number, and asked her to call him when she woke up and wanted to go to breakfast.

Munster and Thompson flew to Scranton, Pennsylvania, on January 11. They arrived at the Victoria Inn just before noon and were met by Henry. The three of them then joined Ty in a conference room. When she met the two Florida cops, Ty began crying, visibly shaking, her narrow eyes darting back and forth. Bruce immediately soothed her down, pulled a card from his jacket, and read her her Miranda rights. Ty waived her right to an attorney and said, "I just want to get this all straight. Okay?"

Munster and Thompson put on their best fatherly faces and nodded their understanding. Munster pulled a chair out from the table in the motel's conference room and Moore sat down. Thompson turned on his recorder.

"Ty—do you mind if I call you Ty? . . ." Munster asked.

"No, that's what everybody calls me."

"Do you understand what perjury is?"

"It means that we lie," sniffled Moore.

"If you . . . if you lie, and you're caught lying, knowingly, you could be brought up on charges."

"Okay."

Munster then swore her in.

"I met her in a gay bar in South Daytona in June of 1986," Tyria began. "We lived together for four years and started out as lovers and later we were just like sisters. We weren't into a lover relationship anymore. But we did continue to live together and still slept in the same bed and everything, but we just . . . were more like sisters than lovers.

"When Lee came home . . . well, I call her Lee . . . she came home one morning with this car. It had tinted windows and it had a Florida Gator tag on the front of it and it was a two-door Cadillac . . . this was in December of '89 . . . and we were livin' at the Ocean Shores motel in Ormond Beach, and she brought the car home and had it parked outside and we used that car to move to Burleigh Avenue.

"It was early in the morning, probably approximately six or seven in the morning . . . well, she was drunk. I know that. She was very drunk . . . we weren't moving until she came home with the car, and then she said that we were gonna move . . . we had planned on moving to this apartment. We had already talked to the people about it before she'd come in with this vehicle . . . and then, it was supposed to be a few days later, but when she came out with this vehicle, she decided to use it to move us that day.

"We were sitting on the living-room floor, and she openly confessed that she had shot and killed a man that day. And at first I didn't believe her 'cause she lies about a lot of things, but I saw it about a week later on the news. I heard it . . . I know I had seen the name Richard on a piece of paper before I heard it on the news. We were just sitting around talkin' and she just came right out of the blue and said she had somethin' to tell me, and she told me that she had shot and killed a guy that day.

"She told me that she covered his body with a piece of carpet. She didn't tell me that that was the car . . . but when I saw it on the news they showed a picture of the car and of the man that they had found with the carpet lying over him, and so I put two and two together."

Ty fingered her thick chin and looked at the carpet.

"What did you tell Lee when she told you about this homicide?" asked Munster. "That she had killed this guy. What did you tell her?"

"I told her I didn't want to hear about it," Moore quickly responded, glancing up nervously. "And then any time she would come home after that and say certain things, tellin' me about where she got somethin', I'd say I don't want to hear it. And she never . . . never would say anything."

"Did you suspect that she was killing again?"

"Not right away, no. Like I said, not until I . . . in July when I wrecked that car and she told me to run for it the second time and I knew it must've been a stolen car. I kind of suspected . . . but I didn't know . . ." Ty stared back down at her boots.

"Is there any particular reason why you didn't come forward at that time to the authorities?"

"I was just scared, that's all . . . Yeah, she always

said she'd never hurt me, but then, you can't believe her, so I don't know what she would've done . . ."

Moore agreed to accompany Munster and Thompson back to Daytona to assist further in the investigation. Before leaving on January 12, Moore took the detectives to her sister's house and handed them luggage and a burgundy briefcase that Wuornos had given her. Munster recognized the briefcase as the one Dick Humphreys was last seen carrying on September 11, 1990. Tyria also gave them a letter from Lee, dated January 7, two days before her arrest. Munster studied the well-formed handwriting, evenly spaced with occasional capitalization in block print, and parentheses and brackets. It was his first contact with Wuornos, his first glimpse into her mind. He read carefully.

Lee began with the hope that Ty had received twenty dollars and a handmade clown doll she had picked up in a roadside bar. She promised she would send more money from time to time, complaining that money was "really *hard* to make." Then Wuornos went on with a whining bid for forgiveness, regretting what she had done in her life. Throughout the letter she pleaded her "crazed love" for Ty and her desire to get back together. "I was just head-over-heels for you," she wrote. "Your on my mind day and night."

Lee complained of financial stress, of being "screwed up" and "broken down," of the "idiotic bullshit" she'd done, of how she "lost her head." But she added she was now "*harmless* forever." After more heartfelt declarations of love, Wuornos closed with a promise she would save her money, "at least 2 or 3 thousand" and that she'd write back with a post-office box number as soon as she got one.

The letter revealed just how much Wuornos felt for Ty. Moore was the leverage the investigation needed to open up Wuornos, get her talking. If it could be worked just right Wuornos would confess. All they had to do was get Lee on the phone with Tyria, have Moore work on Wuornos's willingness to get her one-time lover off the hook. It was right there in the letter: "Your my left and right arm, my breath, I'd die for you."

During the flight to Florida, Munster and Thompson presented their plan to Tyria. They wanted to put her in a motel room in Daytona, have her write a letter to Lee asking her to call her at the motel. "Tell her that you got some money from your mom, came down to get the rest of your things, and found out she was in jail," said Munster. "Then, we'll have the conversations taped. We just want you to get her talking, okay?"

Sitting between the two detectives, Ty didn't need to have anything spelled out further for her. The police hadn't charged her with anything, but then, they'd never promised they would not. Nobody'd said anything about immunity, or accessory after the fact. Tyria Jolene Moore hadn't been to college and didn't know much about law, but she sure as hell knew what that phrase meant.

"Okay. Whatever. Sure."

Upon arriving at the Daytona airport, the detectives drove Moore west on Highway 92, past the huge Speedway, the greyhound track, and the jai-alai fronton to the Quality Inn hard by Interstate 95. Up in the room, they handed Ty a sheet of paper, and a pen and envelope and told her to make it short and sweet: "Call me. I'm in room 160, Quality Inn."

"Jerry Thompson, Binegar, and Munster were the original stimulus on that plan," Jake Ehrhart recalls. "So we tried to get the letter postmarked at the post office, but they wouldn't do it. The post office policy is, if they postmark it, they take it right away, and you can't get it back. We wanted to put it in the jail that day . . . so we postmarked it ourselves. We wanted the letter to look genuine. There was a notary seal on my desk, a red rubber stamp. I stamped it, smeared it, twisted it, and 'posted' it. She bought it."

"The time is 3:32. Your News Talk 1150, WNBB weather forecast . . . pretty good chance of rain this weekend and cooler weather on the way. Be ready to bundle up. Our high is only in the mid-sixties . . ."

Munster hit STOP on the recorder. Satisfied that the machine was working, he punched the RECORD button.

"This is Bruce Munster of the Marion County Sheriff's Office. This listening device is placed on the telephone in room 160. The date is January 14, 1991." *Everything is set at this end*, thought Bruce. *Now it's up to Lee.*

Munster sat by the nightstand in Tyria's room scanning the pages of the *Daytona Beach News-Journal*. Ty Moore lounged on the bed making small talk with the two female FDLE agents who'd been assigned to her. Thompson was in the adjacent room, the door between them ajar.

The phone on the nightstand rang. Munster pointed at the receiver, and Ty answered.

"Hello."

"Hi, we have a collect call to room 160 from Lee."

WUORNOS: Hey, Ty?

MOORE: (dully) Yeah.

WUORNOS: (upbeat) What are you doin'?

MOORE: Nothin'. What the hell are you doin'?

WUORNOS: Nothing. I'm sitting here in jail.

MOORE: I came down here to see what the hell's happenin'.

WUORNOS: Everything's copacetic. I'm in here for a . . . a . . . carryin' a concealed weapon back in '86 . . . six . . . and a traffic ticket.

MOORE: Really?

WUORNOS: Uh-huh.

MOORE: 'Cause there's been officials up at my parents' house askin' some questions.

WUORNOS: Oh-oh.

MOORE: And I'm gettin' scared.

WUORNOS: Hmmmm. Well, you know, I don't think there should be anything to worry about.

MOORE: Well, I'm pretty damned worried.

WUORNOS: Well, all I can say is just, uh, you know . . . don't. Okay?

MOORE: Don't what?

WUORNOS: Just nothing. Don't.

MOORE: Don't what?

WUORNOS: Don't . . . don't worry . . . about anything, all right?

MOORE: Don't worry? It's kind of hard. I know damned well it's not gonna be long before they . . .

WUORNOS: Huh? I can't hear you. What?

MOORE: I mean if they've been to my parents' house asking questions and lookin' for me, it's not gonna be long.

WUORNOS: Well, what were they saying?

MOORE: I don't know. My mom wouldn't tell me.

WUORNOS: Huh! Well, I'll tell you what. I think that they're . . . they got things all mixed up, Ty. You know what I mean?

To Thompson, monitoring the conversation in the other room, it wasn't much of a beginning. Promising, but . . .

WUORNOS: This . . . you know, this phone . . . they listen to everything you say on the phone, too.

MOORE: Do they?

WUORNOS: Mmmm . . . mmm. Uh, I know that, you know, whatever . . . Why . . . Why were they . . . oh. You don't know. Well, I don't think there's anything to worry about . . . Just do me a favor.

MOORE: What?

WUORNOS: Just don't worry and, you know, shut. You know?

MOORE: Whatever.

WUORNOS: Okay? Don't . . . don't . . .

MOORE: Whatever.

WUORNOS: . . . Worry about nothing, okay?

MOORE: Yeah.

WUORNOS: And I'm only here for that concealed weapons charge in '86 and a traffic ticket and I tell you what, man, I . . . I . . . read the newspaper . . . and I wasn't one of those little suspects. And I tell you what, man, did you . . . it said that I wasn't one of those suspects, you know? And I'm gettin' really

WUORNOS: pissed off, them accusing us . . . uh, me. You know?

MOORE: Yeah.

WUORNOS: 'Cause just . . . you know, if . . . if . . . I'll . . . I'll . . . I'll . . . I'll have a lawsuit out.

MOORE: Will ya?

WUORNOS: In a heartbeat.

MOORE: Hmmmm. Well . . .

WUORNOS: Ty, Ty . . .

MOORE: What?

WUORNOS: The storage?

MOORE: Mmmmm . . .

WUORNOS: Forget it. It's over. I threw . . . the storage is gone. I got rid of it, okay?

Four more calls by Wuornos followed on January 14, their times dictated by the periods she was free to have telephone privileges. In these, Wuornos speculated that one of Moore's coworkers at a Daytona Beach motel where Ty cleaned rooms had fingered the two as suspects. Wuornos also continued to suspect that the police were monitoring their conversations, and made an effort to lay out alibis, often speaking with innuendo and improvised code words.

WUORNOS: Yeah. Listen, Ty, this is all a case of mistaken identity. I think what happened, see, there was pictures in the newspaper . . .

MOORE: Mmmm . . . hmmm.

WUORNOS: . . . And . . . and it was a case of mistaken identity. And I think somebody at work, where you worked at . . . said something that it looked like us. And it isn't us.

See? ... And ... and ... it's a case of mistaken identity, so somebody musta said at work, "Oh, wait this looks like, you know, maybe Ty or ... Lee." And I ... they're ... you know, of course, they're wrong. And that's what I was thinkin'. 'Cause when I looked at the pictures I said, "Shit, man, isn't this somethin' how it ..."

MOORE: (in a flat monotone) Mmmmmm ...

WUORNOS: But it's not us, you know, what I'm tryin' to say? And they've got it all wrong. So what's the deal with you? Did they ... did they talk to you or anything? ...

MOORE: No. Not yet, but I'm ... I tell you, I'm waitin'.

WUORNOS: Well, all I can say is that I think ... I think it's a total case of mistaken identity.

MOORE: Well, I just know I didn't fuckin' do anything and I don't want to get ...

WUORNOS: I know you didn't. I know *I* didn't do anything either. Right?

MOORE: I don't want to get into any shit.

WUORNOS: You're not going to get in any shit, 'cause we didn't do anything.

MOORE: I don't want my life messed up because of somethin' that you did.

WUORNOS: 'Cause of somethin' what?

MOORE: That you did. I mean, that's just not right.

WUORNOS: (slowly, with emphasis) Tyria, I didn't do anything.

MOORE: Lee ...

WUORNOS: What, Ty?

MOORE: ... Don't lie. I mean ...

WUORNOS: I'm not gonna lie. I didn't do anything, Ty.

MOORE: You know damned well that I've seen some of the cars and heard it on the news.

WUORNOS: Ty . . . uh-uh. Wrong. No way. I didn't . . . you know I did a lot of hitchhikin' and I've been in a lot of cars but I'da never . . . No.

MOORE: Aww, don't lie about it.

WUORNOS: Ty, I'm not lying. I'm *telling* you.

MOORE: You're just making it harder on yourself. Your life's gonna be misery.

WUORNOS: *Tyria* . . .

MOORE: *Leee* . . .

WUORNOS: Lookit. I'm not gonna go to some prison for something I did not do. You just tell 'em you don't know anything about it and I'm gonna tell 'em I don't know anything about it because we don't. Right?

MOORE: (heavy sigh) Well, I ain't gonna lie. I mean, I can't.

WUORNOS: Tyria.

MOORE: What?

WUORNOS: (begins crying) Just . . . I'm telling you. You can . . .

MOORE: (flatly) What's wrong?

WUORNOS: I'm cryin' my ass off 'cause this is a bunch of bullshit.

MOORE: I don't think so. I think the best thing for you to do is just . . .

WUORNOS: . . . What?

MOORE: . . . Do what you think is right.

WUORNOS: I'm gonna tell . . . I don't know anything about this now, dammit, and you knew . . . not either. Now this is a bunch of fuckin' bull!

MOORE: Why do you want to lie about it?

WUORNOS: I don't need to *lie* about it, Ty. I don't . . . I didn't do anything.

MOORE: Now you know damned well you've told me before. I don't wanna . . .

WUORNOS: Ty, I didn't tell you nothin'.

MOORE: Don't lie.

WUORNOS: (pronounced sigh) What is this shit? . . . You got somebody there listenin'? . . .

MOORE: No, I do not have anybody sittin' in here.

WUORNOS: Huh? What? I can't hear you.

MOORE: No, I do not have anybody sitting in here.

WUORNOS: *Tyria* . . .

MOORE: What?

WUORNOS: . . . I'm telling you. Any . . . any kind of car that I ever borrowed from somebody was a car because I borrowed it. But that is a long, damned time ago. I do not know anything about this *shit*!

MOORE: Okay.

WUORNOS: And neither do you. So . . . right?

MOORE: (heavy sigh)

WUORNOS: You know we're not the people. This is a bunch of fuckin' bull. Are you tryin' to tell me that you're gonna say something to them that I am fuckin' . . .

MOORE: To save my ass? You're damned right I will. 'Cause I'm not gonna go to fuckin' prison for somethin' that you did. No way.

WUORNOS: Well, all I can say is you do what you think is right, but . . . whatever.

MOORE: I don't think it's fair for me to have to screw up my life.

WUORNOS: You're not . . . your life isn't screwed up, 'cause you didn't do anything.

MOORE: I know I didn't.

WUORNOS: You didn't do anything at all. Matter of fact, you didn't do one thing.

MOORE: I know I didn't.

WUORNOS: I know that, too. I know that I'm in here for a stinkin', fuckin' little . . . concealed weapons charge.

Later in the conversation, Wuornos shifted her tone from suspicion and defiance to affection and regret. It was a pattern that marked the entire series of calls throughout three days. Wuornos's abrupt mood swings were dramatic—at one moment angry, the next joking, from tears to laughter to tears to banal chatter to fierce anger to self-pity. As time went on, Aileen Wuornos's quicksilver, erratic mental gymnastics would be seen by psychologists not as a result of momentary stress, but as her fundamental behavior.

WUORNOS: It really hurt, man, when you left. That . . . (sobbing) . . . that . . . I understand why you left, man, but . . . 'Cause that really did scare me, too, when it, you know, and I thought, well, this is fuckin' weird, you know, and I understand. But it's not true. And I . . . you were workin' all the time, twenty-four . . . yeah, all you did was work, eat, and sleep and stay home.

MOORE: Yeah.

WUORNOS: So . . . all I did was work, eat, and sleep and stay home . . . usually.

MOORE: Basically.

WUORNOS: Yeah.

MOORE: Oh.

WUORNOS: When . . . You're not cryin', are you?

MOORE: Oh, I was when you were cryin'. I hate to hear people cry.

WUORNOS: Oh, honey, I'm sorry. I'll always care about you. You're my best friend.

MOORE: I know that.

WUORNOS: And I'll always love you . . . but I know damned well that you didn't do not one little iota of thing . . . And, you know, don't blow everything out of proportion or anything, you know, like go . . . go say . . . say you know, don't . . . 'cause you know I might still have that stupid warrant out that I don't know if I have it or not . . . I don't know the statute of limitations out in the Keys [the forgery charges], okay? And I, you know, I just wanna get this over with and get out and get back, get another job and just go do what I usually, normally do, just be a good person and do what I have to do.

WUORNOS: There is nothing to discuss. I know what I did. I know that I . . . I know what I had to do, you know, to get money.

MOORE: Mmmm . . . mmm.

WUORNOS: And I did it very cleanly. And very honestly . . . and after that pressure cleaner was lost . . . and you know, there's nothing to worry about. I honestly think this is a case of mistaken identity. 'Cause I know . . . I

know for one, that damned well, there is
no fingerprints or anything about you or
me. It's gotta be . . . 'cause we never, ever . . .
there's . . . there can't be. We don't have anything to do with this. You see what I'm saying? . . . And I'll bet you ten bucks they'll
say, 'Oh! well, we found some fingerprints,'
just to scare the shit outta you to see if you're
gonna say somethin', but it's not true. You see
what I'm saying? I know that they probably
called at work and said, 'Well, that sounded
like you.' I think that's what it is, I really do. I
honestly do. This is a bunch of bull.

MOORE: Well, that car that we wrecked [Peter Siems'
           Sunbird]. I mean, what about that?

WUORNOS: . . . Ty . . . what car that we wrecked?

MOORE: The one that was on the news.

WUORNOS: The one that was on the news?

MOORE: Yes.

WUORNOS: Did you hear somethin' about a car bein'
           wrecked on the news?

Anxiously listening in, Munster and Thompson realized that Wuornos was more than a little suspicious; her
incredulous tone was a bit theatrical. They might have
gone too far in having Moore push this. Wuornos might
clam up at any moment. Munster signaled Ty to stay
calm and easy.

MOORE: Yes, when I . . . right before I left.

WUORNOS: Was that in Min . . . well, when you were up
           there, it was on there?

MOORE: No, down here, right before I left.

WUORNOS: Oh. Honey . . . I don't think . . . I don't . . . I don't think so.

MOORE: You don't think so?

WUORNOS: Remember those two guys? Those . . . remember those two guys that picked us up?

MOORE: No.

WUORNOS: Honey. (emphatically) Remember those two guys that picked us up?

MOORE: Nooooo, I don't.

WUORNOS: Oh, God. I'll bet you ten bucks you got somebody sittin' there and you got a little tape recorder and you're tryin' to pin me with this shit.

Munster ground his jaw and rolled his eyes up to the ceiling. He saw the whole operation collapsing around his ears.

WUORNOS: Just tell me right now. Do you think you would pin me with this shit?

Munster looked at Moore. She stared across the room and spoke without hesitation.

MOORE: If it comes down to my life bein' in jail for the rest of it, yes. I mean, I know what I know. I'd have to tell. I'm sorry, but I would.

WUORNOS: . . . Oh . . . well, I . . . all I can say is I think it's mistaken identity and I think it's bull.

That's all I'm gonna say. Okay? I love you.

MOORE: I know you do.

She's not going to budge and Wuornos knows it,
thought Munster. It was all going to come down to just
how deeply Lee loved Ty. Would she let the girl go
down with her?

WUORNOS: Why would you come all the way down here
to wanna talk on this phone, that you know
they listen and everything . . .

MOORE: I don't know that they listen on that phone.

WUORNOS: Well, just, you know . . . yeah, well they do.
And . . .

MOORE: I just wanted to try to come and see you.

Good work, Ty. Munster allowed himself a little
smile. *Get it back to feelings. Best friends.*

WUORNOS: Honey, I wouldn't put your life in jeopardy
either. You have never done a thing wrong in
your life when you were with me. You
were . . . you . . . you are the best woman I
have ever known. You are the sweetheart . . .

MOORE: I know that.

WUORNOS: You are. You're a living angel.

MOORE: I know that.

WUORNOS: I'm not gonna let you get in trouble.

MOORE: Okay.

WUORNOS: (tearfully) Do you hear me? I'm not gonna
let you get in trouble. But I'll tell you what.
I would die for you.

MOORE: Would you?

WUORNOS: Yes, I would. That's the truth. I'll gladly die for you. And I'll just wait to see you on the other side. But you *didn't* do anything.

MOORE: Don't make me cry.

The calls went on throughout the day, with the final one coming in just before ten o'clock that evening. Back-and-forth small talk, with Wuornos grousing about her bust, about the jail, recalling how she had bought the stuffed clown in a bar—but always threading her way back to how it was "all mistaken identity." Munster and Thompson weren't too pleased with the progress, but it was just the first day. They really didn't expect a dramatic turn this soon. Moore was handling herself all right, but without enthusiasm. They would just have to be patient.

"Hell," said Thompson. "I thought she was wise to us there and was going to hang up. But she didn't."

"Yes. I thought the same thing. I mean, it's funny. I think Wuornos *knows* there might be a tap, but she goes on anyway. She gets right back to it. She's obviously laying some shit down for our benefit. Just in case. The thing is . . . the key here is, she really loves Ty. I believed her when she said she'd die for her. If things work out, she just might."

On January 15, Lee made three calls into the Quality Inn's room 160. As far as the cops were concerned, these were less fruitful than the day before. Tyria was sluggish, hungover from little sleep, anxiety, and too many beers the night before. Lee sidestepped any direct references to the murders or events at the time of the murders, yacking on about how "the fuckin' Volusia County cops" were out to get her, about how "pukey" the colors were in the jail. She railed on about law-suits—"making a million bucks." And then, abruptly adopting a playful, girlish voice, Wuornos got to business. She wanted Ty to have a little gift.

WUORNOS: Yeah. Oh, I thought of somethin', Ty.
MOORE: What?
WUORNOS: I have these two crystal balls. I mean, really pretty little crystal balls . . . in that storage? If you wanna go and get 'em, just take a hacksaw and open it up and get what you want outta there. Okay? And you know that . . . water . . . water pistol I have? [the murder weapon, her .22 revolver, which she had dumped into Rose Bay.]
MOORE: (chuckles)
WUORNOS: I gave that away.
MOORE: Ohhhh. You're so funny.
WUORNOS: I know. You know what I'm talkin' about.
MOORE: I might.
WUORNOS: You can take the pillows and all that other shit you want. You can take that Eagle blanket [taken from Charles Carskaddon]. I mean, why don't you just go down there, get some of the stuff out, and then, you know, just let it go, because . . . what do I need it for? There ain't fuckin' nothin' I need.

Munster and Thompson grinned. Lee was a little late. The day before, a search warrant had been served on Jack's Mini-Warehouse storage unit 43G, down on Nova Road. Ward Schwoob and his FDLE Crime Scene

Unit had already transported its contents to their lab in Tallahassee. Schwoob's inventory report ran to seven pages. It was a banal but telling array of items: Suitcases stuffed with clothing—mostly men's sizes—included a camouflage T-shirt, a sleeveless Detroit Pistons "Bad Boy" shirt, a plaid long-sleeved shirt, and two windbreakers, one a size 42, the other a size 54. A wooden tool box, later identified as the one missing from David Spears's pickup, contained numerous wrenches, several levels, and a measuring tape with an engraved name that had been scratched out. Three *Playboy*s and two other male magazines. Fishing rods and reels. A black Lifetime brand billy club, soon identified as Antonio's.

An Igloo cooler held driver's license receipts for Tyria Moore and Susan Blahovec, and a driver's license, birth certificate, Social Security card, and baptism certificate for Susan Blahovec. A simulated leather wallet, the one Lee had flashed for could-be customers, contained scores of business cards. A pathetic collection of yard-sale kitchenware and dishes. In a brown vinyl case, a Remington MicroScreen razor that had once shaved Richard Mallory's face, and a Polaroid Impulse camera that he would no longer use were also collected.

A Win, Lose or Draw board game, a Scrabble game, three decks of cards, and a cribbage board were stuffed into a cardboard box, along with a fire extinguisher, a wooden parrot, and a black wall-hanging with a unicorn, starburst, and rainbow design. A gold rope chain, a gold ankle bracelet, a Resorts International one-dollar coin, a silver necklace, and a gold heart with "Tyria" engraved upon it. A softball glove. A blue and black dildo vibrator. A Captain Black medallion connected to a handcuff key. And two crystal globes set upon fish-shaped tripods.

WUORNOS: And . . . get those crystal balls. They're so pretty and they're worth a lot of money. Really.

FIFTEEN

"I'm the One"

By the night of January 15, after eight lengthy phone
calls that were slowly leading nowhere, the cops
decided Ty wasn't trying hard enough. They had kept
her as comfortable as security would allow. She had her
Budweiser, access to the telephone—there'd even been
a shopping trip to the mall with her FDLE handlers,
Rose Giansanti and Debbie Crosby. But her perfunctory
performance wasn't moving Wuornos. At one point, Lee
seemed more fretful over the pending war in the Persian
Gulf than her own situation, saying, "You know, tonight
is the beginning of a war? And it'll be eight o'clock in
the morning in Iraq and there's gonna be the bomb-
shelling and they're checking out for terrorists in the
United States because they're probably planted. They're
infiltrated all over the United States and they're just
gonna start some shit."

Thompson advised that it was time to put some fire
into the proceedings. He called in Bucket.

Early the next morning, before Lee was allowed
her first call, Sergeant Joyner sat down with Ty and

proceeded to give the rotund redhead an acting lesson. As an incentive, the streetwise cop reminded Moore of her tenuous position in this multiple-homicide investigation.

"You better get with the program here, Ty. This is no bullshit. You don't have immunity, ya know? If Lee doesn't come through with saving your ass, if she doesn't talk . . . you understand what I'm saying? You understand first-degree murder?"

Moore's freckled face went pale. She nodded.

"Okay. I want you to get with the tears. For real. I mean, it *is* real. When she calls tomorrow, I want you to get right to it. From the get-go. If she loves you, then she's got to do the right thing. Tell her you've just heard from your family, your sister. Say the cops are all over them. Tell her you're fucking freaking out. She gets off in another direction, starts with that 'mistaken identity' shit, you stay right on it . . . cry, freak. Okay? Okay? Say, 'If you love me then you've got to tell the truth.' Right?"

Ty bobbed her head, already near tears. At nine o'clock, the phone jangled.

WUORNOS: Hey, I had to call you early 'cause I didn't know if you were going to leave today or what.

MOORE: (shaky voice) I don't . . . What the hell's goin' on, Lee? They've called . . . they've been up to my parents' again. They've got my sister now, askin' her questions. I don't know what the hell's goin' on.

WUORNOS: Huh! What are they askin' your sister questions for?

MOORE: I don't know. (begins sobbing) They're comin' after me. I know they are.

WUORNOS: No, they're not. How do you know that?

MOORE: (through continuous tears and sniffling) They've got to. Why are they askin' so many questions? . . .

WUORNOS: (sobering, soothing) Honey, listen, listen, listen. Do what you gotta do, okay?

MOORE: I'm gonna have to because I'm not goin' to jail for somethin' that you did. This isn't fair! My family is a nervous wreck up there. My *mom* has been callin' me all the time. She doesn't know what the hell is goin' on.

WUORNOS: Ty. Okay. Do what ya gotta do, okay? Alrighty? Ty? . . . You . . . I'm not gonna let you go to *jail*. You hear me? Ty, listen.

MOORE: Why?

WUORNOS: I . . . Listen, you didn't do anything and I'm . . . I . . . I . . . I will definitely let them know that, okay? Okay?

MOORE: (sharply) You evidently don't love me anymore. You don't trust me or anything. I mean, you're gonna let me get in trouble for somethin' I didn't do.

WUORNOS: Tyria, I said, I'm *not*! Quit cryin' and listen . . . Go ahead and tell 'em what you need to tell 'em, okay? And I . . . I'll do what I can do, but you know, just do what you gotta do. I love you.

MOORE: I'm not so sure anymore.

WUORNOS: *I love you.* I really do. I love you a lot.

MOORE: I don't know whether I should keep on livin' or if I should . . .

WUORNOS: (soothing whisper) No, Ty, Ty, listen. Ty, listen. Just go ahead and let 'em know what you need to know . . . what they wanna know or anything and I will . . . I will cover for you, 'cause you're not in tr . . . You're innocent. I'm not gonna let you go to jail. Listen, if I have to confess, I will.

MOORE: Lee, why in the hell did you do this?

WUORNOS: Huh?

MOORE: Why did you do this?

WUORNOS: Ty, listen to me. I don't know what to say, but all I can say is self-defense. All right? All I can say is that, all right? Did you hear me?

Despite the charged emotions, Lee Wuornos was still alert to the possibility that police were monitoring her conversations. Though she was about to make a confession, Wuornos was being damned sure she was doing it on her terms, according to her script. Then, once more, she was overcome by her feelings, her exhaustion and fear.

WUORNOS: Just hold on to the phone for a little while, please, can you please? Listen, Ty. I'll probably never see you again. Do you know that?

MOORE: Yes.

WUORNOS: I love you. Honey, I'm not gonna let you get in trouble. Awwww. It's the end of the world, I'll have you know. It's this world . . . Tyria, it was self-defense, okay? . . .

MOORE: I don't know that.

WUORNOS: I know. I know you don't know that. And I'm not gonna let you get in trouble for it. If

I have to confess everything just to keep you from gettin' in trouble, I will, 'cause you didn't do anything.

MOORE: I just don't understand why you did it.

WUORNOS: I don't either. I'm telling you, I don't. Tyria, I'm so in love with you, I never wanted to leave you. You know how much I love you . . . Tyria, I'm not going to let you down. I'll go down for ya. 'Cause you're so innocent. You're so kind and loving. It is me. It was only me. Okay, I'm agreeing . . . you know, I know I'm gonna go down. I know I'm gonna die, okay? I love you. . . . You know, I don't give a fuck if I live or die.

Wuornos again reassured Moore she would clear her by confessing and then said she would call back in ten minutes. The second call would be the last time the two former lovers would speak with each other. During this final exchange, Lee Wuornos desperately spun her last words to Ty in bizarre circles of self-pity, outrage, love, and exculpation. Despite her growing loss of control, Lee's well-developed survival instincts continued to function, jockeying for angles, ways of escape, alibis. But she was fundamentally torn; conflicting messages tugged at her: get Ty off the hook . . . keep her own butt out of the electric chair. It was like looking for daylight at the bottom of a coal mine.

WUORNOS: When I die my spirit's gonna follow you, and I'm gonna keep you out of trouble and shit, and if you get in an accident, I'll save your life and everything else. I'll be watchin' you. I

WON'T watch ya when you have sex, though. When you have sex, I won't watch ya, but I'll watch ya every other way, okay? Just know that. And I hope you got the pictures. Don't burn 'em up or anything, okay?

MOORE: Okay.

WUORNOS: Keep my picture. I've got some pictures of you and I'm gonna keep 'em. . . . I don't know what they do to people on death row. Do they keep 'em in a cell all their life, or what? So, keep in contact with me so I can write you letters and tell you what's happening, okay? . . . I'm not gonna let you get in trouble. There's no sense . . . I think you ought to just go home.

Maybe she had found a way out. Maybe if Ty would just get out of Daytona, Lee could get on with dealing with the cops without going all the way. But Ty was under the eyes of Joyner, Munster, and Horzepa. She pushed harder.

MOORE: How about if I just go kill myself . . .

WUORNOS: *No!*

MOORE: . . . So I could go to jail.

WUORNOS: Tyria. Don't . . . There's no reason. You didn't *do anything*! I am the one. I am the one who did everything. And I'm gonna let them know this, all right?

MOORE: Okay.

WUORNOS: And I'll probably die of a broken heart or a heart attack. I probably won't live long, but I don't care. (abruptly brightening) Hey, by the way, I'm gonna go down in history. Yep. I'll be like Bundy.

MOORE: What a way to go down in history.

WUORNOS: It's like that Ted Bundy. If I ever write a book, I'm gonna give you the money. I don't know . . . Let me tell you why I did it, all right? . . . Because I'm so . . . so fuckin' in love with you, that I was so worried about us not havin' an apartment and shit and I was scared that we were gonna lose our place, believin' that we wouldn't be together. I know it sounds crazy, but it's the truth.

MOORE: Yes, it does. It does sound crazy.

WUORNOS: Maybe I am and don't know it. Maybe my head's all fucked up and I don't even know it. I don't know. I . . . I know one thing. I hope I die and go ahead and get . . . I hope I die a natural death and get reincarnated or somethin'. Start a new life over. I just hope you find somebody that loves you as much as I do. I don't want you to live alone the rest of your life. . . . You know, I care about livin', but if my life is all fucked up, it's such a mess, I don't want to keep wandering and wandering. No sense in me wandering any-more. And that's the way it's gonna be. I'm cryin'.

MOORE: You had to cry sooner or later.

WUORNOS: I just want you to get back home, and by the time you get back home and all the confes-sions that I did, you shouldn't have any problem. . . . It's over for me. I'll do what I gotta do and I'm probably not gonna live long 'cause I'll probably die of a heart attack or somethin' . . . Oh, well, I knew that my life was fucked when I left home at fifteen. I've had my glory days. I've had my fuckin' fun. Now it's over. The only thing that hurts me the most is . . . the most . . . the things that hurt the most . . . all the canoe trips and shit we had, the fun we used to have . . . Yeah, I blew my life away. I just wish I never met Tony, 'cause Tony turned me into a lesbian. Then, I fucked up because when I love somebody I love 'em all the way and I love 'em with all my heart and all my soul and all my mind. And I'll do anything. I'll go nuts. I can't have a relationship. I never will have another relationship.

MOORE: I doubt I'll ever have one either.

WUORNOS: Well, that's good. I'm glad to hear that, because I'd just love to know that you're single.

MOORE: You turned me against everybody. I won't trust a person for the rest of my life.

WUORNOS: That's good, Ty, because you know what? *People aren't right* . . . pollution's fuckin' up their heads. The world crisis . . . everything's messin' everybody up. I love you very much. Will you get over me?

MOORE: Yeah. I don't think it will be any problem at all.

WUORNOS: What?

MOORE: I don't think I'll have any problem at all.

Thompson and Joyner sensed that Wuornos was stalling, dragging along in endless repetition. Joyner signaled Moore to get back on track.

MOORE: Take care of it, just do it.

WUORNOS: Yes, I'm gonna take care of it. I know you came down here for me to do that, right? . . . Okay. And just do me a favor. Be good. Don't ever get involved with somebody like me and don't get involved with anybody, because you never now what that person's gonna do. Love does strange things.

MOORE: Yeah.

WUORNOS: And when you fall in love, head over heels with somebody, you're gonna do something strange. And I was head over heels with you. I mean, I loved you to the max.

MOORE: Yeah.

WUORNOS: More than anybody could ever, ever understand. 'Cause you're so damned kind, and I just couldn't believe I found such a good person. And that's what I wanted all my life. I love you.

MOORE: All right.

WUORNOS: . . . Should I tell 'em at three or tell 'em now?

MOORE: You can . . . It's up to you. I mean . . . it's probably better that you get it over with for yourself.

WUORNOS: All right.

MOORE: Okay?

WUORNOS: Thank you very much.

MOORE: All right.

WUORNOS: I'm glad you talked to me.

MOORE: Okay.

WUORNOS: Take care of yourself.

MOORE: I will.

WUORNOS: (smacks a big kiss) And here's a hug. Don't forget me.

MOORE: Okay.

WUORNOS: I'll never forget you, baby.

MOORE: All right.

WUORNOS: Send me pictures and stuff or whatever. I'll probably never get out. I love you.

MOORE: Okay.

WUORNOS: Bye-bye.

MOORE: Bye.

WUORNOS: Bye, Ty.

MOORE: Bye.

In the eleven conversations over those three days, with Wuornos constantly declaring her undying love, Tyria Moore had never once said "I love you, too." Less than an hour after their final good-byes, Lee was escorted down a pale, cold corridor to an office where Larry Horzepa and Bruce Munster were waiting. Meanwhile, Tyria Moore was lying back on the bed in room 160, an opened can of Bud in her hand. As her eyes traced the pattern on the ceiling, a particular snatch of dialogue from that day's conversation continued to resonate.

"I wish there was a way," Lee had said, "I wish there was a way . . . a way . . . but there isn't. If people would forgive you for something like this, you know, but they can't."

"No," Ty had said.

"They just can't," Lee had said. "I mean, I just have to die, you know?"

"I agree," Ty had said.

Sometimes love is strange—sometimes love isn't anything at all.

SIXTEEN

Talk Show

At 10:15, Lee hesitantly stepped into the camera's frame and shook hands with the big, bald-headed cop smiling at her. "Good morning. I'm Sergeant Bruce Munster of the Marion County Sheriff's Office. Remember me? I'm the one who gave you coffee and cigarettes the night you were arrested."

Returning the smile, Lee appeared confused, and turned as another cop came up behind her, a lanky guy with a mustache and glasses, short sleeves, and a tie. "This is Larry Horzepa," said Munster. "He's the one who arrested you." Horzepa shook hands with her, walked over to a desk that was bare but for a cardboard box and a small tape recorder, and sat down in a big vinyl chair. Munster directed Lee to a chair at the corner of the desk facing the video camera, which was rolling tape on the opposite side of the sparsely furnished room.

"I'm here to confess to the murders," Lee said, continuing to stand by the chair. Munster sat down in a large executive chair across from her, just to the left of the camera, and gestured for her to sit. Before Munster began reading her her Miranda rights, Wuornos interrupted.

Dressed in an orange jumpsuit with fresh white sneakers on her feet, and a white plastic ID bracelet on her wrist, Lee sat down, brushed her stringy blond hair back from her moon face, and blurted, "The reason I'm confessin' is there's not another girl. There is no other girl. The girlfriend of mine is just a friend. She is working all the time and she . . . she worked at the Casa Del Mar. She was always working. She was not involved in any of this. Although, the car that got wrecked, she was in the vehicle . . . She did not know it was a murder vehicle and . . . and the person that was murdered . . . She's really, really a good person . . . She's just a real decent person that works a lot. She was my . . . my . . . my roommate."

"Okay," said Horzepa. "So, then what you're telling us is you're voluntarily coming forward to talk to us now."

"Yeah. To let you know that I'm the one that did the killings."

Munster read her her Miranda rights. At first Lee said she didn't need a lawyer, but Munster kept coming back with that right, making damned sure she understood what was going on. She finally agreed that she'd like an attorney present. A call was put in to the public defender's office. Horzepa and Munster asked her nothing about the killings while waiting for the attorney to arrive.

Horzepa left to get her a pack of cigarettes and brought back Newport menthols. Then Munster went for coffees. Wuornos settled in with the video camera. Crinkling up her eyes, she shuddered and complained about how cold it was. Munster came back with coffees and gave her his navy-blue blazer with his police ID clipped to the pocket. The sleeves came down over her hands. Despite her ludicrous outfit, Lee attempted some panache, holding her Newport like Bette Davis, her wrist cocked back, her elbow resting on the arm of her chair. She reached over to the desk for her plastic cup and sipped. Munster watched her, drank from his own cup, and smacked his lips.

"You know, that is a good cup of coffee," Munster said, turning the affair into a midmorning coffee klatch. "They didn't have any cream and sugar over there, so I put in—"

"Truth serum?" cracked Wuornos, giving Munster a cool look over the rim of her cup.

"No." Munster gauged Lee for a second and continued. "What I did was I put in some Sweet'N Low."

Lee took another sip and considered it, as if she were trying some new taste sensation.

After more rapport-building coffee talk, it was Lee who cut to the chase.

"Oh, you guys. Really . . . ." she said, setting her cup down. She flipped a wisp of hair back from her scarred forehead and put her hands in her lap. "You can put me under hypnosis, you can take a lie-detector test, do whatever you can to make me show you that Ty does not know . . ."

The monologue started slowly, but then gathered momentum as Wuornos realized she was the only actor on stage. This was her show.

". . . God, she's in love with me, you know what I'm

sayin'? We didn't have sex hardly. We had sex, I'd say, the first year"—she tapped her cigarette on the ashtray next to her and chatted on as though this were some morning TV gossip show—"maybe three times, and the next years, we didn't have sex together. We were just friends. Just good friends. Huggin', kissin', but we were good friends. You know . . . So. That's why I'm sayin' . . . that's why I'm confessin' . . . I know right now, it's easy for me to confess. I know right now it's easy for me to say everything honestly now—when I get back to the cell I'll probably cry my eyes out. I'll go through a lot of hell, through court and everything else. I'll take a major toll in this. I understand."

Munster rocked back in his big vinyl chair, tapping his teeth with a ballpoint pen. Horzepa simply gazed blandly. Let her talk, their attitude seemed to say. Eventually she'll cover the ground we want her to cover.

"So, I know it's very frightening for me to confess," Lee went on. "'Cause I know I'm possibly lookin' at death, I'm possibly lookin' at life imprisonment. I don't know what I'm looking at, but I know one thing, I just wanna get right with God again and . . . I'll put my trust with the Lord and with the people here so everybody knows. I'm sorry. I mean . . . I realize I don't have a family, so I don't understand. But when I . . . After seein' Ty's family and everything . . . I have never met the family, but noticing how Ty was on the phone and stuff, I realize how badly I used to hurt some families . . ."

Making references to the phone calls, Lee seemed to be probing the detectives for some response, some cues as to how she should proceed. But the cops remained silent, so she simply plunged on.

"Now, these men were older men . . . another thing,

after they were dead that didn't bother me 'cause I thought, Well, they're older. They probably don't have anybody hardly anyway, so it didn't bother me too much. Because I didn't kill them for that reason. I killed 'em because they tried to do somethin' to me. But I did think that— Well, they're old, their father and mother's probably deceased and so why worry about it and stuff? I don't know. Creaky spots in my head, I guess."

Lee shifted in her chair and threw her arms open, her hands supplicant. "I wish to God . . . I wish I hadn't done it. Not that I'm feeling sorry for myself for what I'm gonna pay, I'm sayin' I wish I never had the gun, I wish I never, ever hooked, and I wish I never woulda met these guys. 'Cause I wouldn't've had to do what I did if I hadn't been hookin', see?"

She picked up on this angle, settled in, and worked it. "It's because of hustling. And the guy's gonna physically harm me, that I had to harm him back. You see what I'm sayin'?"

She looked from one to the other. Munster and Horzepa nodded perfunctorily.

"Yeah. 'Cause if I wasn't hustling, if I wasn't hooking around, I woulda never had a physical problem and I wouldn't've never had to hurt anybody. And I do have to say one thing, though, their families must realize that no matter how much they loved the people that died, no matter how much they love 'em, they were bad. They were gonna hurt me. So, they have to realize the fact, that this person, no matter how much they loved 'em or how good they felt they were, this person was either gonna physically beat me up, rape me, or kill me. And I don't know which one. And I just turned around and did my fair play before I could get hurt, see?"

Lee shrugged and flicked her Newport. Munster rolled his pen across his teeth and thought, *Cold. Stone cold.*

"So, I would have to say that to the families. I mean, that guy's gonna . . . 'You stupid bitch, you killed my husband.' Or whatever, you know, or my brother or somethin'. And I'd just have to say to 'em, 'Listen, what they were gonna do to me . . .' I would be probably turning around if I had survived it and say, 'You stupid bastards. You almost killed me, you almost raped me, you almost beat the shit out of me.'

"So, you know, that's how I have to look at it. I have to look at it like that, too. So, I can't really say they were sweet . . ."

Over the next three hours and twenty minutes, Lee gibbered, wept, and chatted, hammering home Ty's innocence while admitting to the killings—all seven—as acts of self-defense.

It was an explanation that was flatly contradicted by the evidence, yet Munster and Horzepa allowed Lee to drone on, hoping she'd eventually tire of the game. Again and again she fudged on details, trying to draw out of them how much they knew, conveniently skirting facts due to "blackouts." She was a real piece of work.

"If you tried to catch her out on something," Munster later said, "she could lie in a heartbeat. Right on the spot, come up with something. But she wasn't all that good. There would be these little slipups, what I called 'Oh, shit!s,' like 'Oh, shit, I shouldn't have said that!' "

At this point, Michael O'Neill, a short, bearded lawyer with a thick Middle Eastern accent, arrived from the Volusia County public defender's office. Munster and Horzepa excused themselves while Wuornos and O'Neill conferred. After a few minutes, O'Neill called them back in. Wuornos was adamant in her wish to make a confession, despite O'Neill's strong objections. The four of them sat back down, and the video camera and tape recorder once again began rolling.

Horzepa swore Wuornos in, Munster again advised her of her Miranda rights, and Lee waived them. Horzepa began with a discussion of Richard Mallory's murder. He showed Lee a photograph of the victim, whom she recognized.

"I was hitchhiking home at night and this guy, he picked me up. I-4, coming out of Tampa going to Daytona. I was underneath the bridge. It was a Cadillac, cream-colored.

"He asked me if I wanted to smoke a joint and I said, Well, I don't really smoke pot. He said, You don't mind if I smoke some? I said, I don't care what you do. Do whatever you feel like doin' . . . it doesn't bother me. So he's smokin' pot and we're goin' down the road and he said, Do you want a drink? And he had, I don't know what it was, it was tonic and some jazz. I don't know what kind of liquor it was. So I said, Sure, that sounds good to me.

"So, we drank and we're drinkin' away and we get past Orlando and we're gettin' pretty drunk now. And we're continually going down the road and I . . . we're gettin' drunk royal. Then I asked him if he wanted to help me make some money 'cause I need some money for rent and everything. He was interested at the time. So, we got out and we stop at this place on US 1, but we spent the whole . . . we got there about twelve at night, but we spent the whole night drinking and . . . you know, havin' fun for a little while.

"What's 'havin' fun'?" asked Horzepa.

"Like . . . just talkin'. He's smokin' pot and I'm drinkin' and we're talking. Then he said, Okay, do you want to make your money now? . . . Around five in the morning, maybe. And I said, Okay. You know. So he's pretty drunk and I'm pretty drunk. We're past I-95, about maybe a half mile up the road and there was a little spot that went in the woods. It was dark. We couldn't really hardly see to get in.

"So we go in the woods. So he gives me the money and I start to disrobe. Now the guy's gettin' really . . . kinda startin' . . . now, he's gonna start gettin' a little, you know, kissin' on me and stuff and . . . anyway, he hasn't disrobed himself at all. So, we're in the front seat. He's huggin' and kissin' on me and all this shit. So then he starts, you know, pushin' me down. And I said, Wait a minute, you know, get cool. You don't have to get rough. This is . . . let's have some fun. This is for fun, you know. And he's tellin' me, Well, baby, I've been waitin' for this all night long, and stuff like that."

"Where are you when this is occurring?" interrupted Horzepa.

"In the front seat."

"And you're sitting where?"

"On the passenger side."

"And he's sitting where?"

"In the driver's seat going against me. The doors are open. Okay. So, then he's gettin' really heavy, you know, on me, you know, and stuff, and I'm goin' like, now he's gettin' to where he just wants to just . . . you know. Unzipped his pants, not take his pants off or anything.

Just start havin' sex and stuff. And I said, Well, why don't you just disrobe or somethin', you know? I mean, why do you have to have your clothes still on?"

Lee sounded more like an offended deb on prom night than the 'professional prostitute' she claimed to be. A curiously demure attitude for a woman who outrageously boasted of having had sex with a quarter of a million men over the course of twenty years—an almost impossible physical feat that required having sexual intercourse thirty-five times per day.

"Then he started gettin' violent with me. So we're fightin' a little bit, and I had my purse right on the passenger floor."

"What kind of purse did you have?"

"A . . . a brown purse."

"Is that the same purse that you . . ."

"Oh, no. Wait. I didn't have my brown purse. No, it's not the one I had. I had a . . . a . . . a . . . a blue bag, and it had a zip on the side. Okay. And it was unzipped 'cause I . . . I wanted to make sure if anything happened I . . . I could use my gun. Things are startin' to happen where he was gonna . . . I think he was gonna roll me, take my money back, beat me up, or whatever the heck he was gonna do. So, I jumped out of the car with my bag . . ."

Wuornos became more animated as she got into the tale, gesturing with her hands.

"And I grabbed the gun and I said, Get outta the car. And he said, What . . . what's goin' on? And I said, You son of a bitch, I knew you were gonna rape me! He said, No, I wasn't, no, I wasn't. I said, Ohhh, yes, you were. You know you were gonna try to rape me, man. So, anyway, I told him to step away from the car."

Lee, realizing she'd just made a mistake, changed gears.

"Oh. No, no, no. I didn't. All this and another thing. Okay. I know what happ . . . okay, I took . . . I got . . . I jumped out of the car. Yeah. He was startin' to physically do stuff to me. Aww. This is a different story. God, see, it's so long ago."

Horzepa came in on another tack. "What type of gun did you have?"

"Nine . . .22. Nine-shot. You know? Like about this big." Lee spread her hands apart about ten inches. "It's a . . . pistol that has nine bullets that go into it." She described a cylinder in the air and poked her finger in a circle.

"Where did you get the gun from?"

"I stole it from a guy in a house."

"Okay," said Horzepa. "So, you're back there. You jump out of the car . . ."

"I jumped outta the car 'cause he was phys . . . physically starting to abuse me. And I remember now. He didn't even give me any money. This was another guy. This guy, he said, Well, I'll give . . . no, I said, Well I always take the money first. He said, Well, I want to see how the merchandise is first. So, I said, Well, since I been talkin' to you all night long, I think you seem like a pretty nice guy, so, okay . . . let's . . . let's go have fun. So, I started to lay down and he was gonna, you know, unzip his pants. Why don't you take your clothes off? My God, you know. I said, well it hurt, hurt to do that. Then he got pissed, callin' me . . . he said, Fuck you, baby, I'm gonna screw you right here and now . . . somethin' like that.

"And I said, Nooo, no, you're not gonna just fuck me. You gotta pay me. And he said, Oh, bullshit. And *that's* when he got pissed. Now, I'm comin' back to recollection. Okay. So, then we started fightin' and everything else and I jumped out . . ."

Lee was now on her feet, reenacting her drama.

"He grabbed my bag and I grabbed my bag and the arm busted and I got the bag again and I pulled it out of his hand and that's when I grabbed the pistol out, and when I grabbed the pistol out, I just shot 'im. In the front seat."

"So, he was in the front seat of the car?" Horzepa asked flatly.

Wuornos sat down and struck a match to another cigarette. "Mmmm . . . mmm."

"Okay. Do you know where that bullet struck?"

"God." Lee cast her head to the side, demonstrating thoughtful recollection.

"Did he react when you shot the gun?"

"Did I react?"

"Did he?"

"Yeah. He . . . he just went like, Ooooo. You know? I think I hit him on the side."

"The right side of his body?"

"Yeah. Okay . . . then he proceeded to get outta the car. And I ran around to the front . . . of the car. And he started comin' toward me. And I thought to myself . . ."

At this point, O'Neill got up and left the room. Munster thought it likely this attorney of hers was on his way to a telephone to call the public defender's office. They'd no doubt freak and advise O'Neill to pull Wuornos out of the interview. She could be shut up in just a matter of minutes, and they hadn't gotten any further than Mallory, which might be fine for Horzepa, but there were six other unsolved homicides on the table. Munster jumped in as soon as O'Neill closed the door.

"Can I interrupt for just a second?" He quickly locked eyes with Horzepa, who then eased back in his chair. Munster leaned toward Lee. "You said that there were six guys. Do you remember which six there were?"

"I don't even know their names. I just . . ."

"Which cars were they?"

"Oh, God . . . let's see. There was the Cadillac."

Munster hopped from one victim's vehicle to another, establishing Wuornos's familiarity with each one. The first Cadillac, Mallory. The second Cadillac, Carskaddon's. David Spears's pickup truck. Burress's sausage truck.

"The guy in the sausage truck was gonna kill you?" asked Munster.

"Oh, yeah . . ."

"How many times did you shoot him?"

"God, let me see. Let me see." Lee took her thumbs and pressed them to her temples, a melodramatic piece of business. "I shot . . . I shot . . . he was . . . he physically attacked me, and he laughed. He pulled out a ten-dollar bill and said, This is all you fuckin' deserve, you fuckin' whore . . . like that." Lee waved an imaginary bill in the air.

"And I . . . I said, Wait . . . and then he just . . . he . . . he threw the fuckin' money down, and I was standing in front of the truck here, and he had the door open here, and he just came . . . he didn't know I had a gun or anything. He came at me. We were fighting. I mean, we went all the way into the weeds and everything. Fighting. And, uh, when I got away from him, and I ran back to the truck and I had my gun in the back, and I ran in the back real quick, and he . . . now, we're still fighting . . ." Lee was almost breathless in her delivery.

"And he realizes I got a gun. Now, I finally got a . . . fighting, and somehow he . . . I kicked him or somethin'. He backed away or something or I pushed him or somethin' like that, and he backed away, and I pulled my gun out and I said, You bastard. And I think I shot him right in the stomach or somethin'." She stopped and took a drag on her menthol.

"Okay," said Munster. "Did you shoot him after that?"

"Yeah. 'Cause he . . . Oh, yeah, I shot 'im. And he turned around . . . turned around, and he was gonna start runnin', and so I shot him again in the back. If I remember right."

"So," said Horzepa. "All these men that you've killed, did you use the same gun each time?"

Lee bobbed her head and brushed her hair back.

"Mmmm-hmmm."

"Where is that gun?"

"Okay. Yeah. That gun should be . . . there's a bridge . . . uh, let's see, I don't . . ."

"There's a bridge over by the Fairview."

"Yeah, that's it. Headin' south. On the right-hand side headin' south. I threw it in the water there. Holster and all. I threw a pair of handcuffs and I think a . . . flashlight."

"Did you ever have a badge? A police badge?" asked Horzepa.

"No. Was one of these guys, by the way, a police officer?"

"Two of the guys had been police officers." Munster tapped his briefcase, which was lying in his lap.

"Oh, I thought those were fake badges when I saw 'em."

"What happened with the guy that worked at HRS? Where did you pick him up? Or, where did he pick you up?"

"Past Wildwood, goin' that way. He picked me up on 44. I asked him if he was interested and he said, Yeah. Okay, so . . . when I . . . when I . . . when we got to the spot on 484, he took his badge out and he said, I'm gonna have you arrested for prostitution. I said, Bullshit, you are. So, he grabbed my hand . . . my arm and he said, No, better yet, how would you like to suck my dick and I won't do anything, but you're not gettin' any money for it.

"I said, I'm not gonna do anything. You're not gonna arrest me. I'm not goin' anywhere and you can't prove anything." Lee snapped back in the chair, punctuating her recollection with an arrogant sneer.

"So, he was out of the car. He was at the back, 'cause he told me to come over here to the back of the trunk. He said, Honey if you suck my dick, you can get off scot-free. You don't have to worry about nothin'. I said, I'm not gonna do it. So, I sat in the front seat and he grabbed my arm and pulled me out of the front seat and I pushed him back. And as he pushed . . . went punchin' back, there's like this grill thing on the ground and I grabbed my gun and that's when I shot him."

"While he was on the ground?"

"No, he stepped back and he started to stumble and he fell. He got back up and I shot him from there."

"When he got back up you shot him?"

"Yeah. I shot him from there and he . . . then he went back and started goin' toward the trunk, and I shot him again. Then he went back over toward the thing, if I remember right. Okay . . ."

"How many times did you shoot him?" Munster glanced down at his briefcase, on which rested his notes on Dick Humphreys.

"I think I shot him three times."

Munster looked up. "Three times?"

Lee hesitated. "I think. Oh, yeah, he stumbled and fell . . . Oh, yeah, I remember, 'cause he pissed me off and everything."

A picture of Dick Humphreys's body lying on the autopsy table sprang up in Munster's mind. Seven bullets. Seven wounds. The grass stains on his pants, evidence that Humphreys had writhed upon the ground. The bruise on his abdomen where a .22-caliber gun barrel had pressed into his flesh. The powder burns around the kill shot to his heart. "He pissed you off?"

"Yeah. 'Cause I . . ."

"Yeah?"

". . . I knew what he was gonna do, you know? And I think I shot 'im near the neck. I'm not sure."

Munster blandly looked her in the eyes. "Okay, you shot him some more times then?"

Lee put a quizzical wrinkle on her face. "Uh, no, I don't *think* I did. I think I shot him three times."

"Okay. What did you do then? After you shot him?"

"I . . . I . . . uh . . . I got his wallet out, I . . . oh, I went to look for his keys. I found his keys in his pocket . . ."

"Is that when you took his wallet out too?"

"Yeah. I got his wallet . . . and I ran back to the car.

And I think . . . I think that's all I did. And I ran back to the car and I hurried up and got in the car and started the car up and I drove away. I started toward Longwood and then . . . I . . . I went back to Daytona."

"Did you get rid of his wallet or do anything to the car?"

"Oh, yeah. I was always scared, so I'd get rid of everything and I'd try to wipe everything down 'cause I was really fri . . . you know? What I did . . . I knew I had killed somebody and I knew that, man, you know, Look what you've . . . you've done!" Lee flipped her palms up as if to indicate that an impossible predicament had suddenly fallen upon her that September afternoon, an unforeseen calamity that could have happened to anybody. "And I knew all the time, all the time I was killin' somebody, I knew—Look what you've done. But I was doin' it and . . . it just happened."

Lee shook her head, but her rueful expression fell far short of remorse. "A year . . ." She waved her hand, shooing back the time. "Everything was goin' fine, but next . . . this last year, people just started messin' with me is what I'm tryin' to say. They just started comin' like flies on shit, startin' to mess with me. So . . . now I've been raped nine times but never killed."

Horzepa's eyebrows shot up at this odd observation, and he stared at her. She wasn't even remotely aware of what she'd just said.

"I've been beat up so bad you couldn't describe me. So I got to the point where I needed a gun and that's why I got this gun . . . I was makin' all the money. I was meetin' people left and right every moment of the day. That's what I'm sayin'. I mighta had eight guys that day who never even messed with me, and then one guy would come up and mess with me."

She had to be settled down. They needed corroboration from this unpredictable woman. Horzepa rested his forearms on the desk separating them and put his fingers together. "I'll tell you what we need to do. Okay? 'Cause I know this is a lot on you. Okay? And I apologize. You know, what we need to try to do is try to get this in chronological order. Step by step. Just go over the basics, okay?"

"Right." Lee nodded and gathered herself, smoothing out the orange pant leg covering her knee.

"Don't go into a whole lot of detail, right up front, okay?"

"Okay."

"How many men have you actually shot and murdered?" Horzepa quickly corrected himself. "Shot and killed?"

"Six. All I can remember."

Munster slipped in. "You forgot about the one that was in the pickup truck. That makes seven."

"No. 'Cause I only did six."

This wasn't the time to get into a pissing match with her, thought Horzepa. "Okay."

"Well," said Munster, "we'll go over those six first."

"I think there's only six," she continued. "I know. I think it's six. I'm bein' very honest with you, as much as possible."

What the hell did that mean? thought Munster.

"I mean I am telling you the absolute, honest to God, so help me Lord, strike me with lightning in my heart right now, if I'm not telling you the truth."

Right. Of course. She crossed her heart and raised her

right hand. Lee had an advantage here. There were only eight people who knew what actually had happened out in those woods, and seven of them were dead. Fifteen months later she would stand up in court and declare, "*I* am the truth. *I* am the fact." Who was going to contradict her? As far as Lee Wuornos was concerned, no matter what the cops threw at her—evidence, fingerprints, autopsies—*she* was sticking by her version, and there wasn't nothing the motherfuckers could do about it.

And with that, Wuornos launched into a third version of the Mallory murder. "Okay, we're back to the struggle," Horzepa offered. "You get out of the car. You fired one round. You struck him in the side. He was behind the steering wheel?"

"Right. He got outta the car and he was comin' toward me and I shot him again. I think in the stomach or in the chest or somewhere around that area. Then he fell to the ground and then . . . no, wait . . . I'm not sure, but I think, if I remember right, I just kept shootin' 'im."

Then she started playing games with the two investigators. Did she take a radar detector? No. He didn't have one, did he? She was too seasoned a criminal to give anything up to these cops. If they wanted something, they could front it. Yes, he did have a radar detector. Okay, then I sold it. Did he have a camera? Yes. Okay, I sold that.

"He had two cameras," said Horzepa. "He had a 35-mm camera and he had a Polaroid. Purplish in color."

"Oh. A lot of those items I just basically threw away. I just threw them in the woods and stuff. Like in garbage Dumpsters and everything."

Horzepa rocked back in his chair. "We've gone into your bin."

"To my what?"

"To your bin in Jack's Mini-Warehouse."

"Oh, yes." She seemed to suddenly recall this as if it were a long-forgotten minor detail.

"We got a search warrant. And we obtained everything out of there. Are there items in that bin that belong to any of your victims?"

"That I don't know." Lee shook her head. " 'Cause I have so much stuff. I think . . . Oh. He had a maroon . . . uh . . . Polaroid? Yeah." She nodded vigorously. "Yeah, okay. I have that stuff in that room. Okay. Right, yeah I did keep that, I did keep that . . . but I never *used* it."

In Lee's juvenile code of ethics, a self-exculpatory recipe that seemed to run on a kind of point system, not using Richard Mallory's camera after she killed him somehow diminished the seriousness of her crime.

By this time her public defender had returned. For the past ten minutes he had sat crumpled in a chair next to Munster as Lee prattled on about the murders. He had heard enough. He asked for a break so he could speak with his client. Munster and Horzepa turned off the recorders and left the room. A few minutes later, O'Neill, appearing befuddled and crestfallen, called the detectives back into the room.

"There's no control over what she said, and she keeps telling me that she wants to protect her friend, she doesn't worry about herself," said O'Neill wearily. "I keep telling her, well, maybe you *should* worry about yourself. This will be in a court of law and investigators cannot ask leading questions. There's no way I can object to questioning or anything like that, so basically, I told her I feel very uncomfortable in a situation like that because I would generally tell the people, well, you don't say anything. Remain silent. I . . . I even said to her, do you want me here . . ."

Lee burst in. "And I told *you,* I don't care if you're here or not. I just wanna let them understand that Tyria is very innocent. I'll tell everything I did from blow to blow as much as I can . . . I don't care about me." Lee emphatically sliced the air with both hands. "I . . . deserve . . . to . . . die. This person does not deserve anything 'cause this person is innocent. I've given up my life because . . . I . . . I . . ." She shook her head, groping for the words. "I took a life . . . I am willing to give up my life because I had killed six people, which maybe it was self-defense. Maybe it was stupid. Just off the wall, shoot, maybe I could've got away with it, maybe I . . . I mean, I . . . got away from them and ran or whatever, but you know . . . I feel guilty. I am guilty. I'm willing to pay the punishment for that . . . do you understand? I'm putting myself on the cross because I don't . . . I need . . . I deserve it."

"Do you realize these guys are cops?" O'Neill's shoulders sagged.

"I know. And they wanted to hang me. And that's cool, because maybe, man, I deserve it. I just want to get this over with."

Lee's self-sacrificing bravado may have fired her will to continue, but her words would come back hard when they played to the jury a year later. *"I took a life . . . I am willing to give up my life because I had killed six people . . ." "I deserve to die."*

Munster took a look at his watch. It was twelve-thirty, they were about two hours along. Time to get to David Spears, the one she'd said she couldn't remember. "All right," he said. "Let's go back. After Mallory. Okay?

What was the next one? Do you remember the case up in Chassahowitzka, with the guy with the pickup truck?"

"Oh, yeah. Okay. I remember him. He was . . . while we're talkin', you know, drivin'? He kept tellin' me he was some kind of mechanic or somethin', and he was kind of a rough dude, too. Tall guy with a beard. And we were nude and everything, and we were screwin' around and all that stuff, gettin' drunk and everything and then, uh, he wanted to go in the back of the truck, and all I remember is that, I think there was some kind of lead pipe or somethin' like that. And when I got back there, he started gettin' vicious with me and I jumped out of the truck and he jumped outta the truck, ran to the . . . to the door. Opened the door, grabbed my bag . . ."

As in every description she gave of the murders, Wuornos scored her dramatic vignettes with gesticulating abandon, whipping her long hands through the air as she mimed her quick-draw, cocking her thumb and forefinger in approximation of her Double Nine.

". . . Grabbed the gun out, and . . . I shot him. Quick as possible. I shot him at the tailgate of the truck. And then he ran around to the driver's side, tryin' to get in the truck towards me, which was weird, towards me. And I just ran into the truck towards him and I thought, What the hell you think you're doin', dude? You know . . . I'm gonna kill you 'cause you were tryin' to do whatever you could with me. And I shot him through the door and then he was kinda . . . went back, and I went right through the driver's side and shot 'im again and he fell back."

The autopsy report showed that Spears had been shot six times, twice in the back. At some point, David Spears had turned and run away from the barrel of her .22.

"What was he wearing when you shot him?"

"Nothing. He was nude. We were both nude."

Munster plucked an eight-by-ten glossy from his briefcase and handed it to Wuornos.

"Is that him? God!" She handed back the photo. "He had tools and I kept the tools. Brought 'em back to the house, told Ty I borrowed somebody's vehicle again and then took off. The next morning I drove around for a while and I dropped the truck on Orange City and Irvine."

"By I-75?"

"Yeah."

"Do you remember a ceramic panther in there, looked like it was crawling?"

"Don't remember anything like that."

The panther was not among Wuornos's considerable booty discovered in her storage unit. It was never found.

"Did you take the radio out of that truck?"

"Yeah, I believe I did."

"Who's the next one?"

"Let's see . . ." Lee puffed her cigarette and gazed at the fluorescent tubes above her. "Third guy . . . I think the next one's the one . . . he was a Christian guy or somethin'? I . . . I didn't know he was a Christian guy. He was nude. This is the one in Georgia, I think. He took a sleepin' bag . . . took it out in the woods and when we got nude, I had taken my bag with me that time, 'cause I said we're goin' out in the woods. I'm not gonna give him an opportunity to rape me. And that's the time this guy gave me a problem, too. And, so, I whipped out my gun." Lee cocked her thumb and pointed her finger toward Horzepa's hairline. "And I said, you know . . . I . . . I . . . I don't want to shoot you.

He said . . . he didn't say anything, he just looked at me and he said, you fuckin' bitch. And I said, No, I know you were gonna rape me. 'Cause he was gettin' physical with me again and I knew. And he said . . . Fuck you, bitch, and started to come at me, and he was tryin' to get the gun from me. We struggled on that one." Lee became more animated, waving her arms and twisting from side to side.

"We're strugglin' with the gun and everything else and a couple a bullets shot up in the air and finally I ripped it away and I had the gun in my left hand and I put it back in my right hand and I shot him immediately."

Lee's version of Peter Siems's murder played more like a schoolboy's wild re-creation of an action movie, with flourishes of skillful gunplay and triumph, rather than an unvarnished account of actual events. Thus far, each killing, according to Wuornos, was the result of an attack on her, in which she managed to gain the upper hand. She was stretching credibility beyond acceptance. Munster knew Peter Siems had had no sleeping bag with him when he left his home on June 7, 1990. From what he knew of the committed Christian missionary, it was extremely unlikely Siems would have stopped to buy this woman beer. He might have picked her up along I-95 as a Good Samaritan, listened to her hard-luck story, nodded sympathetically when she showed him the pictures of "her kids," and then found himself under the muzzle of her .22. The same likely scenario that Dick Humphreys and Troy Burress fell for, and died for.

Munster slipped his pen from between his lips. "Where'd you hit him at?"

"I think I probably . . . I always shot somebody, if I could, you know, fast as I could. It would always hit around this area . . ." Lee waved her hand up and down her torso, from her stomach to her collarbones. "Up here. I always went to the midsection, so I knew I shot 'em." She seemed like a student who had just correctly answered a test question, leaving an unspoken expression on her face as if to say, "Isn't that the right way to do it?"

"When I took the car and went through his shit I noticed he had some Bibles underneath his seat, and I said, God. You know? This guy's religious or what? 'Cause I was lookin' in the Bible to see if he was a reverend or whatever, but that never said nothin'. Was he, by the way?"

"Yeah. He was a missionary."

"Aww, God."

"Did you get some money from him?"

"Yes, I found some money in his suitcase. I think he had . . . three or four hundred dollars."

"Where's his body?"

"I don't know . . . he took me way the fuck out in the wilderness somewhere."

"Up in Georgia? Off the interstate?"

"Yeah."

"Okay. The guy with the .45 that you told me about, is this before or after?"

"Before. He was the second guy. I shot more than nine times 'cause I was pissed when I found the .45 on top of the car. I reloaded and I shot him some more. He told me he was a drug dealer. I told him to stop where we'd do our hustlin' trick on 52, near a lake . . . no, on 301. We were way out in the boonies. He crawled in the back seat and he said, You fuckin' bitch, you're gonna die. I said, You fuckin' bastard, you were gonna blow my brains out, and I shot him. He was totally naked. I always stripped first. After I shot the guy, he crawled in the back seat. I reloaded and shot him some more. If it was in Western days, they'd put me in a noose and watch . . . let the town watch me die."

Munster nodded. "Now, the last one . . ."

"When Ty left and I got constantly drunk 'cause I was bummed out that she was up there and I . . . I was lonely. And I went hitchhikin' to make some money. I don't know where I picked him up. I was drunk as shit. This is a blackout, man."

"Well, do you remember having his ring afterwards? The man's ring? You gave it to a pawnshop. Nice big flashlight? Badge?"

"Oh . . . I remember. All right, all right. He was an older fella, a little short guy. I musta had a case a beer on this one. I was drunk as could be and again, this guy . . . I'm askin' if I can make some money and he said, Sure. And we go way out in the woods. We were *way* out in the woods . . . some, oh, God . . . somewhere way, *way, WAY* out in the woods. And we stripped on that one, and then he got his pants out and was startin' to come toward me to do my little deed that I'm supposed to do, hustling and everything. He got out his little . . . he had his wallet out of his back pants pocket and said he was a cop. Uh-huh."

Her lip curled and she rolled her eyes. "Same thing. You know, like I'm a cop. And he said, If you . . . I could arrest you and everything like this but if you want to, you can have sex with me for free and I'm gonna let you go and all this other jazz and shit like this. I said . . ." Lee jabbed her finger and blustered. "I am sick and tired of people comin' up to me and tellin' me they're a cop and *I don't think you're a cop*. He said, Yes, I am a cop. I said, No, you can get a badge like that in a detective magazine. So, anyway, I started to get outta the back seat and he got outta the back seat and he ran around in front of me and said, Listen, man, you are going to suck my dick or you're gonna have sex with me. You're gonna do something. I said, No, I'm not. And that's when he started to struggle with me and struggle, I almost dropped my gun on that one. After I whipped out my gun . . ." Once again, Lee mimed her studied quick-draw with a flurry of hands. "And then I shot him."

"How many times did you shoot him?" asked Munster.

"Twice, I think."

Four times, thought Munster, four times. Three in the back, one in the head. Cold, cold, cold.

"Okay. Now, how did you feel when you thought he was a cop?"

"At first, I . . . 'cause that one guy, that HRS guy tellin' me he was a cop, I said to myself, this is another faker. He's just tryin' to get a free piece of ass."

"Yeah. Well, when you shot him, what did he do?"

"Mmm . . . well, when we were strugglin' with the gun and everything else, again, he fell on the ground and he started to run back . . . run away. And I shot 'im right in the back. He just kinda looked at me for a second and he said . . . he said something like . . . what did he say?" Lee cast her eyes back and forth. "I think he said, You cunt . . . or somethin' like that. And I said, You bastard and I shot him again. Then I just got in the car and took off."

"Did you shoot him someplace else?"

"I think I shot 'im in the back one more time. Mmmm . . . mmmmm. Shot him near the head or somethin' like that. I just kinda randomly shot."

Random? Two bullets on either side of his spine and one straight through. One to the base of the skull. All at close range. *Random, my ass.* Munster kept his eyes on his notes.

"Did he survive?" she asked.

"No."

"Awwwww." Lee shook her head as if she'd just gotten some disappointing news. What was she doing with this lame act? She knew damned well Antonio had been dead when she left him by that tree stump.

Lee suddenly asked, "What was he?"

"He had been a reserve cop down in Brevard County." Munster then came back with a question that had been gnawing at him for months. "What happened to his teeth?"

"I took everything outta his car and just threw everything out in the woods."

"His *teeth?*"

"Yeah, everything."

Bullshit, thought Munster. "He still had sex with you and he didn't have his teeth in?"

"No, he didn't have his teeth in at all. They were in his glove box."

She didn't want to get into this. Either she had taken his teeth as a souvenir and gotten rid of them for some reason, or she had taken them to slow identification of the body. Or both. With this one, anything was possible. Munster pressed on.

"Is this the guy whose ring you took to pawn?"

"No, I don't remember that. I don't remember at all. I don't know whose ring it was."

"All right . . ."

"Oh!"

Munster looked at her without expression. "Oh, what?" She had just fallen into another "Oh, shit!"

"There was. Yeah. Okay." Lee waved her hands, as if she were calling time-out in some school-yard game. "Okay, he had a gold chain and ring. He took that off and, uh, stuck it on the seat."

With an incredulous wrinkle on his brow, Munster leaned toward her. "He took it off and stuck it on the seat? Why did he do that?"

"Because . . ." She stalled. "I mean, I took the ring off his finger, but he took his gold chain and stuck it on the seat. Yeah." She actually seemed satisfied with that answer.

"All right. You took the ring off while he was alive or dead?"

"Uh . . ." Lee was at sea. She didn't seem to know which way to go. Should he be dead or alive? What did it all mean? ". . . my God . . . I think he was . . . not dead. I don't think he was dead when I did it. I . . ."

"Had you already shot him when you took the ring off?"

"I don't think so."

Munster stared. "Okay."

"And like I said," Lee gushed. "I probably said somethin' back there, as drunk as I was in my mind, I would probably say somethin' like this . . . Why, you fuckin' bastard, let me get somethin' outta this. You know, somethin' like that."

Something like first-degree murder, mused Horzepa. Something like that.

Munster was thinking along the same track. Premeditated. Cold and calculated. Heinous and atrocious. All those aggravators that went with capital murder. He switched gears. "Now you said that on the HRS guy, you said that he gurgled a little bit and you shot him to put him out of his misery. Did he ever ask you not to shoot him again? Did he ever say, I'm sorry, please don't shoot me?"

"Uh-uh. No. He just cussed at me."

"They always cussed at you?"

"They . . . they were cussing at me."

"Each and every one of 'em?"

"Oh, no. Uh . . . not all of 'em. Just . . . I think the two that you say were police officers, they just called me whores and cunts and everything."

"How about the other guys? Did they ask you stuff while you were shootin' at 'em?"

"They never said anything. They just . . . I . . . I shot so fast."

Horzepa wiped his hand across his nose and pushed up the bridge of his glasses. "Let me ask you something, Lee. You said that you carried the gun for protection. Is that correct?"

Lee turned to face him. "Yeah. Yes."

"Okay. From all the shootings you have told us about, for the most part, you've always gotten the drop on these guys. You've been able to get your gun and point it at 'em."

"Uh-huh." Lee blithely followed.

"Right?"

"Right."

"Okay. At that particular time, you were in control. Why didn't you just run? Why didn't you . . ."

She had the answer ready. "Because I was always basically totally nude with my shoes off and everything and I wasn't gonna run through the woods and briars and . . ."

Horzepa raised his palm. "No, but still, like I say. You're in control. You could go ahead and get dressed while you had, you know, them do whatever you basically wanted." He rested back in his chair. "Why did you go ahead and . . . and shoot these people?"

Lee became agitated. "Because they physically fought with me and I was . . . well, I guess I was afraid, 'cause they were physically fightin' with me and I . . . what am I supposed to do, you know, hold the gun there until I get dressed and now I'm gonna walk outta here?" Her expression said *How stupid!* "When the guy, you know, might . . . you know, run me over with his truck or might come back when I'm walking out of the woods or somethin' . . . uh, have a gun on him, too, or somethin'. I didn't know if they had a gun or not."

"So was it . . ." Horzepa went on: "Was it your intent, during each of these times, to kill this person so that they couldn't come back at you later?"

She nodded affirmatively. "'Cause I didn't know if they had a gun or anything. I . . . once I got my gun, I was like, Hey, man, I've gotta shoot you 'cause I think you're gonna kill me. See?" She flipped her arms out at the elbows.

"What about the ones who didn't have a gun, like Mr. Mallory?"

"I didn't know they had . . . didn't have a gun."

"Okay. So you were taking no chances."

"Right. I didn't know if they had it under the seat, close by 'em, or what. I didn't know if they were in arm's reach of a weapon or what. See?"

"What made you take property . . . a lot of property or a little property from some and not from others? Was there anything there that motivated you to . . ."

"I guess it was after. It was pure hatred. Yeah, I think afterward, it was like, You bastard, you woulda hurt me and, uh . . . I'll take the stuff and get my money's worth because some of 'em didn't even hardly have any money. They were gonna . . . they were . . . some of 'em didn't have *any* money. Like that guy, the drug dealer guy . . . he had twenty bucks, and he wasn't gonna give me any more money."

"So, then you just started living off of the items they had?" probed Horzepa. "Is that what you were doing?"

"No. I think I took 'em just for the fact that, You bastards, you were gonna hurt me, you were gonna rape me, or whatever you were gonna do. Well, I'll just, you know, keep these little items so I don't have to buy 'em or somethin'. I don't know. I just . . ."

"It was like final revenge?"

"Yeah." She bobbed her head, liking that prompt by the cop. "Okay. That would do. Mmm-hmm."

Munster stepped in. "Lee, after you shot one time, I mean, you could've left. You could've taken their stuff and . . ."

"I didn't want to do that because I was afraid that if I shot 'em one time and they survived, my face and all that description of me would be all over the place and the only way I could make money was to hustle. And I knew these guys would probably . . . would rat on me if they survived and all this stuff. I was hoping, after what

I had to do, that I wouldn't have gotten caught for it because I figured these guys deserved it. Because these guys were either gonna rape, kill . . . I don't know what they were gonna do to me. See what I'm sayin'?"

"So, you continued to kill these men to cover up . . . when you shot these men," Horzepa came back. "Mallory was the first, is that correct?"

"Mmm-hmm."

"You had to go ahead and kill these men so that they couldn't testify against you and have it backtracked from body to body, then."

"Oh, no." Lee waved her hand and explained. "I didn't even think that either. I shot 'em 'cause it was like to me a self-defending thing, because I felt if I didn't shoot 'em and I didn't kill 'em, first of all . . . if they survived, my ass would be gettin' in trouble for attempted murder, so I'm up shit's creek on that one anyway, and . . . and if I didn't kill 'em, you know, of course, I mean I *had* to kill 'em . . . or it's like retaliation, too. It's like, You bastards. You were gonna hurt me."

"So now I'm gonna hurt you."

"Yeah."

"All of these guys that you shot, they seem to be older guys. Over the age of forty." Munster waggled his pen between his fingers. "Why is that?"

"Because all the guys that I dealt with were that age. Every guy."

"You were dead wood for younger guys?"

"No. Every guy I dealt with on the road was anywhere from thirty-seven and up. See, I don't do drugs or anything, and I wanted to deal with people who didn't do drugs. I was lookin' for clean and decent people. But like I say, it just happened that the last year, that I kept

meetin' guys that were turning out to be ugly guys . . .
to me."

Munster considered Wuornos's story and the facts.
Her prostitution career had clearly been on the skids.
She'd made no efforts at grooming when she went out,
no makeup, no sexy dresses. She didn't even own a dress.
This dishwater blond with a beer gut had hit the highways in a pair of cut-off jeans, a Marine camo T-shirt, a
ball cap, and a pair of sneakers, toting a plastic bag
loaded down with a ten-inch nine-shot revolver. Not the
usual attire, even for a truck-stop hooker. And not the
kind of weapon prostitutes packed for self-protection. It
was too damned big and heavy. Hell, in twenty years,
Wuornos had never been busted for solicitation. But she
was right about one thing—she was a hustler. That's what
she did. She hustled. Hustled at pool, hustled at forgery,
even hustled a convenience-store robbery. And when
each of them went bad for her, she tried something else.
These seven guys had just had the bad fortune to step
into her latest hustle, one that had ended in murder.

Horzepa pushed a little harder. "So, after all these . . .
incidents . . . had occurred and all these men were shot,
none of this was planned?"

"No."

"But when you decided to pull that gun, that person
was gonna die. I mean, you weren't just gonna shoot
'em . . ."

"Oh, I was definitely gonna shoot 'em to let 'em die.
Because they were either gonna rape me, kill me, strangle me, make me . . ."

Horzepa cut off her litany. "Okay, that's what I'm
trying to get at. That's the line they crossed as far as you
were concerned."

"Yeah. They were crossing my line as far as, like, they were gonna rape me, kill me, I don't know if they were gonna strangle me . . ."

"But when they crossed that line with you, that was the time you pulled out that weapon and that's the only time you used that weapon . . ."

"Right."

"But when you did, you made sure that person was dead."

"I . . . I . . . I was going . . . I shot 'em. Oh, well, yeah. I remember the missionary guy. I shot him once and I thought to myself that I, you know, I don't really wanna do this to you, guy, but I'm gonna have to because if you live, if I let you live, you're gonna tell. And all this other jazz and I'd probably get caught, you know. But it was also in bitterness of what you were doing to me. See what I'm saying? Like, Hey dude, you're gonna rape me, you're gonna kill me, whatever you're gonna do . . . it's not gonna happen 'cause now I'm on the other end of the stick now, see?"

"You're in control."

"Yeah."

Wuornos kept insisting she'd killed only six men. She'd decided, likely because the police had not found Siems's body, that she'd cop only to the murders the detectives put to her. Not once in the confession did she offer details, apart from her self-defense script. If they wanted to know about this or that killing, they'd better show some evidence. After she denied, for the third time, she had killed more than six, Munster slipped several photographs from his briefcase.

"Let me show you these . . . we talked about the white pickup truck with that guy out in the woods who did it in the back and stuff . . . ? Would you look at these and see if that's the guy?"

Lee studied David Spears's photograph, a smiling guy with a reddish beard and thinning curly hair. "It doesn't look like him. I thought he had silver hair . . . or blondish hair or somethin'. It doesn't look like him."

"How about . . ." He handed her a picture of Spears's abandoned truck. "Look at the truck."

"You know one thing that makes me think it might be him is 'cause of that rope on that steering wheel. Was this the one with the radio taken out?"

"Yeah."

"Okay. Then that's him."

"Why do you say that?"

"Because I took the radio."

Munster frowned. "The radio?"

"Mmm-hmm. He was on 27. He said he was goin' somewhere . . . and he decided to take me over to Homosassa Springs. 'Cause I told him I lived there, which I didn't live there. I knew I could make money out there, so I wanted to be out there. So that's where we wound up at night, on Highway 19 . . . I know the roads out there. It was at night. Late. I'd say eleven, twelve, maybe one, two, somethin' like that. He had a metal pipe in the back of the truck, and he asked me to come to the back of the truck and lay on that damned bed that had no blankets or nothin'. Then, uh, when he grabbed the pipe and was going to fight with me, that's when I jumped out the . . . over on the ground, ran to the door, grabbed my gun out and shot him."

"And what did he do when you shot him?"

"Man, he ran around to the driver's side and tried to get in the truck . . ."

"Think he wanted to drive?" asked Munster blandly.

"Yeah, I think he probably woulda done that. I don't know. But I ran to the passenger's side and shot him through the driver's side."

Munster looked puzzled. "Across the seat?"

"Across the seat. Then, I ran . . . I mean, I crawled into the truck."

"Still naked?"

"Yeah, still naked, with the gun in my hand, and he was going kinda like, back. Going to walk backwards, and I shot 'im again."

"What did he say?"

"Nothing. He didn't say nothing. Nothing at all."

"How many more times did you shoot him? Twice more?"

"I think that's all I did, was three times. I think. One . . ." Lee began counting on her fingers. "Two . . . I mighta shot him one more time to make sure that he died or something."

"Was he tryin' to get away, crawl away or something?"

"No. He just fell backwards after that, and I just got in the truck and drove away."

Munster took back his pictures and slid them away.

"Okay, that about wraps it up. All right now, I'm gonna turn the tape off, and it is 2:21 in the afternoon."

"Can I ask you somethin'?" Lee stood up, facing Munster.

"You certainly can."

"Do you mind if I keep these cigarettes? 'Cause I don't have any cigarettes at all."

"You are quite welcome to them, and I'm glad you didn't ask to keep my jacket."

"Oh, yeah." Lee slipped out of Munster's blazer and handed it to him. "That was warm. Thank you."

"Sure, no problem."

The jailer walked into the room. Wuornos glanced around, started out the door, and then turned back. "I'm very sorry . . ." Munster and Horzepa looked at her impassively. When she had left the room, the two detectives broke out in laughter. "Oh, man!" Bruce said. "Larry . . . we got her!" He raised a big palm and the two cops slapped a victorious high five. "Got her!"

SEVENTEEN

Side Show

That Wednesday morning, as Lee was prattling on to Horzepa and Munster about her murders, President George H. W. Bush launched the first wave of air assaults in the Persian Gulf War. Though upstaged by the war she'd been fretting about for months, Wuornos still managed to make the front pages. In some Florida papers her arraignment photograph and accompanying headlines topped the news from the Gulf.

On Thursday, January 17, a press conference was held at the Marion County Sheriff's Office. Sheriff Bob Vogel choppered in from Volusia County; Department of Law Enforcement Commissioner Tim Moore came down from Tallahassee. They joined the lead detectives at tables arranged in the MCSO's ample conference room to face several TV cameras and a pack of photographers and reporters. Attired in an FBI-correct blue suit and crisp white shirt, Binegar took the microphone and made the announcement of Wuornos's arrest. "I believe Ms. Wuornos is a killer who robs, not a robber who kills. There was some money taken in most of the cases, but it didn't seem necessary to take the lives of these men. We believe she pretty much meets the guidelines of a serial killer. We have physical evidence linking Ms. Wuornos to every one of the victims. She did not clam up, that's not her style. She is a very verbose, very aggressive individual. I really don't detect any remorse."

Back in the Volusia County correctional facility, Wuornos watched the news that evening with excitement. The next morning she was taken to medical segregation, where she proceeded to run her mouth in the presence of a medic and a correctional officer.

The medic held up a copy of the *Daytona Beach News-Journal* and said, "Is any of this stuff true?"

Lee jabbed the front page with her finger. "They got this stuff all wrong. My girlfriend and I were only together four years, not six. He doesn't know anything about this stuff."

Lee handed the paper back to the medic, who asked, "Are you *really* a working girl?"

"Shit, I've had over 250,000 men in the last eight years. Yeah, I'm a professional call girl."

Wuornos again picked up the newspaper. "All this shit's all wrong. Listen to this: they say here, 'This is a killer who robs, not a robber who kills.' That's crap. Sure I shot them, but it was self-defense. I've been raped nine times in the last eight years and I'm just sick of it. So I got this gun and was carrying it around. Soon as I got the gun, it got worse. So if I didn't kill all those guys I would've been raped a total of twenty times or killed. No, but I got them first. Shit. They were gonna hurt me. This one guy, the missionary . . . shit, I didn't even know he was a missionary until I killed him. He sure didn't act like no missionary. He was gonna rape me. Maybe even kill me. That's no missionary. After I had to kill him I was going through his shit and that's when I found this suitcase of Bibles. He was just like those two ministers who raped that fourteen-year-old girl. Nobody would've believed he hurt me, so I killed him. This other guy, he had a .45 and he would've used it on me, but I got him."

Lee was rolling. "See, I was outside his car getting undressed. I always undress first so they know I'm not going to run or fake them out. I don't have to undress if all they want is head. If they want all the way, I undress first. Well, while I was bending to get into the back seat, I thought I saw him put something on the hood. But I didn't look and see. He got in the back seat with me but we started fighting 'cause he wanted rough sex. I managed to crawl up front and get my gun out of my bag. I would always unzip my purse first, just in case, you know?

"Well, I took the gun and shot him, and he crawled to the front so I shot him again, and he crawled into the back again. When I got out I saw the .45 on the hood and I got pissed. He was gonna use it on me. When I saw that, I got so fuckin' pissed I shot him again. Then I reloaded and kept shooting. He fuckin' pissed me off. I went through his shit too. After he was dead I took his .45 and shot it a couple of times. The thing sounds like a fuckin' cannon! It made this huge noise. Like, BOOM!

"I never did this to rob people. But afterwards I knew they weren't gonna pay me, so if they had a stereo, radar detector or something, good—I'd take it. One guy wasn't dead after I shot him. He just fell down and was sayin', 'I'm gonna die. Oh, my God! I'm dying.' I said, 'Yeah, motherfucker, so what?' And I shot him a couple a more times. I figured if these guys lived and I got fried for attempted murder—fuck it, I might as well get fried for murder instead. You know, after I killed the first couple I thought about quitting, but I had to make money to pay the bills and I figured I was at least doing some good killing these guys, because if I didn't kill them they would've hurt someone else."

Wuornos turned to the guard, Officer Hansen, and blurted, "You're not gonna tell anyone this stuff, are you?"

Hansen simply shrugged and raised her hands.

"Hell," said Lee. "Well, what the fuck, I already talked to the cops anyway." She started reading her press once again.

"This stuff about Ty being an ex-housekeeper who killed those guys out of state is crazy. She's the sweetest thing in the world. She never knew nothing about any of this stuff. That guy Mallory, after I did him and put the carpet over him, well one day I was really drunk and I told her that while I was riding my bike I found this dead guy under a rug. She didn't know it was me that did it. This stuff about him being a video-store owner, they got that all wrong. He owned like a TV store. I went through his shit afterwards and it wasn't no video store. Get the facts straight. And if the cops really had me under close observation for so long, then how come the last time I did this guy they didn't stop the rape or me from killing him? It was a cop and he was trying to get me to go with him. Me and Ty were sitting around one night watching HBO, and Roseanne Barr was on . . . you know her?"

Hansen simply nodded as Lee plunged on.

"Well, she was talking about how nobody freaked out any more about male serial killers because they kind of expect it, but if a woman is a serial killer, man, people freak out and call her a man-hater. I thought all that stuff was so funny 'cause I'm sitting there thinking, "She's talking about *me*.

"I wish I had never gotten that gun, because none of this would have never happened. I got it from this guy with a huge Rottweiler. He went to get some beer and left me with his dog. I made friends with the dog so he wouldn't attack me when I went in the bedroom to get the gun. He didn't. Of course, I thought I would be dead instead of them. Hooking made me bad because I'm really a nice person. Sure, I killed these seven guys, but they deserved it. My attorney's gonna kill me for telling you all this. I don't care though. He's just trying to get his name in the paper. You know, when I think about what I've done, sometimes I get upset. I killed so many guys, like I feel guilty, you know? And at other times, I'm happy, I feel good. Like a hero. 'Cause I've done some good. I'm a killer of rapists. Shit, they were dicks, you know? If this was the olden days I'd be hung already, but at least I don't think I was wrong for doing this, because if I didn't kill them they would've hurt someone else. You know, I really shouldn't be telling you this. My attorney said not to talk to anyone. What the fuck, I'm gonna fry anyway. You're the only person I've told all this stuff to. No matter what I say they're just gonna believe I'm just a man-hater. If I had wanted to kill just anybody, I had lots of chances, you know?

"My normal day would be going out around seven in the morning and getting home around five or six at night. I never went out after dark. I had lots of guys, maybe ten to twelve a day. I could've killed all of them but I didn't want to. I'm really just a nice person. I'm describing a normal day to you here. But a killing day might be just the same, almost. On a normal day we would just do it by the side of the road if they just wanted head or behind a building or off the road in the woods if they wanted it all, but I could always see a road.

"I always used rubbers—even if they wanted to just get head, I still used one. No way was I having sex without a rubber. Those guys always wanted to go way, way back in the woods, but I wasn't scared, you know, because they were always so nice. I trusted them. I mean, we went so far back in the woods there weren't even any roads. Now I know why they did it, they were going to hurt me. Most of the time that's why I took their cars, to get back out of the woods we were so far away in. I always made sure I wiped the cars clean afterwards, you know?

"The cops could've got me months ago," she sneered. "I left a thumbprint on this thing I sold at a pawn shop. Of course, *now* the cops probably got all this shit I got from these guys anyway. It was in storage and you know the cops took all that. Cops suck, you know. No matter what I say, they're gonna fry me 'cause I got one of their own. I shouldn't be telling you any of this, but get this— I had these two guys who said they were cops, or at least they flashed their badges at me. They picked me up and wanted sex but they didn't want to pay, said if I didn't do it they'd turn me in. One grabbed my hair and pushed me toward his dick. We really started fighting then, so I killed him.

"Afterwards I looked at their badges, and one was a reservist cop and the other worked for like the IRS. I don't remember for sure. Shit, you can get fake badges anywhere now. The guy with the cop badge was older, like a retired cop or something, but the cops will hate me anyway. It would've been like that trooper who killed that lady. No one wanted to believe that two cops raped me. Well they can't hurt anyone now. Cops really can get away with murder. I was gonna be a cop once and go to school, but I didn't have the tuition."

Two things were likely at work in Lee's head as she delivered this monologue: one was to enjoy her celebrity in front of an audience, and the other was to further drive home her excuses for killing. Wuornos was not naive about the workings of correctional institutions. She had done two and a half years at the Broward Correctional Facility for Women on her armed robbery conviction, and she knew that Officer Hansen would have to make a report. Wuornos meant to get her self-defense scenario on record. In her mind, the more times it was said, the more substance it gathered. Despite evidence to the contrary.

In the following weeks, the national media focused on the Wuornos case, with features appearing on national television and in major dailies. The tabloid TV shows were quickest to respond—"A Current Affair," "Inside Edition," "Hard Copy," "Geraldo"—as the story was tailor-made for their spin . . . Highway Hooker. Lesbian Killer. Damsel of Death.

Almost immediately, in nearly all of the stories, Lee was erroneously tagged as "the first female serial killer." The FBI's spokesperson, Kelley Cibulas, gave this mistaken description credence by saying Lee's was "the first female textbook case of a serial killer."

In fact, Aileen Wuornos was the thirty-fifth documented female serial killer in United States criminal history. The difference with Lee was that she targeted adult male strangers as her victims and dispatched them with a firearm. Most female serial murderers chose to kill members of their families, persons in their care, or close acquaintances, and usually dispatched them with poison. Typically, they were "quiet killers," working within the confines of their home, a hospital, or an elderly-care facility. Lee was certainly not "quiet" and searched out her victims, all strangers, along the highways of central Florida.

Regardless, the media response to her and her crimes was dramatic. She was a seemingly sinister package of sex and violence—kinky, calculating, and blond. Lee Wuornos was perfect for exploitation. In 1991 two of the biggest movie successes were *The Silence of the Lambs* and *Thelma and Louise*. With Aileen Wuornos and her saga, it appeared Hollywood had an opportunity to combine the two in a real-life drama.

Within two weeks of her arrest, Wuornos, along with her new attorneys, signed over movie rights to Jackelyn Giroux, a one-time starlet turned producer. At the same time, Binegar, Munster, and Henry had an attorney, Rob Bradshaw, a longtime buddy and former sheriff's deputy, field all the prospective deals coming their way from movie and television producers. The calls began in December, before Wuornos was arrested, and reached a fever pitch just after the press conference on January 17. The willingness of the three cops to listen to proposals would eventually lead to a state attorney's investigation, endless speculation in the press as to their motives, and a virtual blackout of information from the other four participating law-enforcement jurisdictions. In a short time, it raised a huge stink that just wouldn't go away, and that lingered long after Wuornos's trial and conviction.

Lee took up a jailhouse ballpoint on January 24, to write Tyria a letter that offered Moore some financial compensation as well as renewed declarations of love.

Lee led off by acknowledging that Moore was to be a witness against her, demurring with a "do what you think is best." After marking time with renewed assurances of her love for Ty and a few pleas for forgiveness, Wuornos cut to the chase. She nudged her former lover with the news that people were interested in her life story and will "pay me I'm sure quite well. If you know what I mean." Lee then offered Moore seventy-five per cent of any money she might make from books and movie deals and capped that by saying she wanted Ty as beneficiary in her will.

"You definitely deserve all," she postscripted. The letter closed with a drawing of a 'smiley' face.

About the time Moore received Lee's generous offer, she was contacted by Bruce Munster with the suggestion to get in touch with Ocala attorney Rob Bradshaw, who was representing Bruce, along with Binegar and Henry.

According to a state attorney's investigation report issued six months later, "On January 30, Tyria Moore contacted Bradshaw and asked him to represent her in negotiations with those interested in the movie version of the case. Moore stated . . . that she had received a call from Munster suggesting that if she contacted Bradshaw he could put together a package deal for her and the three deputies that would be worth more money than each person acting alone. She said she contacted Bradshaw the day Munster called, or possibly the next day."

The day after Ty spoke with Bradshaw, he and the three officers "took a lunch meeting," as they say in L.A. Bradshaw told the trio he had received an offer from Republic Pictures for their rights that could pay out a possible $115,000 if the movie were shot and they worked as consultants. Binegar and Henry went to their boss, Sheriff Moreland, two days later to advise him of the situation. Beneath the sheriff's outdated flattop was a politically astute thinking apparatus that had kept him in office for nearly two decades. He immediately instructed his two deputies that any proceeds from a movie deal must go directly to the taxpayers of the county. Binegar then suggested that a trust fund for crime victims be set up with the money from the deal.

However, the state attorney's report said that "the initial discussion was that the movie proceeds be placed in the trust fund and the deputies would later decide if the payment for personal services would be retained by them or donated to the fund." At any rate, on February 16, all attempts by the officers and their lawyer to finalize a deal with Republic were abandoned, according to the report. A month later, Tyria Moore called Bradshaw to let him know his services were no longer needed.

"It started with pure intentions," Binegar recalled. "We were only guilty of wanting to portray the story as accurately as possible. If there was money to be made it would go to a victims' fund. Then it took on a negative angle, there were people who were green with envy. There was a lot of jealousy for whatever reasons."

One who acted as if he might be jealous was Sergeant Brian Jarvis, the Major Crimes Unit supervisor who'd run afoul of Binegar some months earlier and found himself transferred to road patrol. (Binegar had put Jarvis on a five-day suspension after Jarvis came in and removed five programs from the CID secretary's computer. Binegar had put Jarvis's computer off limits, saying it was because Jarvis was always "in front of the computer when he was supposed to be out in the field with the robbery squad.")

Jarvis took a leave of absence and soon left the Marion County Sheriff's Office altogether, moving to Tampa. There, Jarvis got in touch with a Miami freelance writer, Mike McCarthy, and signed a waiver of rights with him for development of a book or movie based on Jarvis's life story. Jarvis paid McCarthy five hundred dollars to act as his agent and, in return, Jarvis received one dollar for the waiver. Then the two of them went public with allegations regarding Binegar, Munster, Henry, and Moore—that the quartet were in bed together on a movie deal. But Jarvis went further, alleging that evidence was being overlooked that implicated Moore in some of the murders. Jarvis appeared on tabloid TV shows, in newspapers, and in the pages of *Premiere,* a magazine covering the movie industry, repeating his charges against the three officers. In November, Jarvis made a wild allegation that Binegar, Munster, and Henry had burglarized his home in Tampa, supposedly looking for documents implicating them in a cover-up. Hillsborough County sheriff's deputies investigated the alleged burglary and then brought in the FDLE, which asked Jarvis to take a polygraph regarding his statements. After Jarvis showed deception patterns on questions regarding a "staged burglary," nothing more was heard from him.

Capping this, the state attorney's investigation found "no evidence to support Jarvis's suggestion of improper motive . . . the only signed agreement or payment of money was that involving Brian Jarvis. There is absolutely no evidence that the other deputies, or any other person, has signed any contract or been paid any money."

As the Persian Gulf War wound down, media interest in Lee accelerated. Wuornos had her deal with Giroux, and openly bragged how she was going to get $3 million out of it. But Giroux and Wuornos were obviously ignorant of Florida's so-called "Son of Sam" law, which prohibited criminals from receiving money for portrayals of their crimes. The contract, signed by Lee and her attorney at the time, Russell Armstrong, was prima facie invalid. It read, "Ms. Wuornos agrees to grant and provide information about her life to Ms. Giroux for accuracy and story content or to any other writer who assists her. For this, Ms. Wuornos will be granted a consultant screen/manuscript and/or novel credit and additional compensation which will be negotiated by all involved parties, in good faith, upon each sale in any media. However, this life story shall not be marketed or sold to any distributor for a sum less than $150,000 . . . this document should be signed for the good faith option payment of $60.00 a month to be placed into the inmate account."

Giroux also pursued Lee's relatives, childhood pals, and assorted witnesses, offering them money in an effort to sign up as many rights as possible. Lori Grody, Lee's aunt and adoptive sister, signed a deal memorandum with Giroux in February 1991 that set a "minimum payment of $50,000" to Grody, plus "25% of the producer's net profit from the distribution of a motion picture or television program based upon the life of Aileen Carol Wuornos." The deal also promised another fifty thousand to Grody for any literary work.

In the middle of all this dealing, another woman sprang to Lee's side. Mrs. Arlene Pralle, a twinkly-eyed forty-four-year-old born-again Christian, had seen Lee's photograph in a newspaper while visiting her hospitalized father and had immediately written Wuornos.

"Dear Aileen," she wrote. "My name is Arlene Pralle, I'm born-again. You're going to think I'm crazy but Jesus told me to write you . . ." Pralle gave Lee her phone number at Maranatha Meadows, the small horse-breeding and -boarding farm north of Ocala she and her husband, Bob, ran. On January 30, Lee and Arlene had their first phone conversation. Wuornos's collect calls would soon run into the thousands of dollars, since she called Pralle almost daily. Pralle became the most important person in Lee's life. Everyone had turned on her, even the love of her life, yet here came this elfin woman out of nowhere who accepted Lee unconditionally. From this point on, Arlene Pralle was the dominant figure in Lee's life, her champion, her apologist, her press liaison.

As soon as Pralle entered the picture, Lee turned on her attorneys and Jackelyn Giroux. They quickly learned that pernicious turbulence was Aileen Wuornos's normal behavior. On her birthday—on that odd-date-out, February 29—Aileen stood before Seventh Circuit Judge Gayle Graziano and pounded the podium, demanding new attorneys. She claimed her public defenders were more interested in movie and book deals than in defending her on the charge of murdering Richard Mallory. "They are violating my rights," she blared. "I demand new attorneys and I'm going to get them. To me, they're just a clan of people trying to make money, not trying to make a case." Wuornos claimed she hadn't known what she was signing when she put her name to the Giroux deal memorandum. Her January 24 letter to Tyria clearly reads otherwise. But for Wuornos, reality consisted of her own version of events, facts to the contrary.

The Pralles contacted a high-profile Atlanta lawyer, and president of the Georgia ACLU, Michael Hauptman, seeking to have him defend their new friend. But Wuornos waved aside their offer, saying she didn't want them spending their money.

Three days later Judge Graziano granted Lee's request and appointed Fifth Circuit Assistant Public Defender Tricia Jenkins, who was already slated to defend Wuornos in Ocala on the murders of Burress and Humphreys.

Through the efforts of Pralle, Lee learned of her aunt/sister Lori Grody's deal with Giroux. Wuornos snapped. On March 3, she scratched out a raging screed, boiling with venom.

Wuornos swung out by calling Lori a "sorry bitch" for signing on with producer Jackelyn Giroux and then railed on for three pages, lambasting—"cunt Giroux" and her former attorney "crooked ass Russell Armstrong." Lee told Lori she was being "suckered into this by a pack of lies," said she never wanted to see her adoptive brother Barry ever again and not to bother coming to her funeral. "Arlene is going to take care of all that," she scrawled. "I wouldn't want you two to bury me. It would be a shit ass cheap one." She reserved a whole page for a rant on how she was going to sue Giroux and then capped it off by declaring she was "a *Real Good Person*. Inside and out."

Six days later, Pralle followed up with her own shot to Lori Grody. But Pralle's prose style reflected a different background than Lee's. While Wuornos blustered and cursed, Pralle poured overwrought syntax and pure saccharine.

Pralle described Lee as a "very caring, compassionate, loving and sensitive human being" who deserved to be "treated with some consideration and understanding." She went on to compare her background to Lee's, pointing out she was adopted "just like Lee." Pralle closed by denouncing Giroux as a liar "out to make some quick money" and with a cautionary word to Lori that she should not wait until too late to see Lee as "very beautiful, caring and loving."

Pralle soon took her message to television and magazine reporters, bringing the good news about herself and Aileen Wuornos to the world. She told *Vanity Fair*'s Mark McNamara she had never loved anyone as much as she did Lee. "No, absolutely not. Not even my husband. But it's not like that. People are going to try and make it into a 'sexual perversion,' but it's not like that at all. It's a soul binding. We're like Jonathan and David in the Bible . . . It's as though part of me is trapped in jail with her. We always know what the other is feeling and thinking. I just wish I was Houdini—I would get her out of there. If there was a way, I would do it, and we could go and be vagabonds forever."

To Barbara Nevins of CNBC's "The Real Story," Pralle continued the biblical theme. "God brought me into this to specifically befriend Aileen Wuornos. We took a covenant, like Jonathan and David. I consider her a soul mate. It's a very special relationship, a spiritual bond. It has no homosexuality . . . If the world could know the real Aileen Wuornos, there's not a jury that would convict her."

Pralle arranged phone interviews with Lee for those reporters she thought sympathetic to Wuornos. To Kevlin Haire of the *Orlando Sentinel*, Wuornos complained, "The media has discredited me so much, making me look like a creep. I'm not a man-hater. I'm not a verbal or physical fighter. I like to be tranquil and at ease and enjoy life. I have lots of love in me, but I never got a chance to give it to somebody because every time I gave it to somebody, they took from me. I'm a decent person." Lee closed off by taking a swing at Moore. "Now I'm still alive and sitting here rotting in jail, and she's going ahead and making money. It upsets me that she did that dirty trick to me."

With *Vanity Fair*'s McNamara, Wuornos laid the blame on Ty even more thickly. "The only reason I hustled so hard all those years was to support her. I did what I had to do to pay the bills, because I didn't have another choice: I've got warrants out for my arrest. I loved her too much . . . the problem was I wasn't supporting her as richly as she wanted. She always wanted a brand-new car or a rented one. She wanted clothes, she wanted an apartment with plush furniture . . . So materialistic."

Yet, it was Moore who had worked as a motel maid—at least, until she duked it out with her boss and got fired. Wuornos's records show that she had been on the hustle long before Tyria Moore entered the picture—forgery, grand theft, robbery. Oddly enough, the one thing missing from Lee's file was an arrest for the criminal activity she professed to be so familiar with—prostitution.

Regarding Moore, Binegar said, "She's no angel, this is no nun here. The whole thing was like letting the little devil go to get the big devil. Ty was in what I call the Mafia-wife syndrome. She likely knew [the murders] were going on, saw those cars showing up out of nowhere and all that stuff coming in. Wuornos already told her about Mallory. She just blocked all that out. 'I don't want to hear about it.'"

Speculations and suspicions shadowed the Marion County investigators throughout the year, despite the state attorney's report. Even when the grisly discoveries inside Jeffrey Dahmer's Milwaukee apartment shoved Lee from national attention, Florida media included in each Wuornos story a mention of the deputies' alleged movie deal. Wuornos, Pralle, and Lee's public defender, Tricia Jenkins, kept the heat up on Binegar, Munster, Henry, and Moore throughout the summer and through the fall. It reached a point where investigators from Citrus, Pasco, Volusia, and Dixie refused to speak about the case—to anybody, including their colleagues in the Marion County Sheriff's Office. With paranoia spreading, Binegar, Munster, and Henry found themselves isolated, pariahs in the law-enforcement community. The case of a lifetime, a multiagency serial-murder investigation carried out on a highwire lighted by national publicity, had suddenly become a nightmare for the trio. "It was just dumb," said Binegar. "We thought we were doing the right thing, but we were naive about all of it."

Law-enforcement officers are no more immune to the

media's allure than politicians, religious leaders, or the neighbor next door. Homicide detectives, by nature and necessity, have well-developed, sensitized egos. You work homicide, you are at the top of the profession. And working on the case of a female serial killer betrayed by her lesbian lover vaults you to a higher level still. No one involved in Aileen Wuornos's case was indifferent, especially Aileen herself, to the big American opportunity—celebrity.

Certainly not Arlene Pralle, who became a near-regular on the talk-show and tabloid TV circuit. With her pale blue eyes twinkling beneath heavy lashes, Pralle sweetly portrayed Lee as a misunderstood angel, a victim of child abuse, the streets, Ty Moore, lying money-hungry detectives, and an unfair system, couching her defense in Christian homilies. On "A Current Affair," Pralle's defense of Lee was countered by Dick Humphreys's widow, Shirley. Mrs. Humphreys minced no words in her assessment of Wuornos and Pralle.

"[Pralle] is off in la-la land, this born-again Christian. I attend church, but for this to happen? I can't fathom. She's despicable, they're both despicable. Wuornos slayed a man that was warm and loving with his family. This witch took from us. And you have this Pralle woman saying there's an ounce of good in her, but I'm not going looking for it. Why doesn't she go out and do something for the victims' families, if she's such a born-again Christian?"

Then, Shirley Humphreys locked eyes with her interviewer and said, "I hope she meets up with Old Sparky. You know who Old Sparky is. And if the other lady so wishes, she can stand there and hold her hand as far as I'm concerned."

• • •

Pralle came to take advice from the ultimate celebrity arbiter. According to her, it was God who moved her to legally adopt the accused multiple murderer. The Pralles retained an attorney, Steve Glazer, a huge hirsute fellow with a phone number that read DR. LEGAL, to begin adoption proceedings. On November 22, the adoption was finalized and Lee Wuornos had a new mom and dad, her third set of parents. And with this fresh twist, Arlene Pralle once again traipsed before the cameras, smiling and chatting up the virtues of her daughter.

EIGHTEEN

Looking Back

While media crews made pilgrimages to Pralle's
Maranatha Meadows and chased after phantom movie
deals between Los Angeles and Ocala, the prosecution
and defense focused on Wuornos's pending trial for the
murder of Richard Mallory. Tricia Jenkins, assisted by
Billy Nolas—a specialist in capital cases—and William
Miller, along with investigator Don Sanchez, a former
New York cop, found themselves up against heavy odds.
As public defenders they were already overloaded with
cases, especially homicides. Among their clients was
the suspect in the Gainesville student murders, Danny
Rolling, as well as a crew charged in a botched hit that
had left four people senselessly slaughtered, plus an
itinerant arsonist suspected in dozens of church fires.
Then, there was Wuornos. A difficult client at best—
having confessed to her crimes—Lee was red hot
in the press and on television as "the first female serial
killer in history," taking pretrial publicity way beyond
the norm.

Doing battle for the prosecution were two assistants

out of Seventh Circuit State Attorney John Tanner's office in Daytona, David Damore and Sean Daley. Damore and Daley had reputations for being lean and mean. Decked out in their blue-black suits, the two dark-haired attorneys came on in the courtroom like a pair of Dobermans. Throughout the summer of 1991, Nolas and Daley snarled at each other in pretrial hearings before Judge Gayle Graziano. Their animosity hailed back to the time they'd faced off against each other in Tallahassee, when Nolas worked for the Capital Collateral Review and Daley was with the attorney general's office. In one hearing, a disgusted Graziano simply got up, adjourned, and left the two young lawyers nattering away at each other.

While these pretrial legal brawls continued, investigations into Lee's personal history were being conducted. Wuornos's version was filled with sexual and physical abuse, rape, and betrayal, and while confirmation was eventually obtained for some of her stories, others proved outrageously exaggerated. Always, Lee's main theme was, "*I* was the victim." And, to be sure, Aileen Carol Wuornos had been born into a world of neglect, anger, regret, and alcoholism, an ideal atmosphere for the development of a sociopath.

It was 1954 when fourteen-year-old Diane Wuornos first coupled with Leo Dale Pittman. A suburban Detroit rebel without a clue, Leo Dale was an eighteen-year-old unbridled sociopath with a pair of dice tattooed on his pink forearm, a thick thatch of red hair slicked back from his freckled face, and a penchant for felonies and prepubescent girls. Diane was the daughter of Lauri and Britta Wuornos, both Michigan natives of Finnish descent. Lauri was a control engineer at the Pontiac plant, Britta was a housewife. There were two other children—Barry, born in 1944, and Lori, born in 1953. Theirs was a blue-collar middle-class life.

Diane's younger brother, Barry, remembered Leo Dale cruising Cadmus Street, where the Wuornos family lived in Rochester, Michigan. "My father hated Pittman," Barry said. "He would run him off the property whenever he came around. Pittman was a real hood who thought he was tough. Always had a couple of guns in the back seat of his car. And Diane was kind of wild back then, had a lot of boyfriends. All she wanted to do was leave home and start her own life with nobody to tell her what to do."

On June 3, 1954, two months shy of her fifteenth birthday, Diane married Leo Dale Pittman, much to the dismay of Lauri and Britta. Nine months later she gave birth to a boy, Keith Edward. In another nine months Diane would divorce Pittman, but not before he left another child growing within her. In 1956, on that four-year afterthought of the calendar, February 29, Aileen Carol Pittman was born in the Oakland County Hospital.

"She was real late," Diane recalls, thirty-five years later from her home in Texas. "It was an unusual birth. Breach. Bottom first. She was possibly conceived at the time of a horrible beating. It's the day I left him."

When Diane broke off the marriage, she told her brother that she was deathly afraid of Pittman and was certain "at one time or another" he would reenter her life. Diane found herself living in the upper apartment of a two-story duplex in Troy, Michigan, an unskilled, unmarried teenage mother with two small children and a growing sense of panic. "I was working and trying to take care of those two children and stuff. I just remember being tired all the time and not getting enough sleep. But all new mothers are that way.

"The thing that keeps coming in my mind is she was a very unhappy baby. Both Keith and Aileen were unhappy, crying babies. I've often thought about that even before this case came up because, you know, when I see other children, when I see happy children—I was so happy to see *them* happy. And I believe they were both feeling the stress that . . . Keith of course was there when I lived with my husband . . . and he just cried all the time. All the time. It was like colicky and sick and crying and then Aileen was of the same disposition and I was under so much stress coming out of a battered relationship and then arguing with my parents."

By this time, Leo Dale Pittman was in the ranks of the United States Army, having enlisted the same month his divorce was decreed. Pittman did his two-year hitch, married another reckless woman, returned to Michigan, and then hotfooted it to California, where his sister lived in Sacramento. Leo worked as a shoe salesman, one of several brief interludes of employment before he headed back east. As he drifted across the country, he was arrested for assault, furnishing alcohol to a minor, breaking and entering, and speeding. He molested children whenever he could, slipping the system by jumping jurisdictions. Pittman served short jail terms until 1959, when he was brought up on auto theft and found himself in an Ohio federal institution, just three years after being divorced by Diane.

Back in Michigan, Diane had reached the end of her maternal tether. It finally snapped one night in 1960. Diane called her aunt, Carol Connell, to see if she could baby-sit Keith and Aileen while she went out for dinner. Mrs. Connell agreed. Later that night, the telephone rang at the home of Bernhard and Alma Kuopus. It was their niece Diane asking them to pick up the kids and Aunt Carol at her apartment and take them to her parents. "I'm leaving town," she said. "And I'm not coming back." The Kuopuses had always been close to their niece and had grown only more so since Diane's disastrous marriage that had estranged her from her parents. They got in their car and drove to the little apartment where Aunt Carol, Keith, and Aileen were still waiting for Diane to return. Years later Keith told a friend he thought he could remember the last time he had seen his mother—he was standing behind a screen door watching her drive away. He said he remembered a wind blowing on his face.

"I gave her up when she was six months old," recalled Diane. "I was living with my mother and father and then I lived with myself with the children and there was no one who lived with me. I gave them up for adoption so they would live under good conditions. But they never lived under bad conditions with me."

On March 18, 1960, new birth certificates were issued for Aileen and Keith, listing their parents as Lauri and Britta Wuornos. "I believe Diane still carries a lot of guilt for what happened," said Barry. Every time he spoke with his sister in the years that followed she would tell him how badly she felt and would blame herself for the way things had turned out.

Keith and Aileen came to their grandparents' house at 1429 Cadmus in Rochester as two outsiders. Their uncle, Barry, was sixteen when his parents legally adopted their daughter's children in 1960. Barry's sister Lori was closer in age to Keith and Aileen, just three years older than her new sister. But years later, when testifying against Lee in the penalty phase of her trial, Barry Wuornos said Keith's and Aileen's adoption "was always a sore spot in the family." A strange but telling thing to say in a proceeding that would determine life or death for a member of one's family. Apparently the resentments ran long and deep in the house on Cadmus Street.

Leo Pittman was now out of prison, and he kept a relatively low profile until June 8, 1962, when Pontiac, Michigan, police received a report of indecent liberties being taken with two ten-year-old girls. The girls' description of their molester fit that of Leo Pittman, who happened to choose that date—June 8—to change the address of his driver's license. Two other men who seemed to fit the description were picked up, but later released. Leo was on his way to Wichita, Kansas.

Once there, Pittman inveigled himself into a common-law relationship with a woman who had a motel outside Wichita. On November 23, 1962, Leo Pittman was charged with the kidnapping and rape of a seven-year-old girl. He was committed to the Larned State Hospital for the Criminally Insane. Six months later, Leo escaped and fled back to Michigan. He holed up in Casnovia, working as a mechanic. But Leo couldn't keep his head down, and the Kent County Sheriff picked him up as a parole violator from Ohio. The news hit the papers, and Kansas called for his return to face the possibility of hanging by the neck until dead on the kidnapping and rape charges. But Michigan police wanted him on the molestation of the two girls in Pontiac.

Leo ended up in Oakland County, Michigan, where a sanity hearing resulted in his incarceration at Ionia State Hospital on June 4, 1964.

An Ionia report on Leo's background determined he "was always lacking in emotional support, physical supervision and that he had little chance to incorporate socially acceptable behavior into his personality." Leo had not only the usual childhood diseases, but also a severe bout with scarlet fever that had left him with earaches. He was also a bedwetter until he turned thirteen. Leo dropped out of school after the ninth grade. He told the psychiatrists he had to leave school in order to support the family, because his grandfather was terminally ill with throat cancer. But Leo's work record belies this altruistic move. Most likely he simply had gotten fed up with school and taken to the streets as a juvenile delinquent, thief, and rapist.

Leo's sexual initiation, according to the Ionia report, "occurred at age ten with the next-door neighbor girl [who] was older than he." Leo also told his interviewers that he had had no homosexual experiences, and admitted to "enjoying" fellatio and that "if some girl wanted to perform this on him, he would not object."

Leo Pittman was a pedophile and violent sexual predator. He was also a remorseless sociopath, quick on his feet with a lie and totally immersed in denial. His daughter, Aileen, later showed the same proclivities. Regarding the rape of the seven-year-old Kansas girl, Leo told his interviewers that he was not guilty, "that he had gone to the store to buy pop for his wife." Pittman's embroidered explanation spoke of "a friend of his who had asked him to come to his place." This man had a bottle of whiskey, Pittman explained, and although he claimed he didn't care for whiskey, he did have a few drinks with his friend. As the story went, the man drank most of the whiskey, and after a while fell on the floor shaking and having some kind of spell. He asked Pittman to get a bottle of red pills for him from the medicine cabinet. Pittman got the pills, and the man took some. Later, Pittman said he himself had a headache, and when he mentioned it, his friend told him to take two of the red pills and it would fix him up. Pittman said he did and that his headache left him. He did not know if these pills, together with the whiskey, had affected him or not.

They just didn't understand, Pittman told the authorities at Ionia. It was not his fault what happened to the little Wichita girl. It was his friend, it was the whiskey, it was the little red pills. He wasn't even there. He couldn't remember. Years later, his daughter's confession echoed the same lame denial, the same excuses: "I don't remember . . . I was drunk . . . drunk royal . . ."

Pittman was extradited to Kansas in September 1965. He was tried, found guilty of kidnapping, rape, and sodomy, and was sentenced to life plus additional terms of one to twenty-one years and ten years in the state prison at Lansing, Kansas. On January 15, 1969, Leo was found strangling in his cell, a length of bedsheet wound tightly around his throat. He was taken to the prison hospital and then the University of Kansas Medical Center in Kansas City. He died fifteen days later without regaining consciousness. Whether Leo Dale Pittman committed suicide or was killed by other inmates was never determined. Nobody really cared one way or the other.

"I don't think [Aileen] even remembered him," recalled Barry. "I can't see how she possibly could've, she was just a baby in a crib when we picked her up, you know?"

The fire that scarred Lee's forehead had occurred when she was six years old. She and Lori were watching Keith start fires out in back of their house. The girls made a line with lighter fluid leading from a little hut the kids had tacked together, struck a match to the fluid, and then ran back into the hut. The fire chased them and Lee was burned. She was taken to the hospital by her grandfather, treated, and released. As a teenager she learned to style her blond hair over the permanent welts on her forehead.

Aileen was not told of her true father and mother until she was twelve. She may have learned of her parents through Keith and others in the neighborhood. Regardless, when she did, her personality altered. She once confronted her grandfather as he was about to spank her. "You can't spank me!" she cried. "You're not my father!" Lauri and Britta were forced to admit the circumstances of Lee and Keith's adoption. From this point on, Lee and Keith became incorrigible. They would run away at every opportunity, roaming the neighborhood and crashing with friends whenever they could. Lee's school attendance became erratic. Then she became pregnant.

Lee learned quite quickly how to use sex for more than kicks. Boys were good for money. They wanted sex and they were willing to give something for it—cigarettes, beer, dope. But the boys didn't have much money. Money was with the men. At age thirteen, according to several stories, including one of Lee's, she got into the cab of a pickup driven by one of Lauri's buddies. The man took her out into the woods bordering Troy and they had sex. Prior to her trial, Lee told authorities that as a young girl she'd had sex with her brother, Keith, but his friends told investigators this was not likely, saying Keith just kind of tolerated her presence and would ignore her when she hung out with him and his buddies.

Lee was rejected totally by her grandfather when she became pregnant. He refused to have her in the house. A caseworker at the Michigan Childrens Aid Society, Patricia Verduin, met with Aileen and her grandmother the first week in January 1971. Mrs. Wuornos told Verduin that her husband had been out of work for three months and had forbidden Aileen to enroll in school because of her pregnancy. They had decided, both grandparents and Aileen, that the baby should be put up for adoption. "He doesn't want Aileen in the house," said Mrs. Wuornos. "He says it brings disgrace on us. But he's not a bad man, he's strict but not bad. But when he says something, he expects it to be done. He only means best for the children. He loves them."

In an interview with Detective Sergeant Leonard Goretski of the Michigan State Police, Lori became "very emotional when speaking about her mother. [She] acknowledged the fact that her father was an alcoholic, further adding her father drank everywhere he went, even when driving in the car he would take a bottle with him." Lauri Wuornos's drink of choice was wine; he would go through two or three bottles a day. Lori told Goretski that alcohol also played a role in her mother's life, but that Britta had quit drinking a couple of years before her death. Lori told Goretski that when her mother found out about Aileen's pregnancy "it really broke her heart." Aileen claimed she was raped. She repeated this story to Verduin at the maternity hospital, describing her assailant as a white male with black hair and brown eyes, thirty to forty years old, medium build, about 145 pounds, and of Irish descent. Aileen said she had been walking to a gas station to buy a soft drink, and that it was raining. This man stopped and—after taking her to the gas station, where he bought her a soft drink— took her out, raped her and then drove her home.

Verduin noticed that Aileen was very immature, clinging to her grandmother and letting Mrs. Wuornos do all the talking. "She only believed in the present," recalled Verduin. "No concern for the future, only what today would bring. All Aileen had to say was, 'I don't want the kid.'"

On January 19, Grandmother Wuornos drove Aileen to Detroit and left her at the Florence Crittenton Maternity Home. She was a nightmare for the staff, who described her as "very uncooperative, very hostile toward her peers and unable to get along with anybody." Not too surprising behavior, given the circumstances the fourteen-year-old found herself in.

On March 23, 1971, Aileen delivered a baby boy, who was taken from her and immediately put up for adoption. She was now fifteen years old, the same age as when her mother had first given birth. Aileen's life underwent further upheaval when on July 7 Britta Wuornos died. The cause of death was listed as liver failure, but her daughter Diane had doubts.

"My father called me and read the statement and told me that I killed my mother and that he was going to kill the children if I didn't come get them. He said he had her cremated. So, I drove from Houston to Michigan. I had a motel in Rochester and I told my daddy I didn't want to stay with him, I said I'd just rather be by myself and he says, 'What's the matter? If you stay, you think I'm going to kill you too?' So that's when I called the coroner and asked how my mother died and he told me that they didn't feel that there was anything wrong with it, but she had bruises all over her body. I watched my mother drink for how many years I lived in that house, and my mother was not a falling-down drunk. She did not get bruises all over her body from drinking."

At the time of her mother's funeral, Diane saw her two children, who were now wards of the court, but did not bring them back to her home in Houston. "They were ambivalent about it. They would want to and then they wouldn't want to. I tried to explain to them. I told them I would be strict and they had to understand, but I wouldn't be harsh and I would love them, and they asked me if when they got here could they smoke marijuana. No. I was really going to set down some rules. They didn't like anything they heard."

Aileen dropped out of school while Keith joined the Army. She took to the streets full time, usually staying with her friend Dawn Nieman. "I remember everybody saying you got to meet this girl Aileen, she carries her mother's ashes around," Dawn later recalled. "I was friends with Lori, and then Aileen started coming around, and since Aileen and I weren't in school, then all of a sudden we started hitchhiking together. Must have been fifteen." Dawn was impressed by Lee's fearlessness, her willingness to go into "Boonie Town," the rough black ghetto area near Detroit, where she would score drugs.

"It's really strange, she would take off and come back and always have her hair neat and stuff like that. I knew she had no place to go, how would she do this? Nobody really liked her, so it wasn't like she could go over to the girlfriend's house and take a shower or whatever because nobody trusted her . . . I got the impression that her dad was pretty mean to her. She didn't like her dad. He was a big fat old drunk . . . I don't think he liked those kids at all. I think Lori was the only one he liked, and I think Keith and Aileen knew that, and once the mother died, you know, here he was with these kids that hated his guts."

Dawn said she never discussed prostitution with Aileen. "I never judged her in that way, she never judged me in my way. I would think 'poor kid,' you know. I don't know why I got the impression she had a bad life, but I used to sit and look at her and think— God, they treat her like shit. She had a terrible life, she had a baby and all that, and I could see it in her face. That's why I never put her under any stress, never put her in a situation, like . . . 'Are you a prostitute?' I already knew this stuff and that's why she liked me, she knew I knew, and I just didn't bring it up because I knew it bothered her."

Dawn Nieman Botkins told investigators that there was no indication that Wuornos was a lesbian. "She couldn't come on to women or men. None of them liked her, except for when she'd go hitchhiking. She really wasn't even interested in boyfriends our age, fourteen, fifteen, sixteen. When Aileen and I were hitchhiking home from the pool hall, we were getting ready to go up and have some lunch and sneak into a bar, and these two guys across the street said, We'll pick you up. We said we don't want these guys, [one of whom] ended up being my husband. We ended up going to the bar, and then on our way back we were just taking the long ride back home [with these two] and she was sitting in the back seat with his cousin. We were sitting in the front seat, me and the guy now who is my husband, and all of a sudden she started screaming and yelling and went completely out of control and we just turned around, like, what the hell is she talking about? This was just going to be my first boyfriend and I was kind of feeling funny around him because this was the first boy I was ever with, and here she is supposed to be so damned experienced and she's having a shit fit in the back seat. I remember getting the impression, now this is really stupid. She's really out of control this time. She just must've clicked and went nuts, you know. 'Just sickening!' that was her word. She always said 'sick-en-ing.' She was just screaming up a storm."

Aileen's sister, Lori, experienced a more violent eruption a few years later, not long before Keith's death from throat cancer and Lauri Wuornos's suicide by carbon monoxide poisoning. "We were at the house of a person

I used to baby-sit for," Lori told investigators. "Aileen was eighteen. I was lying on the couch trying to take a nap, and I don't know what the argument was about, but she ran into the kitchen and got a skewer and came this far from my throat." Lori spread less than an inch between her thumb and finger. "She was yelling and screaming and she was on downers, reds, at the time. She pulled back and I got up and ran out the back door. There was a time in 1978 when I was going to commit her to a mental hospital. We had gotten into another argument and she was kind of scary. I called Barry, and Barry says, well, why don't you do it? I said I don't want to do it and he said I don't have nothing to do with it. I said I'm scared if I do commit her and if she ever gets out, I'm dead meat."

Instead, Aileen Wuornos made her way to Florida, where the young blond was picked up by a septuagenarian fellow named Fell, who was living comfortably in Ormond Beach on his railroad stocks. They married, and Aileen proceeded to squander as much money as Fell would give her. According to Fell, when he balked, Lee would thump him with his cane. When word came down that her brother Keith was dying from throat cancer, the Fells traveled to Michigan.

On July 13, 1976, Aileen Wuornos was arrested shortly after midnight in Bernie's Club, now known as Club 131, in Mancelona, Michigan. She was charged with simple assault, malicious destruction of property, and on various misdemeanors.

One witness said he observed a very attractive young lady at the pool table hustling for money and drinks. During the course of the evening he challenged Aileen to three or four games of pool at five bucks a game. She beat him each time. As the evening went on, she became "louder and louder, shouting obscenities at the person she was playing with, like 'you motherfucker!'" The bartender, a six-foot-two-inch, two-hundred-forty-pound guy named Danny Moore, rumbled over to put a halt to the proceedings. Moore later told the cops that he ran a 'kick ass' bar, meaning that if anybody gave him any trouble he kicked ass and threw them out. Moore said the blond had been threatening the customers, so he'd walked over and begun sweeping the balls together. He said that the pool table was closed. Somebody then yelled 'Duck!' Out of the corner of his eye he glimpsed the blond about to throw the cue ball at his head. Moore ducked as the quarter-pound sphere flew past his skull and imbedded itself in the wall. Someone else said they saw a pistol in the blond's purse. Moore had then made a strategic retreat and called the cops. Fell appeared the next morning at the jail, left the money for Aileen's bail, and returned to Volusia County, where he acquired a restraining order against Wuornos and began annulment proceedings.

Keith passed away at Barry's house on July 17. He'd contracted cancer while in the military, and a sizable sum from his life insurance was dispersed to his brother and sisters. Lee ended up with ten thousand dollars in her pocket. She went on a tear, buying a brand new Pontiac Grand Prix that she soon slammed into a telephone pole.

In less than two months she was broke, and heading south to Florida, where she drifted into the next decade, self-destructing her way through several relationships, trying one scam after another—a stupid forgery down in the Keys, some theft in Dade County, an armed robbery in Edgewater that netted two and a half years in prison.

She also tried suicide, but half-heartedly. And when things got really bad, she would make an attempt at turning tricks. When she met little roly-poly Ty Moore one night in the Zodiac Bar and fell in love, it had seemed like a new game. But the years and the miles, the alcohol and dope and crimes, had taken their toll, and at thirty-three years of age her market value as a sexual product was at bottom. The old hustles didn't work. So she had packed up her .22 Double Nine and hit the highways with something else in mind, something final.

Murder.

NINETEEN

Guilt and Penalty

January 16, 1992. Day three in the *State of Florida* vs. *Aileen Carol Wuornos*. Two counts of Florida Statute 782.04. Murder in the First Degree—the unlawful killing of Richard Mallory, a human being, perpetrated from a premeditated design and committed while engaged in the perpetration of a felony.

All that morning Aileen Wuornos sat at the defense table, fidgeting with a pen and legal pad, as forensic experts from the medical examiner's office and the Florida Department of Law Enforcement testified. Dr. Arthur Botting was taken through his autopsy of Richard Mallory's body by Seventh Judicial Circuit State Attorney John Tanner. Throughout the spring, summer, and fall, Tanner's assistants—David Damore and Sean Daley—worked the trenches preparing the Mallory case, defeating defense motions to suppress Wuornos's confession and managing to have Judge Graziano recuse herself from the trial after the judge made several decisions the prosecution thought were too favorable for the defense.

Wuornos was now before Circuit Court Judge Uriel Blount, Jr., a twenty-two-year veteran brought out of retirement for the proceedings. With considerable media attention focused on the little courtroom in Deland, State Attorney Tanner stepped in to lead the prosecution. Politics had long since become a dynamic in this highly publicized case. Earlier in 1991, investigators had recommended that a special state prosecutor be appointed to handle all six murder charges against Wuornos and to bring all the cases into a single trial. However, her charges were spread over four circuits, involving four different state attorneys, and 1992 was an election year. At one point Wuornos and her attorneys agreed to a plea bargain on all six charges that would have netted her six consecutive life terms with a mandatory twenty-five years on each count—meaning Lee would have had to serve 150 years in prison before she would be eligible for parole. But one state attorney refused to buy in, insisting she be tried and face the death penalty. The deal fell apart, leaving Wuornos listening to Dr. Botting as he vividly detailed Richard Mallory's death to twelve jurors.

"The fatal mechanism was hemorrhaging in the lungs. When the bullet struck, it allowed rapid escape of large amounts of blood, plus there's the fact that once the chest wall and/or the lungs were perforated, this would allow pressurized air to enter the cavity and this would impair respiration. So, you've got two very basic things working against the vital functions. There is a point that is reached that so much blood has been lost that you cannot maintain effective circulation and life ceases. Death is not instantaneous. I would imagine the individual was trying desperately to breathe."

"How long would it take for this person to die?" Tanner drawled. Nolas objected and was overruled.

"Roughly ten to twenty minutes."

Botting was followed by Ward Schwoob, an FDLE evidence technician who identified Mallory's raspberry-colored Polaroid camera, the victim's bloodstained shirt, Wuornos's card wallet containing the business cards of her "clients" as well as the photos of the two children, the Susan Blahovec documents Wuornos had used to provide an alias, and a few other items. Then came Donald Champagne, the twenty-three-year veteran firearms examiner who was on his first day of retirement from the FDLE. A former specialist with the Royal Canadian Mounted Police, Champagne was making his 731st court appearance as an expert witness. Tanner handed him the rusted .22 Double Nine recovered from the waters of Rose Bay, which Champagne identified as the weapon that had fired the CCI .22-caliber hollow-point bullets recovered from Mallory's corpse. Six grooves with a right twist. Champagne referred to the hollow points as "more effective" rounds. Another FDLE firearms expert, Susan Pomar, testified that the powder particles recovered from the holes perforating Mallory's shirt indicated that the weapon had been fired from less than six feet away and from the victim's right. During the morning's testimony, Wuornos whispered into Miller's ear, sneered, grinned, and eyeballed the jury to her immediate left, occasionally glancing over her shoulder to catch the eye of Mrs. Pralle,

very much aware of the nest of cameras just eight feet
behind her.

That Thursday afternoon, one year to the date since Lee
had made her final collect call to Ty's motel room, the
two former lovers faced each other across the small cir-
cular courtroom. Both women had undergone transfor-
mations since their days together at the Fairview Motel.
Deprived of her beer, Wuornos was now some thirty
pounds lighter, and she had been dressed by her adoptive
mother in a cranberry suit jacket, white blouse, and
black skirt, with her thin blond hair flounced on top in an
unsuccessful jailhouse perm. She sat at the end of the
defense table with her attorneys, Jenkins, Nolas, and
Miller, a box of pink Kleenex, and a bag of peppermints
within reach. With her hefty five feet two inches ele-
vated on a pair of tan cowboy boots, Ty Moore swag-
gered into the courtroom, flamboyant in an African print
pants outfit chattering with electric violets, blues,
greens, and reds, her ginger hair trimmed in a radical
brush cut complete with a rat's tail. Lee choked back a
few tears as Ty rolled before the jury on her way to the
witness stand. With her cleft chin thrust upward, Moore
studiously avoided eye contact with Wuornos and evenly,
without emotion, answered prosecutor David Damore's
questions regarding the events following Mallory's
murder.

Moore repeated those details she had already told
to Munster, Thompson, and Horzepa—how Lee had
arrived that December morning at the Ocean Shores
motel with a 1977 Cadillac, how they had moved their
belongings from the motel to their new Burleigh Avenue

apartment in this Cadillac, how Lee had told her that she had shot and killed a man, leaving his body under some carpet out in the woods, how Lee had shown her papers belonging to this man that had the name Richard on them, how Lee had not appeared upset, nervous, or particularly drunk at the time, and how Lee had given her a Members Only jacket and scarf.

William Miller took the cross-examination for the defense and probed Moore's jealousy of the men Lee had encountered out on the highway, which she admitted. Then Miller brought up the alleged movie deal, a tactic that proved fruitless as Ty adamantly repeated that she was not involved in any "deals" with any law-enforcement officers or their attorney. And then she was excused, sauntering past the defense table, where Wuornos cast a baleful eye on her exit.

Next up was Larry Horzepa, looking schoolboyish with his cowlick and glasses as he was sworn in. This was the point where Judge Blount was pressed by the attorneys to rule on the admissibility of testimony and evidence from Wuornos's other admitted murders. In Florida it is called the Williams Rule, and it allows the presentation of evidence to show a similar pattern or scheme. The jury was sequestered, and Horzepa stepped down out of the witness box while Billy Nolas and Sean Daley began their arguments before the judge.

Judge Uriel "Bunky" Blount, a rotund, well-respected jurist with lavish jug ears, bloodhound jowls, and a florid rope of flesh bulging over his knit collar, topped by a rigorously maintained flattop, had already made it known that he was not going to brook any legal maneuverings that engendered delays. On the first day of the trial, Blount, as straightforward and casual as the golf shirts and slacks he wore beneath his robes, advised reporters in his Florida cracker growl that the whole damned thing would be wrapped up in two weeks. Bunky was good to his word. Peering over his narrow glasses, he listened to twenty minutes of arguments between Nolas and Daley, referred to the case law, and quickly ruled in favor of the state.

With Blount's ruling, the jury was brought back in and Horzepa resumed the stand. With this investigator, the state commenced a parade of witnesses and accompanying evidence ranging from Mallory's murder through those of Spears, Carskaddon, Siems, Burress, Humphreys, and Antonio. Horzepa testified to Wuornos's confession regarding all the homicides. Large brown paper bags, ice chests, and plastic bags packed with tagged evidence along with maps and charts were toted in by bailiffs. These accumulated in the space between the prosecution's table and that of the court clerk. From this formidable cache Tanner and Damore presented crime-scene and autopsy photographs, victims' property and clothing, the .22 pistol, bullet casings, spent rounds taken from the victims' bodies, fingerprint cards, and property belonging to Wuornos and Moore. Time and again, forensic specialists, witnesses, and investigators took the stand to identify this or that article or document, their testimony piling fact upon fact until the state's case was like a heavy freight train moving slowly but inexorably down a long straight track, its destination as clear, as certain, as final as a mountain in the desert at midday.

Stefan Siems, the son of Peter Siems, took the stand.

Damore offered the soft-spoken engineer a blue and tan suitcase recovered from Lee's storage bin; Siems identified the suitcase as belonging to his father.

"I used this suitcase myself to go to college," he said.

Damore handed him a tagged pair of scissors.

"Yes. He used them to cut my hair. These would be the scissors he used."

Damore asked Stefan about the last time he had spoken with his father. "He was leaving for New Jersey to visit his sister and then he was coming to Arkansas."

"Did your father make that trip?"

"No, he didn't."

"Did he ever arrive?"

"No, he didn't."

Lee slapped her hands flat on the table, jerked around in her chair, a nasty frown furrowing her brow, and whispered loudly into Miller's ear: "There's just lie after lie after lie!"

Another prosecution witness, Bobby Lee Copas, a pot-bellied trucker from Lakeland, filed up to the witness box to tell of his fateful encounter with Wuornos. Copas recalled how he'd picked up "that lady," pointing a thick finger toward the smirking Wuornos. "Said she had car trouble, said she had to get to her sister's . . . had two kids in day care and had to get to Orlando to pick them up." Copas said the two drove to his bank, where he withdrew cash to make his insurance payment, stuffing the money above the visor.

"She propositioned me, up till then she'd been a perfect lady. She kept glancing up at the envelope. And then I seen what looked to be a small-caliber gun in this bag she had. She kept reaching down and taking this comb out of it and combing her hair. And then she says, 'I'll give you the best damned blow job you ever had in your life.' We were driving by these orange groves and she said we could just pull in over there. I pulled off at I-4 and 27, went into a truck stop, and whipped out this five-dollar bill and told her she could call her sister. When she got out, I reached over and locked the door. That's when she realized I'd taken her. She was mad as hell, started hitting on the window. I drove off and she was screaming, 'I'll kill you like I did those other fat bastards! Copas! I'll get you, you son of a bitch!' "

Copas was just one among some dozen men who related encounters with Lee over the years, men who were able to identify her from photo-pack lineups. One was Pompie Carnley. In the spring of 1990 he had picked her up at I-75 and I-4 "because she didn't appear to be a hooker or street person and because it was raining." She was wearing a yellow blouse and blue jeans and carrying a drawstring bag. Carnley drove her to his Plant City home, they had a few beers, and then they got back on the road. She told him her car had broken down, she needed two hundred dollars, said her girlfriend back in Daytona beat her, said she'd "do anything for the money." He said he had no money, showed her his wallet. She continued badgering him for miles, and then told him to pull off the highway, directing him out on a firebreak road near Highways 19 and 98. They ended up within a few hundred yards of where David Spears's decomposing body would be found a month later. Lee "got out of the Jeep and started to come around . . . I'd been in Korea and Vietnam and was shot before and scared before . . . there was a difference in her now, in her personality and the way she looked . . . it caused the hairs on the back of my neck to stand up . . . I just got out of there, left her out there."

As the prosecution moved inexorably toward the inevitable, Jenkins, Miller, and Nolas hammered hope-filled nails on an appellate case, raising objections with such frequency that it seemed like a chorus to the testimony. There was really little else they had in their tool kit. Wuornos's confession videotapes—at least those excerpts directly related to Mallory's killing—were played before the jury and the court on a quartet of television sets. They watched Lee puffing on her Newports as she chatted up Horzepa and Munster with an even and easy admission to shooting Richard Mallory to death. Several of the twelve Volusia County citizens staring at the screens from the jury box seemed appalled by Lee's video performance. The woman on the tape did not appear to have the slightest remorse, concern, or doubt. She did not appear agitated, considering the seriousness of the crime and her situation. She did not appear drunk or hysterical. The entire twenty-seven minutes ran by as a study in banality, but for the disturbing subject matter. For the defense team, it was bad television. There was their client—on camera—telling her lawyer at the time to be quiet, saying she wanted to confess, saying she had killed the victim, saying she ought to die for what she had done. After the screens had gone blank and bailiffs had switched them off, rolling them away on their carts, the prosecution rested. Court was adjourned for the day, and the jurors filed from the courtroom. Lee stood up and began crying, openly sobbing as the jurors filed by the defense table where she stood in her too-tight purple jacket and black skirt. The seven women and five men pointedly looked straight ahead as they walked by. A reporter observed that Wuornos was about a year late with her tears.

The next day, January 24, Tricia Jenkins reluctantly called the defense's only witness. Against the advice of her counsel and all reason, Lee insisted on her right to take the stand. "Lee is volatile, liquid," said Jenkins afterward. "You have to move her, make her understand on a street level. She doesn't follow legal strategy in its own terms. For her it's like, 'We're renegades, let's run. Let's get them. Get the cops. Fuck with the system. Take the cops down, beat the system.' It was like he broke your doll, let's make 'em pay."

And here in Bunky Blount's courtroom was her big opportunity to go for just that, right at center stage. She had things to say. She had a story to tell, never mind all the evidence, never mind that confession, never mind the witnesses. As Lee so succinctly put it, "I am the truth. I am the fact."

Wearing a blue velour jacket, floral-print skirt, and white blouse, her features softened by eyeliner and blush, Lee took the witness stand. As Jenkins walked her through her history, Wuornos fingered a gold cross hanging at her breasts and looked at the jurors as she spoke to the hushed courtroom.

She said she had become a prostitute at age sixteen. "A lot of guys would pick me up and pay me sixty dollars, a hundred bucks, and it was excellent money and I became a hitchhiking prostitute." She said she had settled in Florida when she was twenty. Tricia asked if she had any children. "I had a son, he should be twenty. I was fourteen, my grandmother made me give him up." Lee was affecting, speaking with convincing emotion, a rueful but realistic woman who had gotten some very bad breaks. Jenkins established Wuornos's prostitution routine, the number of men, the long hours, the danger, and then the attorney led the questioning to Ty.

"In 1986 I met her at the Zodiac, and from the first day we were head over heels . . . the sex part didn't work out and we became like sisters . . . she quit her job because I made $150 a day and she made like $150 a week . . . she wanted me out there . . . the last year she didn't like trailer living, she said I want you to go out there more often and if I didn't she'd break up with me and find somebody else . . . I tried to talk about Richard Mallory, but she didn't want to listen . . . she worked a couple of times, the only solid job she had was Casa Del Mar the last year . . . she got fired . . . she beat up her boss . . . I wanted to save up for a house but she always wanted to go to the mall and buy clothes . . . I saw her spend a hundred dollars on a stuffed animal machine . . . we were always drinking, I drank a lot . . . it was like my tranquilizer . . . Out there I was shy and embarrassed about my body . . . I was scared out there." Tyria Moore was painted as the money-grubbing spouse. Wuornos actually referred to herself as Moore's "white slave."

Jenkins moved on to Wuornos's rapes.

"Two guys raped me . . . I had my Mace gun, but it didn't do any good . . . a guy in Indiana raped me, had a seventh-degree judo black belt and beat me up so bad you couldn't recognize me . . . I learned he'd raped some other girl and it took me two months to recover . . .

"[Prostitution] was the only way, churches couldn't help me . . . I tried to be a police officer but they wanted like three thousand dollars, and I didn't have my GED. I tried to be a corrections officer but didn't have a car, couldn't get into the military because I couldn't pass the tests . . . the only thing I could do was be a prostitute."

Then came the depraved nightmare of rape and torture at the hands of Richard Mallory.

"We both started to get undressed . . . I said Richard, I don't do this without rubbers . . . he went back to the trunk of the car to get some . . . I started to take off my clothes first, I always do this to let them know I was all right, I'm honest . . . I started to take off my jeans . . . he came back . . . helped me arrange the sleeping bag . . . I said its not fair, you still have your clothes on . . . the dome light was on . . . he said 'Hey, not too bad' . . . I was embarrassed, I got this beer belly and stretch marks . . . I said Richard why don't you take off your clothes? . . . he opened the window and it's blowing and cold . . . and he's unzipping his pants . . . then he says he doesn't have the money . . . I had somebody at home to have sex with . . . He said I only got a little for breakfast and gas . . . I said Richard, no way, we've got to call this off and started to get my clothes out of the back . . . and I saw him coming toward me . . . he put a cord around my neck . . . said yes you are, bitch, you're going to do everything I tell you to or I'll kill you . . . done it before . . . your body will still be warm for my huge cock . . . you want to die, slut? Are you gonna do what I tell you to do and I just nodded yes . . . He tied my hands and tied them to the steering wheel . . . he got out of the car and told me to slide up . . . he said he was going to see how much meat he was going to pound in my ass . . . he got undressed and threw his clothes on the floor, he lifted my legs all the way up to where my feet were near the window . . . then he started having anal sex . . . he's doing this in a very violent manner and I don't know whether he came or climaxed and he violently took himself out and violently put himself in my vagina . . . I was crying my brains out . . . he said he loved to hear my pain . . . that my crying turned him on . . . he pretty much bruised my cervix and all, bruised my ribs.

"He got out and took his clothes out to the driver's side . . . put his clothes on the ground and went and got something out of the trunk . . . he got a red cooler and a blue tote bag . . . there were two liter bottles of water, a maroon towel, a bar of soap, tooth brush, a bottle of rubbing alcohol and a bottle of Visine . . . I said to myself, this guy is going to kill me or dissect me . . . I don't know . . . he's totally weird."

Lee's eyes widened and she put her fingers to her temples. "Oh . . . oh, lord . . . my ears are ringing. I'm dizzy . . ." Jenkins suggested she put her head down, but Wuornos waved her off and continued. This moment was not particularly believable.

Lee held the court with her vivid description of Mallory squirting alcohol from the Visine bottle into her rectum, vagina, and nostrils, Mallory strangling her with the cords wrapped around her neck, her breaking free and spitting in his face, their struggle in the front seat of the Cadillac, and finally the fast draw of her trusty .22 and the dispatch of the villain Mallory with three rapid-fire shots.

Lee was on the stand for over an hour with her direct testimony. It was a hell of a performance, a terrifying account of rape, degradation, and self-defense. Like something out of a true-detective magazine or a made-for-TV movie or a second-hand story heard in a highway bar. Then came state attorney John Tanner on cross-examination.

"Ms. Wuornos, you saw the tape of your confession to detectives Horzepa and Munster in the courtroom yesterday, didn't you?"

"Yes."

"You didn't say anything about an anal rape or having alcohol squirted up your rectum, did you, Ms. Wuornos?"

"I . . . I was interrupted. I never got a chance to express myself . . . my main purpose was to confess about Ty's innocence . . . I was hysterical . . . I was in shock . . . I was totally out of it and I couldn't remember."

Tanner hammered away and Lee quickly became belligerent, scratching her head and her nose. "I wasn't in the mood. They forced me to talk about it. They threatened me. They had me set up."

And for the next two hours it was all downhill for Lee, with her testimony a skidding out-of-control truckload of contradiction and inconsistency. Jenkins, Miller, and Nolas seemed to melt into the table, rising only to advise Lee not to answer any questions regarding the other murders. She ended up invoking her Fifth Amendment right twenty-five times. In between she shoved blame onto Ty. "She knows it was self-defense and she's not saying anything because she's involved in books and movies and she's worried about her family. Ty Moore is interested in her five hundred million dollars. All these people have to have my blood. If I get acquitted she doesn't get her multimillions nor does Horzepa or whatever his name is nor Munster nor a lot of you others!"

Lee would veer off into a tirade with each of Tanner's questions. She claimed her jailers and detectives had drugged her with Vistaril. She claimed she had been set up by the cops and the state attorneys. Tanner plucked away at her conflicting accounts, at her claims of anal rape, and she responded by contradicting herself or laying out a lame excuse.

"Hard to keep the stories straight, isn't it?" Tanner drawled sarcastically.

"No," she snapped. "It's hard to remember."

"You'd remember being anally raped, wouldn't you?"

By the time Wuornos left the stand, her direct testimony shredded by Tanner like a chain of paper dolls, she had argued that convicted felons should be allowed to pack guns and accused Tanner of being a law breaker. Lee was so angry it is unlikely she realized she'd just sealed her own fate.

On January 27, the seven women and five men filed out of the box and into the jury room. An hour and a half later they were back with a verdict. When the clerk read out the guilty verdict, a unanimous vote, Wuornos glowered, and then the skin on her face seemed to constrict, drawing tighter against her skull. Billy Nolas eyed her nervously as the jury began filing out of the courtroom. "I'm innocent!" She shoved her palms against the desk. "I was raped! I hope you get raped!" She kicked her chair back. "Scumbags of America!" A deputy put his hand on her and led her away.

* * *

The penalty phase of the trial began the next day, and doubtless Lee's outburst still rang in the jurors' ears. If they needed reminders, Lee sat and glared at them as a quartet of mental-health specialists took turns testifying to Wuornos's personal history and mental disorders. In this proceeding, Billy Nolas took the point for the defense and called Dr. Elizabeth McMahon, a neuropsychologist. McMahon said she had met with Lee five times for a total of twenty-two hours. She spoke of Lee's alcoholism, of her hearing difficulties, which had begun in elementary school, of a trauma to the head when she was fifteen. "[Lee] evidences a mild degree of cortical dysfunction. But if you'd meet her on the street you wouldn't know it . . ." Nolas took McMahon through the results of a battery of tests she had conducted on Lee, as well as those results from tests dating back to her school days. McMahon's conclusion was that Lee suffered from a Borderline Personality Disorder.

"She is classic," said McMahon. "She meets all eight criteria as established by the DSM III-R." The *Diagnostic and Statistical Manual of Mental Disorders* is the standard reference used by clinicians in determining psychological dysfunctions.

It defines the Borderline as "a Personality Disorder in which there is instability in a variety of areas, including interpersonal behavior, mood, and self-image. No single feature is invariably present."

The disorder is most commonly diagnosed in women, but is prevalent throughout the clinical population and is associated with the better-known Antisocial

Personality Disorder. Five of eight criteria are needed for a diagnosis. Lee got a perfect score.

1. Impulsivity or unpredictability in at least two areas that are self-damaging—spending, sex, gambling, substance use, shoplifting, overeating, physically self-damaging acts.
2. A pattern of unstable and intense interpersonal relationships—marked shifts of attitude, idealization, devaluation, manipulation.
3. Inappropriate, intense anger or lack of control of anger.
4. Identity disturbance manifested by uncertainty about . . . self-image, gender identity, longterm goals, friendship patterns, values, loyalties.
5. Affective instability—marked shifts from normal mood to depression, irritability or anxiety, usually lasting only a few hours and only rarely a few days, with a return to normal mood.
6. Intolerance of being alone, frantic efforts to avoid being alone, depressed when alone.
7. Physically self-damaging acts—suicidal gestures, self-mutilation, recurrent accidents or physical fights.
8. Chronic feelings of emptiness or boredom.

Not only did two other defense experts—Drs. Krop and Toomer—concur with this diagnosis, but the state's expert psychiatrist—Dr. Barnard—did as well. However, Barnard testified that the Antisocial Personality diagnosis fits most of the United States criminal population. Yet the hours of expert testimony and the wrangling between

Nolas and Tanner over how this disorder affected Lee in the commission of the murders did not seem to affect the jurors as much as the state's final witness—Barry Wuornos.

Softly featured, balding, wearing glasses, the tubby Wuornos took the stand and described his family and how Lee had come to live with them. He discounted the stories about his father's violence—"He laid down strong rules, a kind of strict disciplinarian . . . [but he] would not beat a child." Barry said his mom "was very quiet, studious, a laid-back kind of woman."

Lee stared at her brother with rage as he told of how she had started getting in trouble around ten or eleven years of age, shoplifting, toying with fire. He talked about his sister Diane and her husband, Lee's father, Leo. "When she got mixed up with Leo Pittman her life turned for the worse. He hung out with hoods, a criminal type. I heard he hung himself in prison." He recalled little Aileen being badly burned, though he was away in the military at the time. "She always did well, up until the ninth grade. She had good grades." Barry knew nothing about any hearing impairment nor about how his mother refused to have Lee tested for hearing loss. What Barry did on the stand was describe two sets of children—Keith and Lee were problems, full of anger and delinquency, while he and his sister Lori were more laid back. He said the adoptions of his niece and nephew were "sore spots in the family." Many in the courtroom wondered if Barry knew that his testimony would be sending his sister to the electric chair; nothing in his expression indicated that, if he did, he would be losing sleep over it.

• • •

Closing arguments came. John Tanner stepped before the twelve, a trial-seasoned expression of sorrow on his lean face. He began carefully and without fire to guide the jury toward the death penalty.

"Mental impairment is the defense of the last resort. Under the law it is not whether Aileen Wuornos is strange or has a sour view of the world, is manipulative and perverted, she is all of those things. *But she knew what she was doing and what she was doing was wrong.* Her mental impairment is almost entirely based on Aileen Wuornos's statements . . . Who is responsible? Aileen Wuornos says it was genetics. Aileen Wuornos says it was her parents that caused this. She'd blame prostitution, but she told us she liked the money. She blamed Ty Moore. She blamed the detectives. She even blamed the victim. This is not a case about forgiveness. You can pray for her soul. Mercy is just another word for sympathy . . . In her own words she said 'After I shot him he said "Oh my god, I'm going to die." I said, "Yeah, motherfucker, so what?" and I shot him a couple more times.' . . . By an act of her will, in fifteen to twenty minutes, she extinguished his life. All that was left were a few pitiful possessions, the junk of life . . . You heard her."

Tanner's voice rose.

"She said 'I'm guilty . . . I deserve to die.' And you know that is the truth. Aileen Wuornos deserves the ultimate penalty."

Tricia Jenkins followed with an impassioned plea for Lee's life. Speaking in her throaty baritone, Jenkins gripped the lectern and bored into the jurors' eyes, hoping to find sympathetic hearts. "I don't know what I can do or say to convince you, but I know I should . . ." Jenkins roamed back over Lee's pathetic life marked by abandonment, neglect, and violence, over all the abuses life had inflicted upon the tense woman sitting before them. "She has been burdened with an impairment that makes her intensely afraid . . . she has no idea who she is. She is always alone, always, always frustrated . . . as you heard Dr. McMahon say, Lee is a damaged primitive child . . . working one exit to the next. She feels persecuted, she has no control. You have seen the mood swings, the intense emotions. You've seen her. When Dr. Krop said she was one point away from retardation, she laughed."

Jenkins then assaulted Barry Wuornos's testimony. "Barry came and testified in a proceeding in which the state is trying to kill her. What does that tell you about how dysfunctional that family was?"

As she closed, two women on the jury had tears tracking their faces. "Do not be deceived that life imprisonment is not punishment. Life in prison is severe . . . she will never know freedom, she will go to sleep in a metal cage, and if she's lucky she will have a window, and every time she looks out she will remember what she did to lose it . . . Lee lost her freedom January of last year, but she thinks somehow everything will be all right, but when she goes from here, she goes without hope. She has already lost her life. You will be giving her the *mere right to exist.*"

Two hours later the jury told Aileen Wuornos that wasn't enough. Again it was a unanimous verdict—twelve to zero—that Lee be delivered to the electric chair. Judge Blount said it was the first unanimous death verdict he'd ever seen.

On the morning of January 30, Wuornos stood between her attorneys before Judge Blount's bench. They were joined by Arlene. Lee spoke. "First I'd like to say I've been labeled as a serial killer, been framed by law enforcement as a serial killer. I'm no serial killer . . . what I did is what anybody else had the right to do . . . I had no intention of killing anyone . . . I told you I was raped and that is what happened in all of them . . . law enforcement framed me for books and movies . . . this is all a *con-spire-acy* . . . State Attorney Tanner was manipulating the jury . . . he lied right through his teeth . . . I was forced to confess . . ." She began hacking the air with her free hand. "I was under duress . . . I was hysterical from alcohol withdrawal . . . I had the deliriums . . . they have to have these convictions to get their money . . . I am not a serial killer."

Blount nodded sagely and thanked her. Then he allowed Pralle to make a statement. Pralle said Lee was "emotionally and psychologically a child, and me and my husband are one hundred percent behind the diagnosis . . . she never got a chance to grow up . . . please give mercy . . . we are willing to pay for counseling . . . we ask for mercy for my daughter's life."

As Blount was about to pronounce sentence, Lee asked if she could speak again. Blount extended a beefy hand and said, "Please."

Lee then took a shot at her attorneys. "I had two clients willing to testify for me. I was surprised when my lawyers said, 'Defense rests.' I had high-school friends I wanted contacted and they were not." She paused, shook her head. "I couldn't believe I just got on that stand myself." Jenkins, Miller, and Nolas simply stared at her.

Judge Blount picked up his pen and ordered Wuornos to be "electrocuted until you are dead. And may God have mercy on your soul."

She seemed to shrink under the words. And then she smiled. The guards brought her to the clerk's bench, where she was fingerprinted for her transfer into state custody. As they led her across the courtroom, she wiped her fingers with a paper towel and smiled out at the cameras before disappearing into a bright yellow passageway. She would be on death row in time for the six o'clock news.

Epilogue

When the Marion County jury returned recommendations for Wuornos's execution on May 7, 1992, on the three counts of homicide she had pled to a month earlier, Judge Thomas Sawaya scheduled her sentencing for the following week. Wuornos had waived her right to appear during the proceedings before the jury, which amounted to nothing more than a walk-through for the prosecution. Her attorney, Steve Glazer, injected the only drama into the affair when he took to his hands and knees in front of the jury box, taping out an eight-by-nine-foot rectangle on the floor to illustrate the dimensions of Wuornos's cell. Suddenly, the mammoth attorney began gasping for breath, floundering on the carpet, unable to lift his bulk from the doglike position he had unwisely assumed. He called out for his heart pills, which were immediately fetched. Sawaya called a two-hour recess, after which Glazer returned with a routine denunciation of the death penalty and rested. The jury went out and came back four hours later to recommend that Lee be sent to the electric chair for the murders of Burress, Humphreys, and Spears.

During this time, Marion County Investigator John Tilley drove down to the Broward County Correctional Facility for Women and interviewed Wuornos. Lee informed Tilley she remembered where she had left Peter Siems's corpse. Off Interstate 95, near an exit to Beaufort, South Carolina. She pointed it out on a map. Law enforcement in South Carolina and Florida scoured the terrain Lee had indicated and came up with nothing. Lee pushed harder, saying that if they would fly her up there she would take them to his body. They complied, much to the dismay of the detectives who had brought her in. They found nothing. But Lee got a trip out of jail, a spatter of publicity, and an opportunity for escape. Wuornos knew where she had left Siems's bullet-riddled body, and it wasn't anywhere near South Carolina. A growing consensus among investigators was that she had killed Siems somewhere north of Jacksonville off Interstate 95, dumping his body in the uninhabited marshes and swamps west of the King's Bay naval station. "Wherever she put that body," said Bruce Munster, "it was somewhere she knew it wouldn't be found. In the ground, in water. That's why she was so comfortable with keeping his car as long as she did. She didn't keep any of the other victims' vehicles very long, a day or two at the most. She kept his car for a month. She *knew* his body wouldn't turn up."

After this wild-goose chase, Lee followed with a one-on-one interview with morning TV talk-show host Montel Williams. Wuornos reveled in the attention, repeating her charges of conspiracy, betrayal, and victimization. Her attorney, Steve Glazer, admitted that Arlene Pralle was paid seventy-five hundred dollars for the interview.

But Wuornos saved her most vitriolic performance for her appearance before Judge Sawaya at her sentencing. Once again she produced a lengthy handwritten script, laced with Christian pieties and protestations of self-defense, from which she inveighed for over an hour against all the "conspirators," meaning everyone involved in her case—excepting herself, her present attorney, and Mrs. Pralle. She closed her awkwardly worded, repetitious diatribe by turning from the podium to level her murderous eye on Assistant State Attorney Ric Ridgway, seated a few feet behind her. Looking directly at Ridgway, she snarled, "I hope your wife and children get raped in the ass!" It was a galvanizing moment for those in the courtroom who'd spent the past eighteen months in the grip of Wuornos's sordid saga of murder and lies. Here was the face her seven victims had taken with them into death, a pale ruined mask boiling with hatred, fear, and satisfaction.

Judge Sawaya then quietly concurred with the jury's recommendations by leveling three more death sentences on Wuornos's head. She responded by saluting Sawaya with an upraised middle finger and a muttered, "Motherfucker." For someone who'd repeatedly declared she wanted to be executed as soon as possible, Lee certainly was not pleased that her wish had been granted.

But then, this was Lee after all. A raging contradiction, but a contradiction so transparent, so infuriatingly childish, that it aroused no sympathetic curiosity. It was just another example of her disordered personality, another tantrum thrown by that "primitive damaged child." However, Aileen Wuornos was no child.

The last time I saw Lee, two deputies were taking her

from the courtroom, and she turned in the doorway and flashed her crooked teeth in a wide grin. She raised her manacled wrists and exuberantly called out, "Come down to death row! Maxwell House coffee for you guys!"

She started to say something more, but just then the deputy closed the steel door and she was gone.

Postmortem

Lee was wide awake just before dawn on Wednesday, October 9, 2002, when the death row officers came to call. She was in a "good mood," they said. She was "ready to go", they said. She'd stayed up until midnight the night before chatting it up with her childhood friend, Dawn Botkin. Four hours remained in her life.

A week earlier Florida Governor Jeb Bush lifted a stay of execution after a panel of psychiatrists ruled that Lee was mentally competent. Wuornos had been fighting for her date with the executioner for ten years. In her last petition to Florida's Supreme Court, Lee wrote, "I'm one who seriously hates human life and would kill again."

Wuornos refused the barbecue chicken dinner along with any religious counsel. No chaplain, no preacher. Certainly not the born-again huckster Arlene Pralle who made her screen debut by taking $10,000 in cash from British filmmaker Nick Broomfield for an interview with Wuornos for his 1993 documentary, *Aileen Wuornos: The Selling of a Serial Killer.* Wuornos later complained that she had received little money from Pralle.

Pralle didn't show up to see Lee off. Neither did Steven Glazer, the pot-smoking attorney from Gainesville Pralle brought in to facilitate Lee's race to the death chamber and arrange interview deals. When contacted by reporters he said he had to be in court that day. "Ob-la-di, Ob-la-da, life goes on," said the bearded Glazer. "You can quote me."

As for Broomfield, the in-your-face filmmaker met Lee for her last interview on Tuesday afternoon but after thirty-five minutes it all went sideways when Wuornos unleashed a string of invectives and stormed out of the room.

Broomfield told waiting reporters outside the prison that "we are executing someone who is mad. Here is someone who has totally lost her mind. My overall impression doing the interview with her is that she was completely insane." He said Lee told him that she was a victim of sonic mind control perpetrated by Florida correction officers whenever she complained. She also bitched about the police investigators who deliberately ignored her killings so that they could make big money off her story.

Her attorney in the Mallory trial, Billy Nolas, agreed with this assessment, naming Lee as "the most disturbed individual I have represented."

One of the Volusia County prosecutors in that case, David Damore, told the *Orlando Sentinel* that "She's really a much more shallow character than she's been portrayed as. She has been made into something she's not. She truly hated men. I think it's a tragedy to make her into some type of heroine figure."

But some did. Carla Lucero, the composer-librettist of the opera *Wuornos*, said, "On a karmic level, it's almost like—and many women would agree with me—Wow, I'm surprised this didn't happen sooner. I don't really condone killing, but you do have to wonder, Why did this take so long? I've always likened it to a boiling pot, and she's the steam that escaped the pot."

Steve Binegar didn't have any metaphors in his view the day before Lee's execution. "She's not a robber who kills, she's a killer who robs," he told reporters. "She's a pathetic creature." As for the motivations in the killings, Binegar said, "I don't think anybody but the victims know."

Volusia County Sheriff's detective Larry Horzepa didn't have time for any comments for the press on Wuornos' execution date. He was busy building a case on another murder suspect, the alleged killer of a 2-year-old boy who had been beaten to death in 2001.

When it came time to climb aboard the execution gurney, Lee offered no resistance. She was strapped down and rolled to an anteroom to the death chamber where IV shunts were placed in her arms that would carry the lethal chemicals into her system. Then she was wheeled into the death chamber where the assembled witnesses waited to watch her die. "Other than her final statement, she made no sounds," said Department of Corrections spokesman Sterling Ivey, who witnessed the execution. "She just closed her eyes and her heart stopped beating."

Her last words from the T-shaped gurney inside the death chamber were an off-kilter fusion of Hollywood celebrity, pop Christianity and murderous revenge. The subject of three movies, two plays and an opera, Lee referenced two films in her final statement: *Independence Day* and *The Terminator*, both apocalyptic action movies filled with massive destruction by alien forces. An oddly articulated summation of the final twelve years of her desperate and damaged life, it was marked by egregious error and capped by a final empty threat.

"I'd just like to say I'm sailing with the Rock and I'll be back like *Independence Day* with Jesus, June 6, like the movie, big mothership and all. I'll be back."

The lethal drugs began to flow and she said nothing more. At 9:47 A.M. Aileen Carole Wuornos, aged 46, was pronounced dead.

On instruction from Lee, Dawn Botkin claimed the body and had it cremated. She carried Lee's ashes aboard a flight back to Michigan where they were scattered at a location known only to the two women. The body of Lee's seventh victim, Peter Siems, remains somewhere in the marshes near the Florida–Georgia state line.